THE GREAT BEER TREK

Revised Edition

Stephen Morris

Illustrated by VANCE SMITH

THE STEPHEN GREENE PRESS
PELHAM BOOKS

THE STEPHEN GREENE PRESS/PELHAM BOOKS

Published by the Penguin Group
Viking Penguin, a division of Penguin Books USA Inc., 40 West 23rd Street,
  New York, New York 10010, U.S.A.
Penguin Books Ltd., 27 Wrights Lane, London W8 5TZ, England
Penguin Books Australia Ltd, Ringwood, Victoria, Australia
Penguin Books Canada Ltd, 2801 John Street, Markham, Ontario, Canada L3R 1B4
Penguin Books (N.Z.) Ltd, 182–190 Wairau Road, Auckland 10, New Zealand

Penguin Books Ltd, Registered Offices: Harmondsworth, Middlesex, England

First published in 1984 by The Stephen Greene Press/Pelham Books
This revised edition published in 1990
Distributed by Viking Penguin, a division of Penguin Books USA Inc.

10 9 8 7 6 5 4 3 2 1

Illustrations by Vance Smith

Library of Congress Cataloging-in-Publication Data

Morris, Stephen
  The great beer trek : a guide to the highlights and lowlights of American beer drinking
/ Stephen Morris : with illustrations by Vance Smith. — Rev. ed.
    p.   cm.
  ISBN 0-8289-0766-8
  1. Beer—United States.   I. Title.
TP577.M672   1990
641.2′3′0973—dc20   89-23409
                                                                        CIP

Printed in the United States of America
Designed by Deborah Schneider
Set in Clearface Roman and Clearface Gothic by Compset
Produced by Unicorn Production Services, Inc.

CONTENTS

PREFACE

TEN YEARS AND TEN THOUSAND BEERS LATER

Just for the halibut, I put pen to paper. Ten years earlier a young man had been struck by the lightning bolt of inspiration. Beer is important! Beer is food! Beer is good for you! Beer provides the window to human souls! Armed with convictions and emboldened by youth, The Great Beer Trek took to the highways of America, determined to visit the ever-dwindling number of beer shrines.

But ten years have passed. Lots of beer has flowed under that bridge. How much? Let's see—ten years times three hundred and sixty-five days, multiplied times three beers a day—that's more than ten thousand beers. And what beers they have been! That is the saga of this sudsworthy decade and the subject of this revised edition of *The Great Beer Trek*.

Beer is a fluid subject. At McSorley's Old Ale House in Lower Manhattan they still serve a crisp ale that goes perfectly with Liederkranz and onion sandwiches. The dust on the wishbones still makes one wonder who has been paid off at the health department. This is the same dust that was there when the Beer Trek van parked outside, festooned with its emblematic bumper stickers proclaiming FOREVER BEER.

Although the beer is the same, it is different, brewed by different hands, from different kettles and even different cities. Rheingold, Ortlieb, or Schmidt. New Bedford, New York, Philadelphia. It makes no difference to the McSorley's quaffer. So long as the ale is fresh and clean, with a little more zing and oomph than Budweiser, and served with respect, it will do nicely.

Perhaps with the renaissance of on-premises brewing, the owners of McSorley's are now considering brewing their own. The circle will then be complete, although from the fluid subject standpoint, it has never been broken. So long as the ale is fresh and clean, with a little more zing—

What has changed at McSorley's are the people. The clientele is hopelessly yuppified. This class had not yet been invented back in the days of the Original Trek, a period best described as an interstadial between oil shortages when the United States looked to get back to the land to regain its balance after the buffeting of Vietnam and Watergate. Back then you saw long hair and backpacks at McSorley's. Beards. People pondered the fate of the planet. Now one sees wing tips and alligator attachés. The discussion is of market indexes and the merits of various sleek cars. Back then they drank ale. Now they drink ale. That's the point.

Special Note
to Original Readers
of the Great Beer Trek

The ideal way to do a Beer Trek is to quit the job, hop in the van, and point toward the nearest malt. Alas, in the intervening decade since the Original Trek, the baggage has gotten heavier; the job has a firmer hold; and there are new considerations, like taking the kids out of school. The landscape has changed as well. The pressing motivation of the first trip was to see many of the fine regional brewers before they slipped beneath the waves of the sea of Budweiser. The trip uncovered a welcome ray of promise for the future, as hardcore sudsophiles like the home brewers (practicing a still-illegal craft at that time) provided the fertile foundation from which grew the robust micro-brewing scene of today.

The nation enters the 1990s with more than three times the number of independent brewers as when the Beer Trek van put 20,000 miles under its wheels in 100 days. The brewing scene is changing so fast that one portrait will be obsolete as soon as it reaches the printed page. The beer world today is like a keg that has just been tapped. There is more foam than substance at first. One must let it settle before judging the beer. No, now is not the time for the Next Great Beer Trek. I will save it for the year 2000 and do it with my sons.

This book, like the first, was written with a beer by my side. But what a difference a decade makes! Ten years ago, unless one dared to break the law and brew at home, the available fare consisted of Bland, Bland Lite, and Bland in a different container. Today the commercial brewers have heeded the consumer's call for quality, purity, and variety. The regional brewers have found new life as contract brewers for entrepreneurs who have everything needed to enter the beer business except for the hardware. And the micros are filling every consumer's greedy pore with brewed exotica. Even the home brewers are in the act with improved equipment and ingredients to make sure that the beer drinker's need for identity need not come at the expense of quality.

While the state of beer may be improved on all fronts, the state of beer drinking is not. Consumption overall is down, and the heat is on. Antialcohol, and therefore antibeer, sentiment has resulted in higher drinking ages, stiffer penalties for drunk driving, and a revival of prohibitionist tendencies. The idea of a Great Beer Trek, simultaneously glorifying beer drinking and the open road, seems as anachronistic as a treatise advocating cigarette smoking as the path to healthfulness.

The text of *The Great Beer Trek*—Revised Edition, as it relates to the original trip, is virtually unchanged. This means that there is a host of quaint anachronisms. Companies change hands; people shave their beards; beers are reformulated. Updating a manuscript so specifically fixed in time is an impossible task that might be compared to fixing an old house. One can drive one-self crazy trying to get all the angles straight. The better route is to relax, have a beer, and appreciate the fine character that the passage of time has lent to the structure.

Each Trekker's Guide, on the other hand, is completely up-to-date to provide beer enthusiasts their more current guide to what is happening in beerland. The sidebars comment, from a contemporary viewpoint, on the State of Beer. And like its predecessor, this revised edition is intended to be read in whole, in part, in sequence, or in the bathtub. It is both a reference and a narrative and should be enjoyed in the company of your favorite brew.

This revision would not have been possible without the efforts of Laura Morris, the Lady of the Trek, who contributed many painstaking hours of work, not to mention a lifetime of patience.

I also thank the many people who by sharing time or intuition were instrumental in the creation of this book. In ten years the Beer Trek has found many friends in the world of malt and hops. I praise you with the simplest gesture of respect I know, the raised glass.

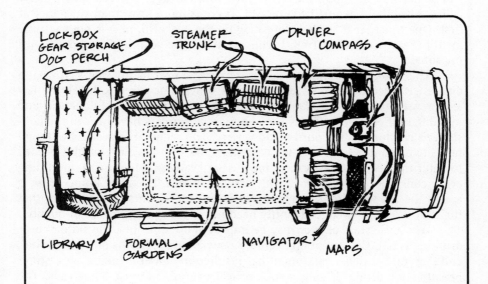

Tactical Planning

The logistical challenge for a Beer Trek has changed by the decade. Ten years ago the trekker had to scramble to as many breweries as possible before they closed. In today's whirlwind world of mushrooming micros, the task is to complete a circuit before a handful of new ones open. Can it be done? Not by car. And beer trekking by Lear jet misses the point. Here are some considerations.

CHARIOT

A van might have been perfect for the latter reaches of hippiedom but not for the 1990s. Just look at today's vans—they're cute, intended more for hauling kids to Little League than professional road flogging. Nor does a van make the proper statement about the seriousness of the venture. The slogan FOREVER BEER, is still suitable for the bumper sticker, but let's attach it to the rear of a stretch limo.

THE DESIGNATED DRIVER

With more and more severe penalties for driving under the influence, one cannot screech from mecca to shrine with even the slightest taint of hops on the breath. The trick is to find someone who, without pay, will drive the stretch limo from tavern to brewery to barley field while you quaff the best and the freshest and think big thoughts about the interrelationship of Humanity, Beer, and the Cosmos. The successful applicant will be sober and understanding with the willpower to resist great brew and the patience to endure your loquacious verbal meanderings. This person will have to love you very much or be of low native intelligence.

LAPTOPS AND OTHER NEAT STUFF

The original Beer Trek van had sturdy wooden cases from the Congress Brewing Company stuffed with files, papers, and notes. There were directories with addresses of beer can collectors and breweriana zealots who might lend a hand along the way, as well as the few published tomes to provide inspiration. This stuff is all obsolete. Pack a laptop computer, a portable FAX machine, and a little tin box into which you place all your electronic gewgaws—dictaphone, 35 mm camera, etc. If you are really smart, you will fit everything into an attaché case and still have room for Michael Jackson's Pocket Guide to Beer.

TELECOMMUNICATIONS

CB radio? Gimme a break! Those things went out with nonfiltered Camels. You need a cellular phone and a modem. And while we are on the subject, forget about atlases and compasses. All that navigational stuff should be built into the dashboard.

CLOTHING

Do not worry about it. A simple business suit will do, along with a power tie. The modern brewer is more businessman than the stereotyped Germanic type with hop oil on his fingers. And he dresses for "doing lunch." Send the suit out to room service for cleaning every night since you have dispensed with this sleeping-in-the-van nonsense and are making the Marriotts of the world your home. Expensive? Forgedaboudit! You do not care about expense because you are protected by—

PLASTIC!!!

Carry at least a three-inch stack of credit cards. Make sure at least half of them are gold and accumulate mileage-plus miles. If you spread yourself thin enough (remember, this is the American way), you can Beer Trek in style for six months or so before they catch up with you.

To my sons, Jake and Patrick
May you grow to love beer—and to respect it

1
BEER DRINKER AMERICANUS

SCITUATE, MASSACHUSETTS

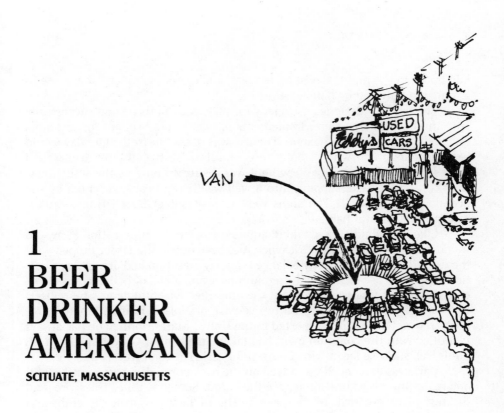

A TWILIGHT OF DARTS

Old friends drift apart, rightfully so. If they meet again, the scars of passions, positions, wives, wars, children, and success obscure once-familiar features. Behind a mask of the present each peers through the other's disguise. Not until the last bit of make-up is gone, the wigs and rubber noses discarded, do old friends become new.

So many of my friendships were formed over beer . . . over six-packs smuggled into football games, over sudsy water swilled from paper cups (one in each hand) at freshman mixers, over carefree pitchers at Rudy's Bar & Grill, over crisp pilsners on ceremonial weekends.

Now I manage to get together with old friends once or twice a year, whenever. The occasion may be a football game, fishing, a business trip, or, as in the instance about to be described, a Fourth of July weekend visit. But the occasion always involves beer.

In the morning there was a parade through town. We awoke to the off-key sound of a drum and bugle corps, followed by a twenty-one-gun salute during which at least three guns misfired. The group that had gathered at odd hours in the night, stayed up too late, and drank too much, now arose to a morning buttered by holiday sunshine.

The day was designed especially for play, each of us having successfully left our shackles elsewhere. Implements of "war" were brought forth: tennis racquets, a croquet set, a canoe. The day was passed in frolic; Monday would be time enough to worry about sore muscles. By twilight the frenzy had passed, and the tranquility of twilight was disturbed only by the soft thunk-thunk-thunk of darts slipping into a well-weathered board, accented by the occasional PCHSSSST! The signs were unmistakable: Beer Drinker Americanus in his natural habitat.

Like a good host I had laid in ample provisions in anticipation of my old friends. Cherrystone clams, Pickwick Ale, beer nuts—the larder bulged with the essentials of the perfectly balanced holiday diet. Bob had driven from Baltimore with a case of National Premium beer and a box of boiled crabs slathered with a curry sauce so hot that the only effective antidote was more beer. Fen came from Montreal with a twelve-pack of Molson Brador, a potent, robust brew not at the time exported to the United States. John, who has always identified with the common man, had taken an all-night Greyhound from St. Louis, his suitcase laden with Coors and Pearl. The man travels in style.

Darkness descended unnoticed on the back porch dart game until someone realized we could no longer see the board. Someone asked the score, and the rest of us groaned. No one cared. The night was warm, the crabs and clams delicious, the moon was yellow, and there was no conceivable way we could run out of beer. We could live forever in this twilight of darts.

The game eventually became incidental to the conversation. The obligatory catching-up had by now been dispensed with, and the floor was given to a profound discussion of The Meaning of Life, a subject that had occupied untold hours in the term of our previous acquaintance. This time our pool of arrogant ease was not so brimming. We retreated into sentimentality, lamenting the absence of those who had shared our concerns, if not our fates. Remember Peter? What the hell do you think happened to Peter?

By midnight "The Meaning of Life" became "the meaning of our lives." We boasted of success, then shut up as we saw our accomplishments in the light of the original goals. Not a single one of us had changed the world, and now, on a warm summer night, on a back porch, bathed by moonlight and gentle sea breezes, it did not seem so much in need of change. What was left to believe in?

The awkward silence was broken by John, master of timing and the well-turned phrase, who stood and repeated the litany we realized had set the rhythm of the entire night: "When in doubt, have another beer. What can I get you: Molson, National, Pickwick, Coors, or Pearl?"

Aha. Perhaps we had been trying too hard. Why worry about cosmic issues beyond our control when we could be enjoying the simplest of pleasures—good food, good company, good beer.

The Great Beer Trek was thus born. The decision came easily once the alternatives were considered. On one hand was the life for which I had been raised—safe, secure, and plush enough to provide all the beer I could conceivably consume (although martinis or chablis were considered more appropriate). This component life, complete with optional extras such as Transcendental Meditation, est, TA, yoga, golf, Pyramid Power, PTA, Jesus, valium, the

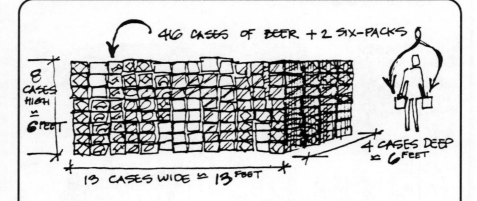

416 CASES OF BEER + 2 SIX-PACKS

8 CASES HIGH ≈ 6 FEET

4 CASES DEEP ≈ 6 FEET

13 CASES WIDE ≈ 13 FEET

Ten Thousand Beers in the Great Scheme of Life

OK. I have consumed more than ten thousand beers in the last ten years. Is that a little or a lot? Obviously it is a function of perspective. Saint or sot? That is the question.

If the beers were consumed evenly over the period—three each evening for instance—there is no time when I could have been found legally drunk. At the same time, in taking the myriad self-help questionnaires regarding alcohol abuse that are so common in Parade and Family Circle, I register as a problem drinker on every one. The American Heart Association would approve. Most of my friends say I am a wimp.

Ten thousand beers is 120,000 ounces, 1,666 six-packs, 3.2 a week. This works out to approximately 28 barrels of beer, the brewer's standard measure, each barrel consisting of 31.2 gallons of fluid. While 28 barrels might be a significant amount to a brewpub (a boutique brewery where the entire output is served on the premises), it would not change the course of events at Anheuser-Busch, the producers of that great beer river. Taking A-B's annual production, making the appropriate conversions, and assuming that their production is spread evenly across the entire year, it has taken me ten years to consume what it takes them 53 seconds to produce.

Well, that's not bad! The idea of Anheuser-Busch's various plants devoted entirely to me, even for less than a minute, is really quite flattering.

Other measurements are more humbling. According to some statistics quoted in an article entitled "Sports and Suds" (Sports Illustrated, August 8, 1988), my 28 barrels would be less than half the beer consumed in Riverfront Stadium in Cincinnati during an average Reds game. What a kick in the teeth! Ten years and those slobs outdrink me during a 2-hour ballgame!

There must be other measures of my achievement. Perhaps this amount of beer could cover the state of Rhode Island to a depth of a quarter-inch or provide enough fluid to float a battleship. Let's see. If a beer can is 5 inches high, then 10,000 placed end to end is . . . 4,166 feet, not even a mile. At $3.50 per six-pack, I spent $5,833 on beer during this period. Had I invested in the stock market, I would be a rich man today.

> *The truth is that 10,000 beers is not really an impressive amount any more than ten years is an impressive length of time. What is impressive is the span of environments, personalities, and tastes that have been part of the 10,000. From the raucousness of the Great American Beer Festival to the anonymity of an airplane to the solitude of my own cellar. Beer Treks operate on the beer standard, as opposed to the gold standard, meaning that 10,000 doppelbocks, pilsners, stouts, and weizen beers translate into 100,000 memories. I am a wealthy man indeed.*

VFW, or even my own shrink, featured a good job, a beautiful wife, a nice home, and a bleak future . . . the American Dream!

I began to perceive, not surprisingly, that the entire country, if not the world, revolved around beer. There was much to learn, but only so much to be learned where I lived. I felt compelled to go out to where the barley was grown. I had to see steelworkers and cowboys chugging. I had to taste the beers of the tiny breweries whose exotic names rang through my sodden brain—Leinenkugel, Yuengling, Anchor, Dixie. I had to learn the Secret of the Suds. I had to go on a Beer Trek.

The idea of a Beer Trek is not new. A popular entertainment in seventeenth-century Germany was beer riding. A young noble loaded a cart with beer and left for the nearest duchy. After sharing the liquid refreshment with his host, he filled his barrels and headed for the next manor, taking with him any revelers who cared to come along. Their performance was repeated so long as people contributed beer and joined in the fun. The well-planned beer ride could last forever, the trip being over only when the beer ran out.

On an entirely unfrivolous level, I realized that by understanding a nation's beer drinking habits, one could understand the nation. The pieces slid into place. My wife, Laura, is, thankfully, a beer drinker who understands that civilizations rise and fall on their beer bellies. Our dog, Guinness (named for the world's finest stout), welcomed the chance to become the most beerwise dog in the annals of American canine history. Thus, it was settled. The three of us would cruise the land, learning about Beer Drinker Americanus, a noble and lofty goal. For a chariot we would ride in a well-used Chevy van with a mere 86,000 miles under its chassis.

If the Lord protects fools and tipplers, then surely The Great Beer Trek would be doubly blessed.

Explanation of the Trekker's Guide

This is the meat of the book, the factual information that allows the reader to plan a Beer Trek. Due to the continual changes in the beer business in the last decade, it is inevitably obsolete as soon as it is complete.

There are no "Order of the Trek" awards to distinguish brews that represent the highest expression of the brewing art. You will have to make those judgments for yourself (lucky you!). With pretension as common as water in today's burgeoning beer world, there is no need for yet another self-styled expert's opinion. In the section called "Buy 'Em If You Can Find 'Em," brews are highlighted that from a regional perspective are just plain interesting. Other features:

BREWERIES

All known breweries and branch plants are listed. Tour information and breweriana availability are included as the information was supplied by the brewery. Brands are listed only once, with the parent company, except in certain cases where the subsidiary is clearly identified with a specific brew. Brewery type is divided into the following categories:

National: *Brands available nationally.*

Independent regional: *A dying breed. Firm's primary products are available within a fixed radius from the brewery, although this is complicated by the increased popularity of contract brewing, whereby a regional brews beer for an independent contractor who might distribute it in an entirely different market from the regional brewer.*

Contract: *Many would-be microbrewers get their feet wet by hiring another firm to brew their beers until their own facility is constructed. Others are content to leave the brewing to others while they concentrate on marketing. Bona-fide micros tend to look down on contract brewers, but the truth is that some of the best beers available today are contract brews.*

Microbrewers: *The new generation. These specialize in handcrafted beers that are available in limited quantities.*

Pub breweries: *These are microbreweries whose products are available only on the premises. The line of distinction between micros and pub breweries is sometimes fuzzy as the micros put in a taproom and the brewpubs start to bottle.*

KINDRED SPIRITS

At one time beer fanatics were a lonely breed. But beer has become a respectable pastime for can aficionados, breweriana devotees, and suds swillers of all form or manner. They all have a common denominator: they like beer and welcome others of like inclination.

GREAT PLACES

No description, no addresses, just the cities and names of bona-fide shrines. Please note that breweries and brewpubs are generally not included; they are listed elsewhere. Their exclusion is due only to the fact that each of them automatically qualifies for inclusion. Anywhere the beer is fresh, the beer is good.

OF NOTE

Everything that did not fit—events, sources of brewing supplies, publications, sites of defunct breweries (RIP), and more.

2
THE
NEW
WORLD

BOSTON, MASSACHUSETTS, TO STRAFFORD, VERMONT
7 DAYS, 820 MILES ON THE ROAD

WHERE HAVE YOU GONE,
KING GAMBRINUS
New Bedford, Massachusetts

Thus was the garden tilled for the Fourth of July seed that would blossom into The Great Beer Trek. Another two years of preparation ensued; in fact, enough time elapsed that it became questionable whether the ship would ever set sail. Nonetheless, preparations began. I made up stationery and wrote letters to everyone in the beer business, from Augie Busch to Ed McMahon. I read every piece of beer-related literature I could find. I tasted every brew available locally. I bought a vehicle (a 1972 Chevrolet Beauville Sportsman with 86,000 miles) destined to become our noble steed, carrying us from beery highlight to lowlight. In short, I became like thousands of other beer fanatics across the country.

Eventually preparations were complete. The van was brewery ready. The itinerary was finalized. Laura and Guinness reported for final inspection. Now came the hardest part—quitting the job and thus cutting the umbilical cord to reality. Reactions included incredulity, sympathy, and pity. Most of the world, it seems, is entangled in an ethic that defines a quest to learn the Secret of the Suds as an exercise in frivolity.

Nothing could be closer to the truth.

An unforeseen twist occurred when we discovered some two weeks prior to departure that Laura was pregnant, an occurrence that would limit her consumption but not her enthusiasm. Oh well, at least there would always be a sober driver.

The Great Beer Trek started with a simple theory—that beer is important, and therefore learning about beer drinking customs and trends would reveal much about society. Minimally we wanted to visit all existing independent breweries and to hit as many highlights as possible in between. We wanted to learn how beer is made and what role it has played historically in America. Then we wanted to put this information together to see if the original theory was correct. There comes a point, however, when the planning must be put aside and the key inserted into the ignition.

On Debarkation Day the first order of business seemed clear enough: let's have a beer. It seemed to be appropriate to make our first stop at one of our long-time favorite watering holes, Jacob Wirth's in Boston. Jake's has changed little since opening in 1868. The place still has the right counterbalance of elegance and grime that allows both the politicians from the State House and the local rummies to feel equally at home. The waiters still wear tuxedos and starched aprons, and yet one need not feel guilty about spilling a few peanut shells from the elephant foot serving bowl. The fixtures are ancient, as are many of the waiters. Although other liquors are served, beer is the only suitable accompaniment for the fare at Jacob Wirth's. The menu relies heavily on unadorned and unmentionable parts of the pig.

I asked our waiter, a dignified old gent, about the beers served; one can choose between Jake's Special Light and Special Dark. He was noncommittal, saying that the manager did not want the brand of beer divulged, but he did reveal that it was a commercial brand locally available. The question obviously had piqued the interest of an employee who had spent many years serving a proud establishment, and he wanted to show off a little:

"Until a few years ago we served a beer specially brewed for us by Dawson. Now that was good beer."

I asked why they stopped serving Dawson.

"Why, they went out of business a few years ago."

I corrected him. I was an occasional Dawson drinker and had purchased a six-pack locally only a few weeks ago. The clouded look on the waiter's face foretold his confusion:

"I dunno, sir. I'm sure they went out of business five or six years ago."

I asked if he knew where the brewery was. Here was a perfect first adventure for the Beer Trek: to solve the mystery of the missing Dawson. We explained our mission to see, feel, and hear nothing but suds for the immediate future. The import of being the first official participant in The Great Beer Trek escaped him, but nonetheless he was polite in his response:

"The brewery was somewhere around here, but I don't know just where. I know who would, though." He fetched another vintage gentleman from behind the bar and explained the Beer Trek to him in terms that were more flattering than I would dare to have used.

"Sure," said the bartender. "New Bedford. That's where Dawson was. But they're gone now." I explained my recent purchase, a phenomenon to which no one could provide an explanation. A silence ended the conversation. It was obviously time for the Beer Trek to set off for New Bedford.

I used the transit time from Boston to the old whaling port of New Bedford to try to find out more about Dawson. The only reference to be found in my mobile library was this short entry in *One Hundred Years of Brewing*: "Benjamin and Joseph Dawson, in 1899, founded this firm, and put their first brew of ale and porter upon the market in May, 1900."

The only mention of any brewery in New Bedford was in an outdated (1976) edition of *Brewer's Digest Annual Buyers' Guide,* which listed a Forrest Brewery division of Rheingold.

Many passers-by and quizzical looks later, we found the one-time site of Dawson's. It proved to be the same address as Forrest. Completely confused, we sought out a liquor store where we might find a six-pack of Dawson's. At the third stop we struck pay dirt, until we read the fine print on the label, Dawson Brewing Company, Hammonton, New Jersey! The Great Confused Beer Trek, some eight hours away from home, consoled itself with its purchase of a six-pack. The mystery of Dawson's, makers of Jake Wirth's Special, would for the moment remain.

NO MATTER WHERE I'M GOING   Cranston, Rhode Island

The trip from New Bedford to Providence is pleasant in full bloom of spring. But when the brown has not yet turned to green, only the bare essentials of life are visible from a passing Beer Trek van. The rivers—Nemasket, Agawam, Passumpsic, Weweantic—provide a historic and geographic orientation. They flow south through the bogs and marshes of southern Massachusetts toward Buzzards Bay. They are tidal rivers whose mud-polished banks glisten and smell at low tide like the wall of an intestine.

The van bounces over roads potholed by the blizzard of '78 and lovingly preserved by the Massachusetts Department of Public Works. The setting is unmistakably and dramatically New England. I am moved to song, spare and simple like the landscape, designed for the untrained voice:

No matter where I'm going
I remember where I've been
And I still like best

The things that seem like home.
Seacoast in the rain, take me there
Green fields from a train, take me there
Take me there.
I can see the sunlight shining
Over Narragansett Bay,
So lift a glass, my friend
And talk to me of home,
Of home.

I do not know if this song is an adaptation of an old whaling tune or the brainchild of an advertising copywriter, but for years this was the theme of Narragansett Beer, a brew that claims to be New England's own. Whether or not the song sold beer, it makes one love New England.

Exposure to Narragansett propaganda started at an early age for me. Curt Gowdy was the announcer for the Red Sox during the lean years of the late 1950s and early 1960s when the home team consistently failed to fulfill our expectations. After every rally-ending double play hit into by Jackie Jensen or two-base error by Don "Double Dribble" Buddin, Curt's reassuring voice would say, "Hi, Neighbor, Have a 'Gansett," and we would remember it was only a game. For all its faults, Narragansett, like the Red Sox, was the home team.

Sighting the brewery provided us with immediate relief. In an era of faceless industrial parks, the brewery is welcome brick, blood-red and teeming with vitality, a perfect location for the creation of frothy lagers and tart ales. King Gambrinus, patron saint of brewers, overlooks what was once an ice pond, the source of necessary refrigeration, to extend the brewing season. Somewhere along the line a master planner filled it in and converted it into a parking lot. A circular stained glass window over the front door states the company policy, "Made with honor, sold on merit."

The Beer Engine

MANUAL ACTION CREATES SUCTION, WHICH PULLS A HALF PINT UP FROM THE CASK IN THE BASEMENT.

The Campaign for Real Ale

Consider it one of the most successful consumer movements of all time, and call it CAMRA—The Campaign for Real Ale.

The spark of CAMRA was genuine outrage. British beer drinkers in the early 1970s surveyed their lot and did not like what they saw. The major brewers were acquiring local brewers, dominating the taps in pubs, and squeezing out traditional, hand-drawn ales in favor of brews that were long on shelf life and eye appeal but lacking the quality that makes beer a beverage worth fighting for—life.

Real Ale is better described than served to Americans. Even the few hardy microbrewers that have dared to produce a true top fermented, English-style ale have quickly retreated to a beverage better suited to the Yank's soda pop concept of beer.

Real Ale is equal parts brewing methods and service. Fermented at high temperatures in open vats, Real Ale is stored in wooden barrels without the intervention of pasteurization, preservatives, or filtering. It is precious stuff, prone to contamination and spoilage unless maintained by a publican who appreciates the fragile nature of this commodity. The resulting brew is mild (in terms of alcoholic content) and flavorful, ranging in color from straw to burnt copper and in flavor from coal mine to fairy princess. Each draught deserves another, and another.

The success of CAMRA is readily apparent to the London visitor today, a decade and a half after the original group of beer drinkers gathered in their local, sipped their preferred ale, threw darts, and got pissed enough to take on the megabreweries. Nearly all pubs offer mild, bitter, and IPA (India Pale Ale) versions of traditional ale. Regional brands such as Ruddles and Greene King, once nearly extinct, are widespread. Most important, a glance around the pub at 10:00 P.M. on Friday night reveals a healthy number of quaffers clutching, with pride, their straight pint glasses of amber life. The beer drinker prevails.

No one has successfully translated either the pub experience or Real Ale to America. The closest cousin is the home brewer, that one-time felon who can now ply the trade with impunity. It is the home brewer who lurks in the cellar, defying the national brewers by working rituals with glass carboys, scrub brushes, malt, and hops. He toils to maintain cleanliness in an environment that seeks equally to prevent it. He holds the fruit of his labor up to the light and sips and marvels at the life in his glass. It is alive!

He admires the color again and listens to his beer. The bubbles whisper, "It just doesn't get any better than this."

On this day, however, the parking lot was empty. A truck driver standing idly by delivered the shocking news: the brewery was closed. Hopefully, temporarily. Production was coming out of the parent company Falstaff's more modern facility in Fort Wayne, Indiana. As to the fate of the Cranston brewery, the driver shrugged:

"They say they're going to reopen it . . ." His voice trailed off into the distance, making his lack of confidence obvious.

The first barrels of Narragansett were released to the public in December 1890. Twenty years later the company had become Rhode Island's largest brewer (225,000 barrels per year) with a thriving West Indies export business to supplement the New England trade. After repeal, theirs was the first beer back on the state market. Narragansett never looked back at local competition.

In the 1930s the firm was purchased by Carl and Rudolph Haffenreffer, prominent Boston brewers whose plans for an empire were cut short by prohibition. Once in Cranston, they began producing their former brands. In succeeding decades, as other local firms succumbed to the pressure of competition, the Haffenreffers were always around to pick up the pieces. Hanley, Croft, Dugan . . . many of the most prominent names in New England brewing found their lease on life in the Narragansett kettles. Still no sign of Dawson, however.

Eventually and inevitably time caught up with Narragansett. Antiquated equipment needed modernizing, unions demanded higher wages, and television provided national breweries with the means to market to the masses. In 1966 the Haffenreffers joined the swelling ranks of ex-family brewers and sold out to Falstaff. At that time Falstaff was a success phenomenon in the brewing industry, a burgeoning company and the leading brand in each of the thirty-eight states where it was sold.

But time has been unkind to Falstaff. The company is now owned by the same people who own General Brewing, a company as faceless as its name. Their business strategy revolves around buying distressed breweries, reducing

The Falstaff Story

At one time this company was the embodiment of success in the beer industry—the first national brand. Falstaff was the leading seller in each of the thirty-eight states in which it was sold. Hell, it even outsold Bud in St. Louis.

The plan was Machiavellian in its simplicity: buy faltering regional breweries, phase out the local brands in favor of inoffensive, bland Falstaff, especially formulated for the median taste, and use the efficiency of the mass media to deliver the message, "Your first one is never your last." Instead of a choice of a dry, hoppy ale or a spritzy pilsner, the beer drinker was offered a 12-ounce can, 12-ounce bottle, 16-ounce can, 16-ounce bottle, etc.

For a long time it seemed as if the Falstaff experiment would work. The brand

"frills" such as marketing expenses, and removing a fair amount of romance from the beer business. Is it any surprise that "New England's Own Beer" is now brewed in Indiana?

To General Brewing's credit, it is apparently more interested in selling beer than creating an empire. This means that Croft Ale, Narragansett Porter, Ballantine India Pale Ale, Haffenreffer Malt Liquor, and Pickwick Ale will be brewed so long as they can be sold. The beer drinker is richer for it, even if the native brews are coming from Fort Wayne rather than Cranston.

The Beer Trek van swung back onto Interstate 95, heading south. There was a prominent billboard greeting us with a hearty, "Hi, Neighbor, Have a 'Gansett," just as Curt Gowdy used to say it.

Someone should have told them the brewery was closed.

originated at the Lemp Brewery in St. Louis, a mere stone's throw from the Anheuser-Busch cathedral. The Griesediecks, a long-time brewing family, took over the company and formulated the national strategy. Before long Falstaff was the third largest and fastest growing brewery in America.

What went wrong? Certainly the obstinate grit of the beer drinker was a factor. More probably, other brewers followed the Falstaff lead and did it a little better. Budweiser, Schlitz, and Pabst built regional facilities that enabled them to compete locally. The TV networks would sell time to anyone. Before long the other breweries developed the promotional techniques that enabled them to take advantage of the efficiencies of national advertising. Falstaff, the great consumer, became one of the consumed. But for a while they were indisputably the hottest show in town.

FROM HULL TO ETERNITY   New Haven, Connecticut

The passions of an intimate relationship come bubbling to the surface when men consider their brews. As in any love affair, there is a courtship period after the initial meeting when a beer's wispy hoppiness or nutty richness is imprinted midway between the drinker's brain and throat. The period of devotion may be months, years, or a lifetime. Some beers are good wives, sharing equally times of exaltation and defeat, providing comfort and companionship, leaving us alone when we need to be left alone. Others are mercurial. They beguile us with tricks, and we become fast friends. As the dazzle fades, so does the marriage. Our eyes wander, we cheat. Soon we walk away, a new brand in hand.

We wear beer as badges. The Cape Verdean fisherman who operates a boat out of New Bedford may drink nothing but familiar 'Gansett on tap whether it is brewed in Cranston or Fort Wayne. His son who drives a sanitation truck for the city may order his wife to buy Bud or Schlitz so that his buddies will not think him a cheapskate when they come over to watch a Bruins' game. His son, a college freshman, buys the cheapo budget brand when away and Michelob at home (when Dad is paying.) The cycle is complete.

I returned to the land of Hull and my bright college years for selfish reasons. As the least expensive beer available, it was the natural first choice as the designated beverage on the mixer scene. Whenever social committees met, the question would be raised whether to serve premium beer or Hull's at college functions. The pros and cons would be brought forth in due parliamentary procedure and argued as strenuously as any debate before the political union. In the end would be left the inescapable fact that if we bought Hull's Export, we could buy much, much, much more beer. Case closed.

"Hull's Export Piss" it was called, but we drank it willingly, liberally, and enthusiastically. On a date, however, or at lunch with a professor, we would snub these simple cans with their low-rent graphics in favor of beers more befitting our fledgling status in the world. We were young, vain, arrogant, mostly young. Now older, wiser, and more worldly, mostly older, I was in a position to make up for earlier thoughtless remonstrances on "Hull's Export Piss."

The early morning hours are arguably New Haven's finest. Thieves, pimps, junkies, and politicians rest in their lairs, while college students dreamily snooze away the excess of the night before. In four years I had seen New Haven in the cleansing stillness of dawn only in the bleary aftermath of an all-nighter. This morning, cruising once-familiar streets, I thought perhaps my memory had been unfair.

The Beer Trek pushed through the schizophrenic downtown looking for Congress Street and the Hull Brewery. Much of New Haven was leveled in the early sixties, decaying shops and storefronts replaced with cement fortress department stores and parking garages. The reconstruction, which enabled the suburbanite to commute or shop without encountering living beings (save through the windshield of an air-conditioned car), was initially hailed as a landmark of urban renewal. For the residents of New Haven, especially the black communities, the moatlike access roads and one-way streets of urban renewal neatly penned their neighborhoods into concentration camps.

We asked directions of a starched and pressed young black man well prepared for another day of upward mobility. "Congress Street?" He sounded a suspicious note. "What part of Congress Street?" The brewery, we replied, confident of the prominence of this local landmark.

He nodded, told us to take a right, a left, and a right, cross over the access road, then proceed up Congress Street until we came to the brewery. "You can't miss it," he assured us. "It looks like it's been bombed." Bombed? Traffic was backing up, so we yelled a quick thanks over our shoulders. But the seed had been planted. Bombed?

Congress Street winds through a neighborhood known as The Hill. Originally an ethnic neighborhood (Italian?), "urban renewal" transformed it to exclusively poor and exclusively black. Even morning is not kind to The Hill. No dew glistens. Children and winos people streets joylessly. The frivolity of The Great Beer Trek produced a flash of guilt, obscuring our nobility of purpose. Suddenly a gigantic glass of beer loomed several hundred yards ahead. The billboard was attached to a large brick building that dominated the street for a city block. As we came nearer we read the line on the billboard, "Connecticut's only brewery."

Omigod.

The brewery had once been handsome. A noble Gambrinus, unmolested on a perch at the building's highest gable, proffered a toast to The Hill. Although the billboard was freshly painted, the building had experienced the equivalent of the bombing of Dresden. Windows were blown out, parking lots had become repositories for abandoned junk cars, doorways were boarded up, and the loading platforms gaped like open wounds, exposing brewery bowels to the entire world.

The air smelled faintly of malt and urine, a stale, dead odor well suited to the surroundings. For hundreds of feet in either direction, the streets were dusted with beer labels, testifying to a wild Friday night confetti party. I picked up a label: "Malta Caribe . . . pasteurizada. A carbonated cereal beverage brewed from water, malt, corn, corn and invert syrup, hops and caramel color." Not even beer. No self-respecting brewery brews a soft drink if they can brew beer. This is what Hull had been reduced to before succumbing. "Cerveceria Caribe, 820 Congress Street, New Haven, CT 06519." The venture did not warrant admission of the company name. This had been the final gasp of a terminally ill business.

The building was intact yet beyond hope. Not long ago that production line had been humming, but the ensuing disintegration had been swift and lethal. I resisted the temptation to go through the open doors, a wise move when we were subsequently apprehended by three men in a city maintenance truck. Expecting a snarl in reply, I explained defensively that we were just

harmless beer freaks taking pictures of the brewery exterior. "What's The Great Beer Trek?" asked the crew boss, a round, balding man of forty-five making a gesture toward the sign on our van. We explained and were rewarded by an unexpected outpouring of friendliness. "Wanna look around inside?" he asked. We did not need a second invitation. "I hope you like bottle caps," he said with a cryptic smirk.

Most of the bottling house equipment was intact, the components deemed of no value by human and animal scavengers. Labels blanketed every horizontal surface, with unthrown bundles waiting for the next party. Some harkened sadly to brews never again to be tasted—Hull's Export Lager, Hull's Bock, Hull's Cream Ale.

Beer experts have spoken highly of these brews. Michael Weiner in his *Taster's Guide to Beer* (Macmillan, 1977) calls Hull's Cream Ale "a real sleeper," while James Robertson's *The Great American Beer Book* (Warner Books, 1980) rates the export lager "one of the best lightly hopped American pilsners."

As for the bottle caps, the crew boss was right—there were passageways where the bottle caps were two feet deep. Footing was simultaneously treacherous and comic. The dim setting was perfect for a horror movie.

"My uncle worked here forty-two years, then just like that it's gone," said our tour guide, a young city worker in his late teens. He punctuated the observation by throwing a handful of caps across a room already knee deep. I asked if he had been a Hull's drinker. "Nah. My uncle said it was good beer, but no one around here drank it much. Said it gave you the shits." I flashed back to Sunday mornings after excessive Saturday nights of encounters of the Hull kind. I had made similar comments when it was the amount, not the quality of the beer, that was at fault.

Outside the boss was telling Laura his opinions on local government. Like any other good city worker, he was not overly anxious to get down to work. "They're going to tear this down. You ask me, it doesn't make much sense. Look around here. This area's crap . . . just a bunch of crap. This brewery's the only decent thing left. They tear this down, sell off the brick, then put up one of these housing projects which won't be built half as good. It's a shame. This building's historical. They made beer here more'n a hundred years." He looked at us for a reaction, but we were still too shell-shocked to register emotion.

"Been gone over pretty good in there, hasn't it?"

"Yeah."

"Yeah. Anything worth anything is long gone. Mazinni here's uncle worked forty-two years in this place."

"Lotta good it did him," piped in Mazinni.

The boss surveyed the surrounding neighborhood. Two little black kids played in the refuse of the labels. Most of the nearby homes were worse off than the brewery. The crew boss knew if he did not say something, it would be time to start work. "It doesn't make sense. This building's good for another hundred years . . ."

It was time for The Great Beer Trek to move on.

We bid adieu.

A CONNECTICUT COWBOY IN KING GAMBRINUS'S COURT
Western Connecticut

From New Haven a stunned Beer Trek turned inland. The morning had soured, beer dregs from last night's party. No need to search deeply for the cause of Hull's ignominious demise. I confess, I murdered Hull. Who scorned the local beer in favor of the more prestigious national brands and imports? Who made jokes about Hull's "Export Piss"? Who assumed there would always be a local beer associated with old school days?

Who?

Me.

For a Beer Trek interpreting America in terms of its brews, so far we had encountered little booze for thought. Could the truth of this odyssey have come so quickly, so easily, and so depressingly? Perhaps there is no beer to trek for. Perhaps we would crisscross landscapes of plastic, neon, and parking lots, meeting only lobotomized swillers of Miller, Schlitz, and Bud.

We continued inland, watching Connecticut's personality change from megalopolis to New England. This diplomatic state maintains schizophrenic gentility in the face of torn loyalties. Is it a suburban and recreational adjunct of New York City or a bona-fide rock and winter piece of Yankee real estate? In the town of Derby we stopped for a sandwich and a beer. Two men at the bar were vehemently arguing the relative merits of the Yankees and Red Sox, an ancient battle whose bloodiest field is Connecticut. The Yankee diehard drank Schaefer, the Red Sox booster Narragansett. Perhaps there was an order to the cosmos. We felt a little better.

Will Anderson's loyalties are worn on his forehead, sleeve, and bumper of his car. ("This is Red Sox Country!") Will Anderson is the dean of American beer writers. Protocol demanded the Beer Trek pay respect and homage.

Will Anderson's five beer books concern breweriana, a term invented to describe the realm of beer advertising collectibles—trays, calendars, lithographs, openers, bottles, cans, signs—anything on which the brewer has affixed his name. As much as anyone else, Will Anderson's work has elevated and defined the field.

As one paying homage, I felt entitled to a gray-haired statesman who could spin endless tales of brewing lore. On the trip from New Haven to western Connecticut, I prepared a list of formal questions designed to provoke thoughtful answers from the contemplative person of my imagination. The list never got out of my notebook.

Will Anderson stands over six feet with brown curly hair, a mustache, and the build of an athlete. ("You should see me on the tennis court or softball field.") He is not modest. He greeted us in baggy white cutoffs, a beer in one hand, a bowl of salad in the other, and french dressing dripping off his mustache. After a hard day on the job as marketing director for a New York publishing company, on top of commuting time, he was not about to put on airs, even for The Great Beer Trek. He made us feel right at home.

Will had a simple beer can collection when he first met his wife, Sonja. Then he graduated to the hard stuff—breweriana. Each new phase of collecting was entered with the uniquely Andersonian form and gusto. As a result they have one of the finest overall breweriana collections in the United States. Not surprisingly, Will's interests go beyond beer to such areas as baseball and rock and roll. In each case, his zeal for collecting is a testament to his passion.

Will's face mirrors the animation in his voice as he digresses from beer long enough to tell us about the excitement of the early days of rock and roll.

He never allows our beer mugs to empty fully. Although one of the better-known beer people in America, Will is not a beer snob. He serves us Fort Schuyler, a budget product of the F. X. Matt Brewing Co., Utica, New York. "This is from one of my favorite breweries," he tells us. As the night wears on, we find the list of Will's favorite breweries to be continually expanding. Fort Schuyler has a fruity taste, clean and not at all unpleasant. Will tells us that this beer can still be had for 99 cents a six-pack. Everyone's mug is topped off and the remainder of the bottle balanced precariously in the freezer. Sonja begins telling us about the perils of Life with Will.

"It can get embarrassing sometimes, especially in restaurants . . ."

Will interrupts. "I order the local beer wherever I am. I always order the local beer. If they don't have any, I ask why not."

"There have been times," continues an unruffled Sonja, "when we've walked out of the restaurant because all they have is Bud, Miller, or Schlitz."

"I'll be damned if I'm going to drink one of the national brands," Will begins stoking up. "I'm not going to support those companies. I'll drink a foreign beer before I'll drink a Miller or a Schlitz. I don't even like Heineken, but I'll order one before any of those others."

The phone rings, but before he answers it, Will directs a speech to me: "In your travels I hope you spend some time asking people why they don't drink the local beer. People with a great brewery right in their own town will drink bland fizzwater from the nationals, and pay more for it . . . Hello."

The conversation is swallowed by the phone, and the three of us in the kitchen eavesdrop on a one-way conversation that sounds like the hatching of some nefarious plot. "Just leave the boxes in back. I'll have the stuff by the weekend. Don't worry about the money. I'll hit you the next time I see you."

When Will rejoins us, I ask if perhaps he has another pastime about which he has not yet informed us. "Oh, that," he says with a laugh toward the phone. "My favorite beer is Stegmaier, made by the Lion Brewery down in Wilkes-Barre, Pennsylvania. I'm the unofficial distributor in this area. A lot of people around here have gotten hooked on it." Will tells about the time he was on the television show, "To Tell the Truth." At the end of the questioning, he was asked the inevitable, "Which beer is best?" to which he answered "Stegmaier." In the following week the brewery received more than two hundred requests for their beer. Will has done his part for local breweries.

More beer is brought out, the old poured atop the new, even though different brands are served. The same qualities that ensure that no one will offer Will a waiter's job at the Ritz ensure that he will never find himself out of place at a backyard barbecue, a post-softball get-together, or a can collector's convention. The second beer is Koehler from a brewery scheduled for a Beer Trek visit in Erie, Pennsylvania. "Don't bother," Will tells me, "they've just closed their doors. Another one bites the dust." I am anxious to taste this brew, but Will obscures the issue by splashing some Fort Schuyler into my mug.

Every room in the Anderson house features breweriana, even the bath-room, where a lithograph of a stern-featured maiden stares down, promoting constipation. The crowning glory of the house is a barnlike addition designed by Will and financed by the success of *The Beer Book* (Pyne Press, 1973). The vaulted ceilings and walls are obscured by displays of bottles, cans, signs, trays, posters, and other beeraphernalia. Most collectors of Will Anderson's magnitude store their treasures in a warehouse for security reasons, but Will is adamant about enjoying his collection. "When it gets to the point where I can't enjoy it," he states simply, "I'll sell it."

Will shows us several trays acquired during a recent vacation to New Bedford (the Andersons tend to choose vacation spots depending upon the proximity to old brewery sites and Fenway Park). The trays are splendid ad-vertising pieces from defunct local breweries, including Dawson's. Each ac-quisition has its own story of dusty back rooms and shady antique dealers. It is clearly the chase, not the kill, that motivates Will.

Between dashes to the kitchen for more beer, we hear about Will's early days in the hobby. No organizations or publications had yet formed to let practitioners know that other collectors shared a pursuit that normal people

"WHO WANTS THE HANDSOME WAITER" SIGN. ALSO A TRAY.

HAMPDEN BREWING CO., 1934

ENAMEL TRAY

DAWSON'S, ISSUED SOON AFTER REPEAL.

Breweriana, COLL. ANDERSON

regarded as being beyond the lunatic fringe. Will started while a student at Cornell. He and a roommate made weekend runs to different brewing towns to procure new beer cans. Beer would be brought back from Baltimore, Boston, or Philadelphia and shared with fraternity brothers on the promise that all cans be bottom opened and returned. Ingenious, even illegal ploys, were used to get new and more exotic cans. Once Will and his roommate drafted a letter ("a masterpiece of commercial copy-writing" he still calls it) to all fellow fraternity chapters around the country. The letter explained that a local beer distributor was staging a contest to see who could collect the greatest number of beer cans. The winner would receive a stereo, an item desperately needed by dear old Phi Beta Delta, or whomever.

The response was spectacular as fraternity chapters rallied to the assistance of a music-deprived brother. Will and his roommate were awash in beer cans from coast to coast. They had made one mistake, however: they had requested only a single can of each type, and now there was no fair way for the two collectors to divide the booty. Finally it was decided that the only honorable way to settle was on the field of combat, specifically a bowling alley. For each ten-point differential in score, the winning bowler could take a can from the pile.

"Being the better bowler I ended up with all the cans," Will chuckles without a trace of humility. His roommate, now a prominent West Coast breweriana collector, doubtless has his own version of the story.

Back in the kitchen, Will announces final call. Although he was still going at 78 rpm, tomorrow would bring another long commute into the city. We took our cue and invited the Andersons to stop by on their next trip to Fenway Park. We said goodnight. As we walked into the night Will's voice drifted after us: "Hey . . . you know the bricks on this walk are from the old Ballantine Brewery."

MOUNTAIN BREW Strafford, Vermont

The fate of Dawson, we had learned from Will, was not unlike hundreds of other local brewers. Prohibition had been survived and even World War II, but the brewer in the postwar era found himself competing in an entirely new world. The big brewers had successfully shipped their product across the ocean to homesick and thirsty GIs (Will had shown us some of the specially designed olive-drab, camouflaged cans). The prospect of shipping across America was no longer imposing.

The country was suddenly more affluent, more cosmopolitan, more mobile. Every home had a refrigerator into which cans fit more easily than bottles. The bigger brewers were able to make the expensive packaging changes. With good, fresh beer available in the fridge, why go to the tavern?

Every household had an automobile. The corner grocer was displaced by the "super" market who could negotiate volume discounts from the big brewers. And eventually every home had a television set. Now the national brewer could deliver his sales message into the intimacy of your own home with more effectiveness than the home-town concern. The fate of the local brewer was sealed. Dawson's lingered until 1966 when it ceased brewing. Their local and loyal consumership was gracelessly sold to a succession of other local brewers struggling to maintain volume levels by purchasing the hard-earned drinkership of less fortunate counterparts. Eastern Brewing in Hammonton, New Jersey, was merely the latest and perhaps last home of Dawson.

The sober reality of the brewery pogrom weighed heavily on The Great Beer Trek as we pulled into the visitors' parking lot of the gleaming steel and tile plant of Anheuser-Busch in Merrimack, New Hampshire. As often happens when one is in a bad mood, the resulting outburst is spontaneous and arbitrary. In this case the unwitting recipient of our abuse was the squeaky-clean, collegiate-looking wimp conducting our tour. He recited his script flawlessly, yet how was he to know that among the tourists in his group were beer trekkers unfairly blaming Anheuser-Busch for the ill fortune of hundreds of local brewers from coast to coast? His recitation of the brewing process was repeatedly interrupted by pointedly embarrassing questions. "Which of the fifty-nine approved FDA additives are contained in Budweiser?" "Has Anheuser-Busch ever employed predatory pricing strategies in order to drive local brewers out of business?" "How much does Anheuser-Busch pay Ed McMahon to push their products on TV?" The guide responded with suitably innocuous gibberish.

After the tour, we sat in the neo-Bavarian plastic splendor of the hospitality room. Acting petty never makes one feel good. And one feels even smaller when one accepts the hospitality and free beer of the recently abused host immediately afterward. It was a low, depressing moment for voyageurs who had set out to find the Secret of the Suds and who now apparently had found that there was no Secret left to find.

"Let's get out of here," I said to Laura.

We were now heading north into the Green Mountains and the hinterlands. Our next stop was Strafford, Vermont, where we were scheduled to meet with Tim Matson, coauthor of a simple tome on home brewing called *Mountain Brew* (Miller Pond Books, Strafford, Vermont, 1975). Would we arrive only to find his rustic cabin to be in the same lame state as Hull or Narragansett?

The serenity of the passing scenery gave time to reflect on the recent stop in Merrimack. One had to give Anheuser-Busch its grudging due. First, the company did not have to give tours at all; that it chose to do so showed a laudable concern for the people who consume their products. Second, the tour was well organized, educational, and professionally executed even if conducted by a callow, pimply tour guide rather than a ruddy-faced brewmaster. And last, the beer is good. One may not like the type of beer that Budweiser is, but for its type there is no better.

The tour depicted a brewery that takes no shortcuts in the brewing process, a series of steps finite in number but infinite in their variation. Grain, preferably barley, is harvested. The grain is allowed to germinate under controlled conditions and then roasted to arrest the process. The grain is steeped in water to extract the soluable sugars, flavored with hops, strained, and cooled. Yeast, an organic mass of minute fungi, is added and multiplies itself by feeding on the available starches and sugars, giving off carbon dioxide and alcohol as by-products. The resulting liquid is beer.

One can laugh at the homespun naiveté of *Mountain Brew,* but to do so is to misunderstand the intentions of this modest book. Once one has the proper orientation, or what Tim Matson would call "spirit," then one can laugh at *Mountain Brew.* Tim Matson confided that commercial wine- and beer-making supply shops hated his book and would not sell it. In his words, "They didn't like *Mountain Brew* because it was against all the bullshit. You know, I've been down the road with all those imported malts and fancy equipment, but here we were just getting loaded on Blue Ribbon Malt you could buy at the grocery store, making really sleazy beer, and having a great time. The beer wasn't great, but it was pretty good."

The book, or more accurately the booklet, was compiled and produced by Tim with no outside financing but lots of help from his friends. It was produced by a local women's collective who knew as much about graphics as Tim did about home brew. The cover was adapted from a drawing by a nine-year-old girl. Tim describes the experience: "It was a very pure thing. No deals, no contracts, no calculations involved. Everyone just grooved along with the idea."

To describe *Mountain Brew* as a guide to home brewing would be misleading. Rather it is a description of a life-style for which home brew is a spiritual center. From the craftsman's standpoint, the book is oversimplified. A hydrometer, the instrument used to measure the unfermented sugars in the wort, is described as "made out of glass" with "numbers and lines on it." Some readers might object to a philosophy typified by statements like, "With food stamps I could make big batches of beer." And some passages in the book defy comprehension:

Technology is going down so fast you can't keep up with it. Or maybe it's the humidity. The greenhouse effect. Except rock. People try hard not to care about the rocks. Since rocks were there first, before the Indians. What do we do with rocks? Gouge them out and run highways through them. Those rocks never grow any corn or hops. And corn and hops make beer.

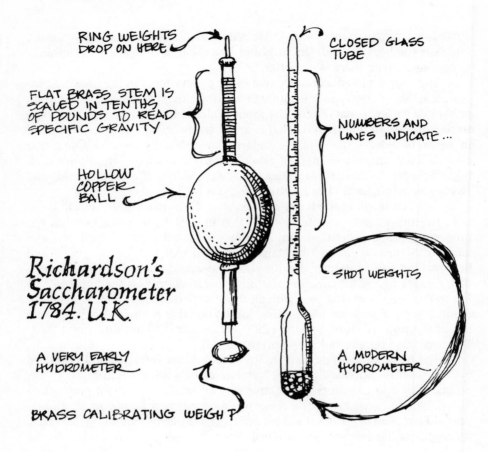

RING WEIGHTS DROP ON HERE

CLOSED GLASS TUBE

FLAT BRASS STEM IS SCALED IN TENTHS OF POUNDS TO READ SPECIFIC GRAVITY

NUMBERS AND LINES INDICATE...

HOLLOW COPPER BALL

Richardson's Saccharometer 1784. U.K.

A VERY EARLY HYDROMETER

SHOT WEIGHTS

A MODERN HYDROMETER

BRASS CALIBRATING WEIGHT

Its shortcomings should not keep one from enjoying the unique perspective of *Mountain Brew*. What the contributors lack in writing skill (in their defense it must be said that no pretensions of literary proficiency were ever claimed), they make up for in ingenuity. Anyone discouraged with the blandness of American beers can look to *Mountain Brew* to learn about brewers who concoct experimental brews with Postum, wormwood, Maxim (to get a beer with caffeine), buckwheat groats, steak bones, chicken heads, maple syrup, and burdock root. There are no mysteries about beer to the Green Mountain brewers. A simple product results from a simple process, which the brewer controls. Some experiments result in improved beers, some in swill, but all will be consumed in a society that cannot afford waste. In Vermont, where winters are harsh and money is scarce, home brew plays the role of balm, nutrient, and sacrament. The role would not be understood by the president of Miller or Schlitz. One of the contributors to *Mountain Brew* comments on beer's elevation to the status of a luxury beverage by saying this about Budweiser:

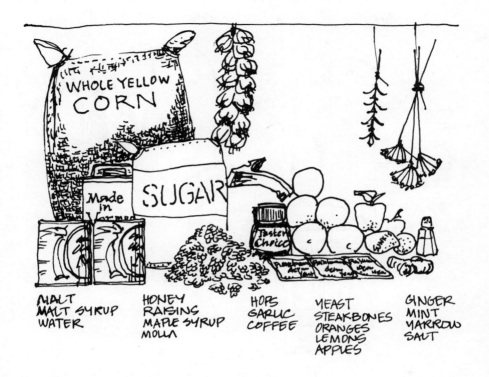

MALT
MALT SYRUP
WATER

HONEY
RAISINS
MAPLE SYRUP
MOLA

HOPS
GARLIC
COFFEE

YEAST
STEAKBONES
ORANGES
LEMONS
APPLES

GINGER
MINT
YARROW
SALT

You know why everybody drinks Budweiser? Because they see the ads and they see the "King of Beers" and they think that if they can't have a little piece of the action at least they can drink the most expensive beer. They may never drive a Cadillac, but Budweiser!

Somewhere an advertising executive reads this, pours a second martini, and gloats over a job well done. In Vermont a flannel-shirted farmer sips on a second pint and feels the pain of a day of hard labor slipping away. Up there, they would say he is "blissed."

Tim Matson, author of *Mountain Brew,* is very much the mountain man on a smaller, more delicate scale. He wears the characteristic plaid wool shirt over a green jersey, blue jeans, and well-worn boots. He has dark, medium-length hair with a few strands of gray, the sign of the transition period between unadulterated youth and middle age. He is polite, friendly, and unpretentious although initially wary of the Beer Trek. An old Vermont proverb says, "Beware of strangers in vans, particularly if their dog is black."

Tim offers tea, which we accept. His first batch of beer of the spring is just fermenting, so he had none to share. We sniff and taste the bubbling wort. It's going to be good. We talk about commercial beers. Tim's favorite is Narragansett Porter served on draft at the local roadhouse. He also likes

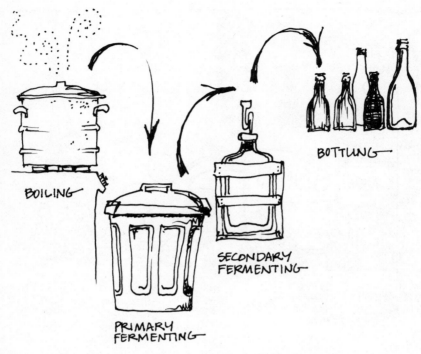

BOILING

PRIMARY FERMENTING

SECONDARY FERMENTING

BOTTLING

I can make my own beer!

Beck's and Busch, the latter not for its taste but for the claim of "no artificial anything." He is suspicious of any claims to purity made by commercial brewers and suggests that we make this a topic of Beer Trek investigation. *"Mountain Brew* was a purity trip, because we all realized how overdosed all the food was. We were trying to get away from all that, to have some control over our lives, some order."

Tim's first experience with home brewing was before he came to Vermont. He and some boarding school friends took cider, added raisins and Fleischmann's yeast, and stored the concoction in their closet. The inevitable explosion occurred on Sunday morning, just before chapel. Tim and his friends had no choice but to show up reeking of home brew. He laughs at the memory. "I think in my subconscious there had always been a feeling of rebellion associated with home brew. Home brewing is rebellion. It is for people who like to get high and people who like to have ceremony. Two pints and you're blissed. The gratification of making home brew is much different than, say, pottery."

Tim tells us about his early days in Vermont, when home brewing played as important a role in daily life as gardening or woodcutting. He and his lady brewed batches of 15 gallons at a time. Friends were pressed into service, especially at bottle washing time. They wound up drinking more than they helped, but that was part of the process. Home brew was used as a form of barter, as no one in the country had any money. It also ranked as the #1 mountain folk house present. Working on the house, doing the garden, fixing the car: these were all passages of life accompanied by the ritual of beer. "Home brewing is like making bread. It's not a matter of knowing how. Many people try it once, then never again. You have to be into the kneading of the dough. Home brewing can be very boring. You have to be into your zen thing—hanging around the kitchen, washing bottles—it's work, and you have to do it with the Spirit."

Head and antlers above the rest.

North of the Border

Free trade has already hit the beer world. Some say you can taste it in the beer. One of the pleasures of crossing the border has long been the availability of beers that offer a masculine appeal appropriate to Sergeant Preston of the Yukon. Now the same exotica is available at the corner store. The Moose is loose, and while familiarity has not bred contempt, another of life's small pleasures is a relic of the past.

Are we better off? It is a question to ponder while sipping a Molson Golden in a Holiday Inn (where the definition of good beer was once Miller Lite served in a frosted mug) while watching Wayne Gretsky slap a puck around for the Los Angeles Kings. Something is disconcertingly out of place here. Add to the equation that Budweiser and Miller High Life are now popular brands in Canada and that nearly all of the Canadian brewers are putting out light versions of their hearty brews. Some say the rivers run faster. Yeah, right. Gimme another Molson.

As for other sudsworthy trends, Canada is squarely in the forefront. The microbrewing and brewpub scenes are active, with Vancouver and Toronto firmly placed among the top ten beer drinking environments in North America. On the negative side, access to beer, from both a cost and availability standpoint, is so limited that beer drinking is becoming a province of the rich. The exhilaration at finding a Brewer's Outlet that carries Upper Canada Bock and Conners Best Bitter is tempered by paying the bill. Even accounting for the exchange rate, be prepared for sticker shock.

Moosehead Lite? Sergeant Preston would hardly approve.

The tea is now gone, and Tim produces a six-pack of Beck's, that salty brew from the port town of Bremen, Germany, which we proceed to devour. The afternoon of the warmest day so far in the spring slips behind us. It becomes impossible to imagine how depressed we were on the morning of this same day. The conversation turns philosophical and then whimsical. The point to life, we somehow agree, is to drink good beer. Towards this end Tim draws up a map to a local roadhouse and promises to meet us later on. There, he promises, this truth will be self-evident.

Trekker's Guide to the New World

The ultimate combination—raw seafood, Red Sox baseball, and great beer—prevails. The Yankee–Red Sox rivalry is undiminished, even if 'Gansett is in its death throes and the beer served under the grandstand is—get this—Stroh Light. There is still a sharp dividing line that bisects this turf.

The sea, alas, is an open sewer, thanks to the Massachusetts Miracle, a phrase that is likely to stick in our craws for some time to come. Another tradition was lost when the Australians won the America's Cup, and the race was held in places like San Diego and Lake Havasu City, Arizona. Newport, however, has not missed a beat, and if you are lucky enough to find a place on a fantail in Narragansett Bay on a warm July evening, you will find the beer selection better than ever. Micros and a bewildering array of imports ensure that even the local 7-11 offers more than Bud and Miller.

The last decade has produced substantial gains for the suds swiller. Microbrewers ply the coast, clipper ships on a foaming sea, bringing the yuppified, health conscious, neo-Yankee his beer the way he wants it: fresh, unpasteurized, and foil collared.

The New World features new brews and exciting places for consumption. (The only drawback is that in too many of them you will feel out of place without a jacket and tie. The common man is all but dead in the New World.)

CONNECTICUT

★ The Connecticut Brewing Co., 175 Main St., Hartford, CT 06106
Type: Contract
Brands: Nathan Hale Golden Lager, "Meg 'n Hale"

KINDRED SPIRITS

Beer Brewers of Central Connecticut, c/o Judy Lawrence, Box 511, Marion, CT 06444
Underground Brewers' Club of South-Eastern Connecticut, c/o Pat Baker, 11 Riverfield Dr., Weston, CT 06883
Can-Ecticut Red Fox Chapter (BCCA), c/o Patrick Rogers, 25 Maplewood Ave., Westport, CT 06880

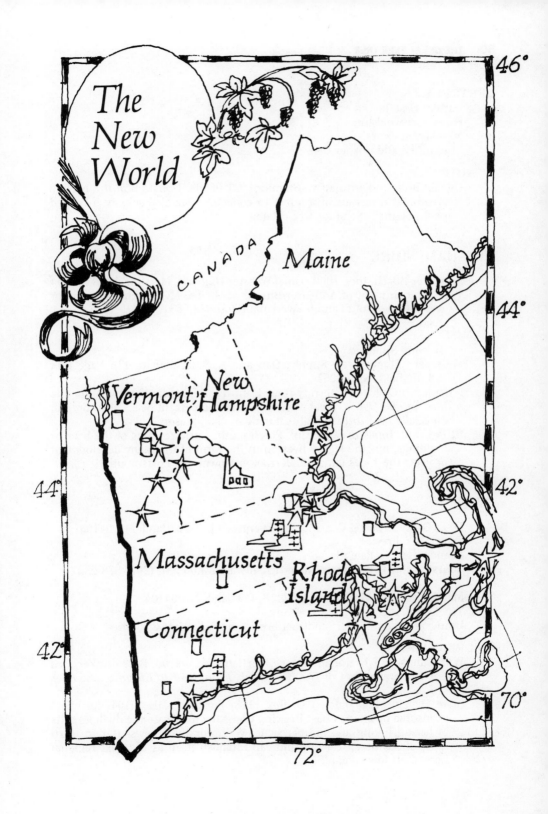

GREAT PLACES
>   Darien: Post Tavern
>   Essex: Griswold Inn
>   New Haven: Mory's
>   Union City: Old Corner Cafe

OF NOTE
>   Donald Bull, 20 Fairway Dr., Stamford, CT 06903. Donald Bull is a prolific creator of materials of interest to collectors. He also sells beer-related books by mail. Send for free catalog.

NEW HAMPSHIRE

> ★ Anheuser-Busch, Inc., 1000 Daniel Webster Highway, Merrimack, NH 03054
> Type: Branch plant of Anheuser-Busch, St. Louis, MO. Contact locally for availability of tours and breweriana: (603) 889-6631.

OF NOTE
>   Brewing Supplies
>   Jasper's Home Brew Supply, Dan and Nancy Callahan, 116 Page Rd., Litchfield, NH 03051
>   Dartmouth College Fraternity Row, Hanover. Reputedly the model for the film *Animal House*. Ideal point to observe adolescent beer consumption, especially on Saturday nights during football season.
>   (RIP) Frank Jones Brewing Co., Portsmouth. Little remains of the beer or buildings, but the legacy lives on in the form of the many development projects the Jones family undertook in downtown Portsmouth.

MAINE

> ★ D. L. Geary Brewing Co., Inc., 38 Evergreen Dr., Portland, ME 04103
> Type: Microbrewery
> Brands: Geary's Pale Ale
> Tours: Available by appointment, usually after 3:00 P.M. (207) 878-2337

> ★ Maine Coast Brewing, P.O. Box 1118, Portland, ME 04104
> Type: Contract
> Brands: Portland Lager (contract brewed by F. X. Matt Co., Utica, NY)

KINDRED SPIRITS
>   Will Anderson, 7 Bramhall Terrace, Portland, ME 04103. Beer drinker, Red Sox fan, and author of *The Beer Book, From Beer to Eternity,* and *Beer U.S.A.*
>   State O'Maine Pig, oinc., P.O. Box 1118, Portland, ME 04104. An effort sponsored by Maine Coast Brewing Company to elevate the dual pursuits of beer drinking and pig barbecue. Write for their newsletter to learn more about how New England can establish itself as the next regional hotbed of slow cookin'.

GREAT PLACES
> Portland: Three Dollar Dewey's

MASSACHUSETTS

★ Boston Beer Co., 30 Germania St., Boston, MA 02130
Type: Contract microbrewer
Brands: Samuel Adams Boston Lager, Lightship Lager (contract brewed by Pittsburgh Brewing Co., Pittsburgh, PA)
Tours: Starting after opening of new brewery, now under construction
Breweriana: T-shirts, posters, caps, coasters, etc.
Slogans: "The Best Beer in America," "The Beer Lover's Light Beer"

★ Commonwealth Brewing Co., 85 Merrimac St., Boston, MA 02114
Type: Pub brewery
Brands: Celtic, Winter-Warmer, Ginger Beer, Commonwealth Gold, Amber, Bitter

★ Mass. Bay Brewing Co., 306 Northern Ave., Boston, MA 02210
Type: Microbrewery
Brands: Harpoon Ale
Tours: Tues., Fri., Sat., 1:00 P.M.

★ Northampton Brewery, Ltd., Brewster Court Bar and Grill, 11 Brewster Ct., P.O. Box 791, Northampton, MA 01060
Type: Pub brewery
Brands: Northampton Lager, Amber, Golden (pilsner), Weizen, and Pile Driver (dark lager)
Tours: Sat., 2:00 P.M.
Breweriana: Coasters, table tents, T-shirts

KINDRED SPIRITS
> Boston Wort Processors Homebrewers Club, c/o Steve Stroud, 15 Dunbar Ave., Medford, MA 02115
> Cape Cod Chapter (BCCA), Ralph Whitcher, 74 Emerson St., Rockland, MA 02370
> Pickwick Chapter (BCCA), Mike Weiss, 1 Endicott St., East Weymouth, MA 02189

GREAT PLACES
> Boston: Eliot Lounge, Fenway Park, Doyle's Cafe, Jake Wirth's
> Cambridge: Plough and Stars, Wursthaus
> Hyannis: Wursthaus
> Springfield: Student Prince/The Fort

OF NOTE
> **Brewing Supplies**
> Beer and Wine Hobby, Karin C. Baker, P.O. Box 3104, Wakefield, MA 01880

Crosby and Baker, Nancy Baker, P.O. Box 3049, 999 Main Rd., Westport, MA 02790

Frozen Wort, Charles Olchowski, 473 Main St., P.O. Box 988, Greenfield, MA 01301

Witches Brew, Ginny and Bob Stokes, 25 Baker St., Foxborough, MA 02035

Cape Cod Brewer's Supply, 126 Middle Rd., South Chatham, MA 02659

Root and Vine, Box 3051, Westport, MA 02790

Operation Brewnet, 999 Main Rd., Westport, MA 02790. A newsletter for the home-brew trade.

Events

New England Homebrew Championship. For details contact the Frozen Wort, 473 Main St., P.O. Box 988, Greenfield, MA 01301

St. Patrick's Day, March 17, South Boston

Brimfield Flea Market. Dates vary. One of the best places for breweriana bargains.

Great Fermentations

Cambridge Brewing Co., Cambridge (new Pub brewery)

RHODE ISLAND

★ Hope Brewing Corp., 669 Elmwood Ave., Providence, RI 02907

Type: Contract

Brands: Hope Lager Beer, Hope Oktoberfest Beer (contract brewed by the Lion, Wilkes-Barre, PA)

Tours: None at present, brewery under construction

Breweriana: T-shirts, aprons, painter's hats, coasters, posters, etc. Write: Hopestuff, 669 Elmwood Ave., Providence, RI 02907

Slogans: "Hope . . . for the Best!"

GREAT PLACES

Providence: Custom House Tavern

VERMONT

★ Vermont Pub and Brewery, 144 College St., Burlington, VT 05401

Type: Pub brewery

Brands: Burly Irish Ale, Original Vermont Lager, Rock Dunder Ale, Gabriel Sedlmayr Oktoberfest, Billybuck Maibock, Grand Slam Baseball Beer, Yule Ale

Tours: Wed., 8:00 P.M., Sat., 2:00 P.M., and 4:00 P.M.

★ Catamount Brewing Co., 58 South Main, White River Junction, VT 05001

Type: Microbrewery

Brands: Catamount Amber, Catamount Gold, Catamount Porter

Tours: Tues. and Sat., 11:00 A.M.; by appointment for groups (802) 296-2248

Breweriana: Mugs, T-shirts, sweatshirts, pipes, caps

Slogan: "Pride of the North Country." The mascot is the Catamount—a species of eastern mountain lion, or cougar or panther (*Felis concolor*) believed by some to be extinct, although many sightings have been reported at the brewery.

KINDRED SPIRITS
Rusty Bunch (BCCA) Mark Radzyminski, 87 Lincoln Ave., St. Albans, VT 05478

GREAT PLACES
Bondville: Bromley View Inn
Burlington: Daily Planet
Killington: McGrath's Irish Pub
Shelburne: Pump House Inn

OF NOTE
Marlboro Morris Ales, Windham County, May. A celebration of traditional dances and traditional beverages.
Tunbridge World's Fair, third weekend in September, Tunbridge. A cross-section of farmers, hippies, and bikers swill brew in the world's least pretentious beer hall. Best on Saturday night, even though rain is guaranteed.

BUY 'EM IF YOU CAN FIND 'EM

Narragansett (Narragansett/General). Lots of memories associated with "New England's Own." Red Sox fans remember Curt Gowdy say, "Hi Neighbor, Have a 'Gansett," after each inning. Today's beer, unfortunately, is as forgettable as the Red Sox team of those days.

Haffenreffer Malt Liquor (Narragansett/General). Sole remaining standard-bearer of the Haffenreffers, once the most prominent of New England brewers. A potent, sweet brew that local teenagers still drink on the rocks with a twist. Sad testament to a great brewer. Maybe the resurrection of Sam Adams in the Haffenreffer plant will set things straight.

Samuel Adams (Boston Beer Co.). One cannot fault this much-decorated brew except on its pedigree. How can Boston's best beer come from Pittsburgh? Hurry up and open that brewery, Jim.

Catamount Amber (Catamount Brewing Co.). World-class beer from an English-trained brewer in White River Junction, VT.

All products from the Vermont Pub and Brewery. Publican Greg Noonan has progressed from home brewer to zealot to author to professional, and his products show it.

3
THE
COLONIES

NEW YORK, NEW YORK, TO BALTIMORE, MARYLAND
19 DAYS, 3,130 MILES ON THE ROAD

A LESSON IN DRAFT

A favorite American pastime is to knock New York—not just the city but the state, its residents, and even its sports teams. From a beer drinker's standpoint, however, New York is a haven. There are plenty of breweries, so the beer is fresh; prices are low; selection is unbeatable; and there is almost no time or place when the thirsty trekker cannot find a brew. The slogan "I love New York" could have been written by The Great Beer Trek.

An evening of pub crawling in Manhattan, however, was less than a resounding success. Beer is a beverage of the common man, and Manhattan is the city of bright lights and Broadway, where everyone wants to be a star. No one, it appears, wants to be common.

We tried. We went to all the right places, spent a small fortune, but encountered beer drinking that could be described only as pretentious. Only McSorley's proved its reliable self. Finally we ran out of time as the bars closed.

Unwilling to give up, we ambled downtown to the Fulton Street Fish Market, where bars have special dispensation to stay open all night to serve the teamsters and stevedores who off-load the products of Maine, Cape Cod, the Chesapeake, and Florida, destined to become the Daily Catch in Manhattan's restaurants and markets. The market bars serve breakfast and beer to sleepy longshoremen, mafia types, and the occasional uptowners out to experience the cacophony of the fishy commerce. The crowd is the same every night; only the people change.

On nice nights like this, old Carmine sits on a folding chair in front of the bar that bears his name. The old lion surveying his domain, everyone says hello, more deferential than jocular. Occasionally someone approaches tentatively and mumbles something in his ear. For years Carmine has been a shop steward with the power to dole out jobs, equivalent to the power of life or death in the working class community.

"So-and-so said I should see you."

Depending on who So-and-so is and when he last did a favor for Carmine, he nods, points, or waves his hand no. We watch the small drama over a mug of Schaefer, the only other choice being, appropriately enough, Rheingold. Twenty years ago Carmine might have offered Knick, Trommer White Label, and several other New York brands, but there is no point in crying over spilt beer.

We move on, fighting our way through throngs of dolly-pushing stevedores who vocalize a steady warning of "watch your back, watch your back." All Seven Ages of Man work in the bustle, each man threading his purposeful way through the stacked crates of hake, fluke, snapper, crab, flounder, mussels, and sea bass. Swordfish are neatly hacked into manageable chunks by men working machetes with the deftness of accountants swinging pencils. When dawn comes, the street will be returned to the day people. Razor-cut businessmen on nearby Wall Street will be oblivious to the nighttime hubbub that takes place in the shadows of their citadels.

We enter the Paris Hotel, the city's oldest operating hostelry, although I am not sure who would want to stay there. The bar combines market functionalism with cut-glass cabinets from a day when the city's elite would meet the dawn in the bar of the Paris. Now a green Formica breakfast counter takes up half the room. The bar is still elbow-polished wood.

The craggy-faced blonde tending bar called constant greeting to passing workers. She had obviously been a market fixture for almost as long as the Paris.

"What will you have?" The voice matched the face perfectly, an edge of compassion that came from a thorough examination of both sides of life.

"What's good?"

"Scrambled eggs," she said disinterestedly.

"O.K. Two scrambles."

"Coffee or beer?"

"Beer. Whaddya got?"

"Schaefer." The waitress was obviously into minimal effort as far as The Great Beer Trek was concerned. No matter, though, the surliness was appropriate for New York and the Fulton Fish Market where, at 4:30 A.M., you gotta be strong to survive. Scrambles and Schaefer. It tastes better than it sounds.

Before we had finished, the men of Fulton Street Fish Market were putting their meathooks into their back pockets and heading for the subway that would take them back to Brooklyn, maybe with the winey hoppiness of Schaefer at the backs of their throats. Across the river a few wispy fingers of gray were trying to pull aside the navy blue curtain of night. The Beer Trek had at last discovered good beer drinking in the Big Apple.

In blue-collar Utica, it was quite another story. Good beer drinking found us in no time at all. We arrived on a suitably bleak Monday morning. The city's heyday has clearly passed. The businesses have moved south and west, as have the job-seeking sons and daughters. Utica is the home of the F. X. Matt Brewing Co., makers of Utica Club, Matt's Premium, and most recently, New Amsterdam beer. This firm is renowned in the beer fanatic circles as a brewery that goes to great length to be hospitable to the beer drinker. They routinely host collectors' conventions, sponsor road races, offer tours, create breweriana, and in countless other ways endear themselves to the consumer.

We anticipated with great pleasure getting to know the F. X. Matt people better. The plan of attack was to take the public tour anonymously in the afternoon, then to return the following morning to talk with company officials. For the time being, however, it was two hours until the first tour, and we had nothing to do.

As we strolled the streets of semideserted, downtown Utica, we passed a small bar on Bleeker Street named the Barn "In" Sider. I paused long enough to read a sign that said "Beer in Mason Jars." A patron spotted our hesitation and scurried outside. "C'mon in!" he bubbled enthusiastically. "This place has the best beer and popcorn in town!"

The man doing the exhorting wore a work uniform with the F. X. Matt logo. If brewery workers drank here, it had to be good. True, it was only 10:30 A.M., but this *was* the Beer Trek. Prejudices against drinking in the morning had to be overcome in the name of research.

We ordered a glass of Matt's Premium. Not that there was any choice— the Barn "In" Sider serves no hard liquor, no bottled beer, and no draft beers except Matt's. The promise of hospitality turned out to be somewhat misleading. Loyal patrons sat silently absorbed in a game show on TV. Individuals would arrive, be served a beer, sit, stare, pay up, and leave with scarcely the exchange of a word. The decor evidenced a warped sense of humor. A handwritten sign on the wall read "Bleeker St.—the street of dreams." Nearby a pair of rubber ears was nailed to the wall. To say the Barn "In" Sider lacked coherent structure was to say that Utica had seen better days. Army recruiting posters adorned walls, while feedbags were draped over fake-Tudor rafters. A separate motif was lent by the shopping bags tacked to the walls.

Our presence had apparently made the regulars uncomfortable, judging from the concentrated television watching. I whispered to Laura that we could chalk this up as a blind alley. The popcorn was fresh and good. Likewise the beer, served in a mason jar, was fresh and lively. I finished my glass and was immediately presented with another, which the bartender explained was compliments of the F. X. Matt worker who had originally asked us inside. I raised my glass in silent salute, but the ice was now broken. The camaraderie of beer had taken over.

Our bartender and the owner of the Barn "In" Sider, Tony Sansoe, originated the idea of using mason jars for beer due to his dissatisfaction with the quality of beer service in competing establishments. The beer drinker, he believes, is entitled to clean hoses, clean glassware, and full measure. Mason jars, with associations of cleanliness and full measure, were chosen as the perfect beer vessels.

"You can be sure in a 16-ounce mason jar that you've got 16 ounces of beer. With the false bottom in glass mugs you don't know whether you've got 9, 10, or 12 ounces of beer. Or take these bell-shaped pilsner glasses. They're supposed to contain 8 ounces, but if you have one-half inch of head at the top where it's wide, you would be surprised at how much beer you're losing."

Tony proved equally fanatical about the proper cleaning of glassware. The slightest bit of grease or detergent, he explained, leaves a film on glass that is ruinous to the head on beer.

"Bartenders think something is wrong when their beer doesn't have any head. They call up the brewery and raise hell, but most of the time the problem is with their glasses. Or maybe the hoses are dirty. Or the beer is so cold it's practically frozen. You know how to tell a clean glass? Sprinkle salt on the inside of the glass. If it's really clean, the salt will stick to the glass."

SALT WILL STICK TO THE SIDE OF <u>REALLY CLEAN</u> GLASSWARE.

"Clean Glassware and Full Measure"
– TONY SANSOE

Tony demonstrated on one of his mason jars. He uses a nondetergent cleaner not available commercially. He discovered the product while on duty in the National Guard and had to write directly to the manufacturer to get a supply.

Tony disappeared to take care of other customers. Upon returning he showed us his half-gallon mason jar. It was big, full, and it was on the house. I gasped. So this is what the Beer Trek would be like—drunk by eleven each morning and dead before I reached the Mississippi. I had never faced a half-gallon of beer. Tony was confident I could handle it. The house record, he pointed out, was nine, held by a gentleman sitting several seats to my right. I turned and asked for confirmation. He was a large man but free of the belly to be expected from a prodigious drinker. He nodded, then spoke calmly, evenly, his reputation carried in the tone of his voice.

"I can do ten."

Tony's assurances notwithstanding, we shared our beer bonanza as well as our mission with the other patrons. The television had been forgotten as the Uticans took advantage of an opportunity to strut their collective beer IQ. After all, this is a brewery town. The regulars of the Barn "In" Sider, hearing we were brewery bound, had been full of who-to-sees and what-to-says. The complaint nationwide may be that local populations do not support hometown breweries, but in Utica, Matt's (the brewery and the family) is an integral part of the community, a source of pride. Its employees and customers are roving ambassadors, not without senses of humor. We left with good-natured instructions to jab the well-placed needle:

"Ask them about Billy Beer. Ooo-oo, that stuff was awful."

"Hey, give them the business about cutting back to two free beers on the tour. Who can get drunk on two beers?"

"Ask them why they don't give out coasters to local businesses."

The gibes were in the spirit that comes after a couple of brews. Not a single malicious word was heard about the brewery or its products.

BREWERY TOURS START HERE

AND MIGHT END AT THE BREWERY SHOP

WESTEND BREWING MPANY

THE HOSPITABLE F. X. Matt Brewing Co.

"See if you can get me fixed up with the babe on the Maximus Super poster."

It was noon, and the lunchtime crowd was starting to arrive. We thanked Tony for the lesson on draft beer and for upholding the beer drinkers' bill of rights. I commented that he must be a beer drinker of repute. "Oh, no," he replied. "I've never tasted the stuff. I'm a teetotaler. I've had people come in here, order two glasses of draft, and offer me as much as fifty dollars to drink one, but I never have."

We thanked him again, then I fell off my stool and crawled to the van. We giggled our way to the Varick Street brewery. Utica's grayness had taken on a golden hue, casting the depressing reality of the city into a temporarily more flattering light. I began to understand why the girls get better looking at closing time.

Matt's is in the business of making friends, a fact self-evident in the obvious care and expense of their tour. The front reception area and hospitality room are furnished in the period decor of the 1890s. Antique advertising memorabilia is showcased on every wall.

Thanks to Tony Sansoe, the normal professionalism of The Great Beer Trek had been suspended. Today I would be a sleazy, semidrunk tourist, there for a free beer. We stumbled through the tour, but upon arrival in the hospitality room found ourselves greeted by West End's publicity director, sales manager, vice-president of operations . . . and more free beer. Someone had detected the presence of The Great Beer Trek and decided to roll out a true F. X. Matt welcome. In classic brewery fashion, mugs were never allowed to empty. We learned about brewing, beer, and the company, although at this point my memory becomes hazy. Apparently the arrival of The Great Beer Trek was an event of enough magnitude for most of the company to take the afternoon off and come by to say hi and to lift a mug.

That's all I can remember. The next morning I noticed the front bumper of the van covered with "Schultz and Dooley [Matt's well-known, talking beer mug spokesmen] Love NY" stickers. Will Anderson called this one of his favorite breweries, and now it was one of ours as well.

A TALE OF THREE BREWERS   Larchmont to Dunkirk

After our overindulgence in Utica, the subsequent few days were long on research and short on beer drinking. In addition to Matt's we visited branch plants for Miller and Schlitz, Genesee in Rochester, and tiny Koch's Brewing Co. in Dunkirk. Additionally we met with Rudolph Schaefer, the legendary brewer whose name is almost synonymous with New York beer. Our knowledge had increased logarithmically, and we looked forward to consolidating conclusions.

Rudolph Schaefer, Jr.

After a false start in which we first contacted Rudolph Schaefer the Fourth, then the Third, The Great Beer Trek finally succeeded in reaching the right number. We met in his well-appointed office across from the Larchmont railroad station. The decor was of dual motif, beer and sailing, with the latter more prominent, a clue to Mr. Schaefer's priorities.

Discard stereotypes when thinking of the late Rudolph Schaefer; he was neither the affable, old world brewmaster nor the high-pressure executive. Even in his eighties, he was fit and perceptive, a testament to the salubrious effects of salt air and beer. His reputation in the beer business was as a straight-shooter, a tough, fair man who made inroads through industriousness and ingenuity. His reputation as a sailor was much the same. He was at once a renowned racer in New York yachting circles and one of the driving forces behind the reconstruction of Old Mystic Seaport. In three generations the Schaefer family progressed from penniless immigrants to pillars of society. Theirs is the classic American success story, and they owe it all to beer.

RUDY SCHAEFER'S
America

AN ALMOST EXACT REPLICA OF THE
1851 AMERICA'S CUP SCHOONER <u>AMERICA</u>

Mr. Schaefer was retired when we spoke with him. He was an interested observer of the brewing industry but no longer a participant. He was a rarity among family brewers in that he was not forced out of the beer business but "escaped" on his own terms. It has been more than twenty years since the family divested themselves of the Schaefer Brewing Co. by selling their shares to the public. Rudy Schaefer looked on the horizon of the sea of suds and saw more than a squall looming. The captain put himself and his family in a life-boat and headed into port. He could not save the ship, and unlike many other brewers, he chose not to go down with it.

During 126 years (1842–1968) of sound family management, Rudy's grandfather Frederick Schaefer's original asset of one dollar was parlayed into New York's premier brewing operation, sixth largest in the nation. Since going public, Schaefer has dropped steadily in the national hierarchy and was recently taken over by Stroh of Detroit, as the relentless process of consolidation in the brewing industry continues.

Twenty-one-year-old Frederick Schaefer emigrated to the United States from Wetzlar, Germany, in 1838. He took a job with a New York brewer and wrote his brother, Maximilian, about life in the New World. The next year he too made the transatlantic leap, bringing with him a treasured recipe for lager beer, a type unknown in the United States where porters and English-style ales were still the norm.

The first American lager was brewed by John Wagner, a Philadelphian who had imported a special strain of lager yeast from his native Bavaria. The Schaefers, although not the first, now lay rightful claim to being the oldest brewers of lager beer in America. In 1844 the two brothers had prospered enough to buy out their employer. By 1848 their lager was perfected and introduced, gaining immediate acceptance. The following year the Schaefers had to move to more spacious facilities, setting a pattern of growth and expansion that continued until the 1960s.

Maximilian's son Rudolph assumed the presidency in 1912. Again expansion was called for, and Rudolph was equal to the task, although his timing could not have been worse. In 1916 in Brooklyn, he opened one of the grandest breweries in America, only to see it emasculated by the Volstead Act less than four years later. The grand brewery was reduced to making near beer.

Rudolph I died in 1923. Control passed to his eldest son, Maximilian, whose tenure was cut short by health problems. In 1927, the same year that Jacob Ruppert's Bronx Bombers were making their owner as famous for baseball as beer, young Rudy Schaefer unexpectedly found himself the youngest brewery president in the United States.

There were growing pains, but Rudy found an unlikely ally in Colonel Jake Ruppert who had been executor of his father's will and his closest friend. The fraternal ties among brewers were obviously stronger than competitive threats. When Prohibition ended, Rudy Junior was ready and able to join the race to recapture America's beer drinkers. He atoned for his father's inability to anticipate the onset of Prohibition by anticipating its end. Before anyone knew for certain that repeal was forthcoming, Rudy mounted an aggressive advertising campaign in the media that reminded the public that Schaefer's hand "had never lost its skill." Once the beer wagons started rolling, Schaefer left the competition in the starting gate. They had the further advantage of one of the finest manufacturing facilities in the nation. Obviously no one had been about to build a new brewery while Prohibition was in effect. While Schaefer had previously been one of several successful brewing companies in New York City, now it became the unquestioned toast of the town. By 1940 young Rudy had passed even his mentor, Colonel Ruppert, in sales.

"— AND THAT HAND IS READY AND WAITING..."
— RUDY SCHAEFER, 1933.

Under the right circumstances, Rudy's sons, William and Rudolph, would now be the fourth generation to manufacture and sell beer to New Yorkers, but by 1960 the company was encountering problems in maintaining profitability. The nationals—Bud, Schlitz, Pabst, Falstaff, and, to a lesser extent, Miller—were now casting hungry eyes at the Northeast market dominated by the "one beer to have when you're having more than one." Vicious price wars ensued. The regional brewers could maintain prices, knowing they would lose the cost-conscious segment of the consumership, or they could meet the unprofitable price, hoping their drinkers would not abandon them in droves once prices returned to normal. The regionals who looked to the courts or government for defense against "selective" or "predatory" pricing were quickly disappointed; no court or government agency wants to rule in favor of higher prices. The nationals' claim that price wars were an expression of free enterprise at its finest held sway. The issue will never be settled until the beer drinker has but a single beer to choose from. What will happen to prices then?

The Schaefers fought the battles and suffered many casualties. Serious family conferences were held to discuss strategy. Meanwhile, their peers—the Ballantines, the Kruegers, the Trommers—capitulated by closing their doors. At one point, the Schaefers took the first step toward going national themselves by buying an Ohio brewery (the one now owned by C. Schmidt) but found it impossible to establish the Schaefer name in virgin territory. Rudy was a brewer, but beyond that he was a businessman. He could face the atrophy that had withered so many of his brewing contemporaries, or he could entrust the family namesake to others for a handsome sum. He chose the latter, and not for a single moment, as he breathed the salt air on Long Island Sound, was it a decision he regretted.

F. X. Matt II

F. X. Matt II speaks of the "mantle of the brewer," which is now his to wear. It was worn by his father and will probably be worn by his son, F. X. Matt III. The undisputed owner of the mantle, however, is, was, and will forever be, his grandfather and namesake, known simply as "The First." He was born in 1859 in Ingelschlatt in Schichthal, Baden. When he died ninety-nine years later, he was chairman of the board. Until the day he died, he went to work every day and was actively involved in all phases of brewery management. More than twenty years after his death, his presence still dominates the brewery on Varick Street.

The F. X. Matt Brewing Co. is in the midst of a crisis, the third of their history. The first two, Prohibition and World War II (when raw materials and machine parts were impossible to procure), were survived through a combination of old-fashioned ingenuity and industry. F. X. Matt II feels the company will survive the crisis of competition from the nationals in the same way.

"My grandfather always said that a business is like a man—'You have to feed him to keep him alive.' We still believe that here. Our business is well fed and healthy. We have to be more efficient than the nationals. Our equipment has been kept up-to-date. We have the flexibility of a private company, and we're small enough that management is integrally involved with all aspects of the product. You don't see that in a big company. Everyone is too specialized. There is no way the nationals can beat us in our own backyard."

In the light of the uncertainties of the contemporary competitive environment, many regional brewers have been reluctant to make capital investments. Although the public image at the F. X. Matt Co. is that of turn-of-the-century hospitality, there is nothing anachronistic about the way they brew, package, and market their beer. But it is undisputedly a family affair: "During World War II, materials were hard to come by. We would drive all over the state trying to convince farmers to grow hops. We would scavenge machine parts; then after church each Sunday, the family would come into the plant to repair machinery."

F. X. Matt is proud of the number of technological innovations pioneered by his company. The question remains as to whether these weapons comprise enough of an arsenal to withstand the national onslaught. In a Beer War between titans, it is possible for a company like theirs to get caught in the crossfire.

F. X. Matt has the lean, Lincolnesque look of one accustomed to adversity. Certainly there is no fear. If the principles of industry and sound management set forth by the man whose portrait is on the wall are faithfully followed, everything should be all right. After all, F. X. III is standing in the wings, ready to inherit the mantle.

John D. Koch

Four hundred miles and one light-year from Larchmont, where Rudy Schaefer, Jr., rules his clan with patrician beneficence lies Dunkirk, New York. In Larchmont the sporting world in the form of the New York Yacht Club acknowledges its debt to the Schaefer legacy. In Dunkirk the sporting world acknowledges that John Koch of the Fred Koch Brewing Co. sponsored a bowling league or little league team. Perhaps he donated the keg for the annual softball banquet, but no one would refer to the Koch legacy.

The Fred Koch Brewery was founded in 1888, the same year F. X. Matt started his company in Utica. There the similarity ends. Whereas in Utica hope springs eternal, in Dunkirk it is realism. F. X. Matt II has the spare look of a Yankee farmer bracing for another winter. John Koch has been given a task he knows impossible to complete successfully. He has examined the statistics, balance sheets, and marketing surveys and knows he is fighting a losing battle. In no way, however, does this mean he will be less tenacious in the defense of his livelihood.

John Koch has the tall, powerful, graying at the temples look suited to an office overlooking a city skyline. Instead he sits tailored and natty in a plain, unpretentious office where the only splashes of color come from an assortment of cans and bottles put out by his competitors. Mr. Koch is a pragmatist, not given to grasping at straws or lamenting his fate. A Beer Trek looks for the fun in beer, the magic of the suds, the offbeat, the obscure, the worthy, the legendary, the humorous, the buried treasure. Such pursuit is of passing concern to John Koch, fighting for survival with an antique brewery in a day of megaplants. During our conversation I made the mistake of expressing passionate yet naive concern for the fate of small brewers. Mr. Koch listened patiently, then laid out the reasons why the days of the small, independent brewer are numbered. By now the story was becoming familiar.

1. Government compliance regulations. Brewers small and large must comply with the dictates of OSHA (Occupational Safety and Health Administration), the EPA (Environmental Protection Agency), and other regulatory agencies. The ability to comply is not equal, however. The small brewer's profit must be plowed back into income-producing equipment to stay competitive. The cash for nonproductive expenditures is not available. Likewise in the case of a dispute, the small brewer does not have the legal or financial resources of a national to contend an issue.

2. Predatory or selective pricing.

3. Increasing importance of media, especially television.

Survival, explained Mr. Koch, is possible but only under optimum circumstances. The brewer must be located in an out-of-the-way place that offers little market potential for the nationals. He must be protected by nondiscriminatory state licensing laws or must make a specialized product as does Anchor Steam in San Francisco. But, he sighed, even these strategies can be ultimately self-defeating. Any sizable growth will create a market profitable for the nationals to invade, and the successful small brewer will be David facing yet another Goliath.

I asked John Koch if he thought free enterprise was dead. He said no, but it was no longer available to the small guy. When government became big after the Depression, business became big to defend itself. The small guy could either crawl off and die or stand his ground, fighting bravely, and then die. His neighbor, the Erie Brewing Co., had closed its doors just weeks before. This was a good company run by smart, nice people who also made good beer. If there were a light at the end of his own company's tunnel, then John Koch could not yet see it. For the time being, however, he would keep making beer the best he could. And if I should come across any yellow brick roads in my travels, he said, be sure to give him a call.

ROOTS—THE ORIGINS OF BEER
Baltimore, Maryland

From New York we penetrated the heart of colonial America. From the highway much of the landscape is a blight of the country's insatiable thirst for growth. We tried our best to plot routes without numbers. This did not prove to be hard, given our suds-determined destinations. The back roads cast the mid-Atlantic states in a completely flattering light, making it easy to understand why this was the first settled section of America. We had also now grown comfortable with life in the van, Laura having discovered innumerable ways to make our rolling metal box a home. Some days our mileage figures were so low we could have covered the same distance in a covered wagon. No day, however, failed to supply an ample quotient of sudsy knowledge from the cradle of American civilization.

Soon after man learned to harvest wild grain, he tried to store it for consumption at a later date. The vessel in which he kept it was rained on and then contaminated by wild yeast. Fermentation began. When man discovered the goopy, bubbling mess, he slurped it down anyway. He became full and at the same time started thinking more kindly toward his neighbor. He belched and slurped down a little more. Thus, with this elementary grain porridge, was beer born.

Throughout history the only limitation on the ability of *Homo sapiens* to brew has been the availability of grain. This is as true of pygmies in Africa as the ancient Teutonic tribes.

Intoxicating beverages necessitate a framework for controlling their abuse. Thus the development of brewing techniques is often paralleled by systems of collective control that we describe loosely as "civilization."

In time, history was recorded, people having invented the written word to catalog recipes, to document brewing technique, to extol the exhilaration of intoxication, and to damn the effects of excess. Early cradles of civilization from Egypt to China contain repeated references to the uses and abuses of fermented grain beverages.

The Britishers who first settled the shores of the New World were indisputably beer drinkers, possessing a genetic aversion to unembellished water. Christina Hole's *The English Housewife in the Seventeenth Century* describes the sudsy traditions of the original North American invaders:

> *Our forfathers' drinks were as varied and plentiful as their food. In the country, home-brewed ale or beer was the normal drink at most meals, including breakfast, and the provision of a sufficient supply was one of the housewife's most important tasks. "Sufficient" in this case meant a good deal, for the daily consumption was heavy and hospitality was generous. Brewing took place once a month in many households and oftener if necessary, and every country bride expected to find her brew house adequately stocked with the barrels, firkins, tubs, coolers, ladles and other necessities for this complicated operation.*

That the Pilgrims brewed immediately upon their arrival in America in 1620 is inarguable. Although there were no professional brewers among them (the first, John Jenny, arrived three years after the *Mayflower* landed), each citizen had a working knowledge of the principles of fermentation. Early inventories indicate they possessed the required "hogsheads, bucking tubs, payles, and firkins" for brewing. John Alden (of Priscilla fame) was by trade a cooper whose duties would have included maintenance of wood beer barrels. And finally, they possessed the necessary motivation, as documented by this entry in the *Mayflower* log:

> *That night we returned again to shipboard, with resolution the next morning to settle on some of these places: so in the morning, after we had called on God for direction, we came to this resolution: to go presently ashore again, and to take a better view of two places, which we thought most fitting for us, for we could not now take time for further search or consideration, our victuals being most spent, especially our beer, and it being now the 19th of December.*

Not surprisingly, the voyagers chose Plymouth as the site for their settlement the next day. The trip is over when the beer runs out.

That first winter the Pilgrims had to slake their thirsts by brewing beers from transported stores of barley or, more probably, Indian maize (as had the Jamestown settlers earlier under the guidance of Captain John Smith). Barley was planted in the first summer's crop, and it is likely that the first Thanksgiving table featured the Pilgrims' finest brew.

Among the first legislative acts of the Massachusetts Bay Colony was a prohibition of the malting of wheat, an act that suggests that the thirst of the early settlers was more powerful than their need for bread. The creation of beer was a simple enough matter, then as now, and the Pilgrims' process makes an interesting comparison with the methods of prehistoric humans or the contemporary brewer.

The first step was to steep the grain (barley, wheat, maize, rye, or any combination thereof) in a cistern for three days or until it was thoroughly soaked. Once germination began, the water was slowly drained and the husks allowed to aerate. For the next month the grain was turned four or five times daily until thoroughly dry. To test for starch-to-sugar conversion, the Pilgrims had none of the sophisticated methods available to the modern brewer. Instead they relied on taste, sight, smell, and feel.

The malt was ground and boiled with water until a pudding-like consistency was achieved. Slowly hot water was percolated through the liquor, or "wort," then drawn off, or "sparged," boiled with hops or whatever other flavoring element was favored, then fermented through the addition of yeast.

Whether the beer of the settlers compared in quality to that of our modern, food-processing brewers, these early brewers must be given their due.

Not only was their beer made without Kelcoloid 0, diatomites, Dinitropheny Chydrazine, or the many unpronounceable substances available to the Schlitz brewmaster, but also, prior to brewing, they malted their own grain (which only a handful of contemporary brewers do) and grew their own grain (which only Coors and Anheuser-Busch do today). Moreover, they cleared the land they stole from Indians, and they crossed the North Atlantic in a leaky wood vessel. Of such true beer-brewing grit is our ancestry.

Alice Morse Earle in her treatise *Colonial Days in Old New York* (Charles Scribner's Sons, 1896) confirms that virtually any occasion was considered important enough to toast with a drink. Farm hands, sailors, cobblers, tailors, and all other members of the working class would not work without drink provided by their employers. Even lawbreakers subject to deprivation and confinement were still allowed small beer as a regular part of their diets. Comparing the New Yorkers to other colonists, Earle says:

> *Of the drinking habits of the Dutch colonists I can say that they were those of all the colonies—excessive. Tempered in their tastes somewhat by the universal brewing and drinking of beer, they did not use as much rum as the Puritans of New England, nor drink as deeply as the Virginia planters, but the use of liquor was universal.*

Indeed many of the most prominent names in colonial history were associated with the brewing trade. William Penn, both a good Quaker and lover of beer, opened the first commercial brewery in Pennsylvania in 1683, just several years after he had founded the colony.

Samuel Adams, the Father of the Revolution, counted among his patriotic credits participation in the Boston Tea Party, signing the Declaration of Independence, a term as governor of Massachusetts, and membership in the First Congress. He was a brewer by trade, as were other members of the Adams family (Jim Koch, president of the company that makes Samuel Adams beer, is a descendant).

General Israel Putnam left his tavern in Brooklyn, New York, to lead the Revolutionary Army to many victories. After the war, he returned to the tavern. George Washington brewed at Mt. Vernon, Thomas Jefferson at Monticello, and James Oglethorpe at Jekyl Island. Alexander Hamilton, John Hancock, Patrick Henry, and James Madison worked actively to promote legislation to encourage the manufacture and consumption of a beverage widely regarded as a temperate alternative to hard liquor.

The English-style beers brewed by the early European settlers were probably similar to the home brews of Tim Matson's Green Mountain men. In the mid-1840s something happened to change the course of American brewing. A Philadelphian, John Wagner, imported a special strain of yeast from his native Bavaria. This yeast fermented the beer wort from the bottom and required cooler temperatures to work correctly. The resulting beer was lighter and livelier than the prevalent types and immediately won converts among the beer drinking consumership. Yet no one could have foreseen the extent of its eventual domination. With scant exception, the only beers available commercially in America today are derivatives of John Wagner's lager. The introduction of this beer type coincided nicely with an influx of Germans, Dutch, Poles, and Lithuanians who came to mine coal from the hills. A brewer could not ask for more willing consumers. Of the hundreds of breweries that arose to serve, only the few strongest remain for the Beer Trekker.

Pennsylvania beers possess a taste characteristic that suggests evolution from a common ancestor. While these brews offer as much variety as is available in any state in the country, each bears the tattoo of its origin in the ferrous waters that have filtered down through the carbonaceous hills. These are unabashedly coal miner beers, regardless of whether one is referring to Schmidt's quaffed in a Philadelphia men's club or Stoney's in the local union hall.

John Koch of the Fred Koch Brewing Co. in Dunkirk, New York, had cited the need for small brewers to have some measure of protection for their markets from incursions by the national brewers. While Pennsylvania has witnessed significant carnage in recent years (Ortlieb, Horlacher, Mt. Carbon, Erie), the passage of time had been kinder, beerwise, to this state than almost any other. Seven state-based brewers still sell their wares, offering the beer drinker an almost unthinkable variety by contemporary standards. They owe their existence to prohibitive distribution laws that limit sales to case lots from specially designated beer outlets. This, combined with the rugged topography and declining yet tenacious population, has made the nationals reluctant to invade the local strongholds of the Yuenglings, Stoneys, Straubs, Stegmaiers, Schmidts, Rolling Rocks, and Iron City's of Pennsylvania.

The Pennsylvania breweries came into and went out of The Great Beer Trek in quick sequence, each leaving an indelible footprint at the back of our throats, having its moment upon the stage, then being seen no more, stealing back into the green hills from whence it came. Of such memories are Beer Treks made.

Straub's, St. Mary's, Pennsylvania

We arrived at night, a fact that camouflaged the town's native blackness. We found no shortage of locals who were willing to tell about the local brew. Straub's has a sweet, pungent taste and an aroma that immediately fills up a room. It is a beer to be drunk in quantity, although locals brag about its strength (4 percent by weight) and after three, one begins to appreciate the subtle personality of St. Mary's. The next morning Gibby Straub himself took us around the brewery. The appearance of any rabid Straub fan (or a Great Beer Trek) is ample excuse to stop work for a few minutes. The archaic, labor-intensive operation is a joke by modern manufacturing standards but not by anyone's beer drinking standards. Gibby confesses they close down for the first week of deer season. Could Anheuser-Busch afford that?

Pittsburgh Brewing Co., Pittsburgh

The business is definitely on the rebound. We tried to experience the magic of "Ahrn" by going to a few joints near the steel mills. One sits on the torn vinyl of a circular stool with tubular stainless legs and tries to appear inconspicuous in an environment as intimate as a stranger's living room. The patrons are veterans of the war between life's expectations and reality. They have fought and lost. Now there is nothing to do but grasp the comfort of Iron City and bide time until the next Steelers' game. As Joseph Lelyveld once said of Iron City in an article entitled "Small Beer" in the *New York Times Magazine* (May 22, 1977), "It's not for dreaming, for changing your lifestyle. It's for remaining the same. Between us it's for drinking. And one more won't hurt." Amen.

Pittsburgh

Jones Brewing Co., Smithton, Pennsylvania

Stoney's is alive and well, thank you, and ruling a tiny corner of the beer world. President W. B. Jones III takes a no-nonsense approach to brewing, which he will pass along to yet another generation.

Rolling Rock, Latrobe, Pennsylvania

The beer is so squeaky clean that one can barely taste the coal dust. We caught the president, James Tito, Jr., just as he was preparing to fly to North Dakota to examine the year's barley crop. A connoisseur of the common man's drinking experience, he was looking forward to revisiting the Lakota Hotel, which is distinguished by the fact that "it has not changed in the last fifty years." Latrobe has not changed in the last twenty-five.

Schmidt's and Ortlieb's, Philadelphia

Ortlieb's was still independent when the Beer Trek passed through. We stopped in the brewery tavern that doubles as the hospitality room and workers' lunchroom. The kid sitting next to us was streaked with sweat, having done combat with a faulty pasteurizer all morning. The problem was acute; a nonfunctioning pasteurizer could eventually bring all production to a halt. Joe Ortlieb, Jr., jammed the last of a sandwich in his mouth, mumbled an apology, and returned to work. Alas, "Joe's Beer," as Ortlieb's has long been known, will never be his beer. The company succumbed to competitive pressures and sold out to nearby rival Schmidt.

D. G. Yuengling and Son, Pottsville, Pennsylvania

Founded in 1829, the nation's oldest brewery, Dick Yuengling keeps one of the nation's most picturesque breweries in a town most notable for being the site of the nation's oldest brewery. Dick confesses that the "and Son" part of the name is not accurate at the moment. His son used to work in the brewery, he says, but "it was terrible! I never knew where anything was." There is a twinkle in his eyes that belies the seriousness of the conflict. "You know," confides Dick, "I was just the same at his age." We sampled first a Chesterfield Ale, then one of their renowned porters, still bottled in the squat "Steinie" bottles obsolete in the rest of the world. Life in Pottsville, we conclude, is made bearable by the availability of Dick's beers.

BUILT ON A MOUNTAINSIDE "LIKE ALL OLD BREWERIES..."

Yuengling's c.1844

The Lion, Wilkes-Barre, Pennsylvania

En route to the Lion we passed the old Stegmaier plant, a magnificent building that stands in Gothic ruin by its railroad siding, awaiting either restoration or the wrecker's ball. Just the slightest squint and one can recreate the might of the brewery during its red brick heyday.

The Survey: The Great Places

Two hundred movers and shakers of the beer world were sent surveys from The Great Beer Trek to determine the best places in America to drink beer. This totally unscientific and admittedly biased study produced the expectedly frothy results:

Of cities cited, Seattle was the most frequently named, followed closely by Portland (Oregon) and San Francisco. Boston, Denver, Chicago, and Milwaukee comprised the second rank, with Santa Fe, New Orleans, and New York completing the top ten.

Among events, the Great American Beer Festival was the runaway winner, followed by the BCCA CANvention and the Microbrewers' Annual Conference.

Pub brewery respondents invariably named their own establishment as the best place to drink beer. The favorite place, however, was at home, which outranked the local tavern, brewpubs, picnics, and baseball games.

Honorable mention to (in no particular order): the Breakers Hotel (Palm Beach, Florida), Siebens (Chicago), Fenway Park (Boston), Wrigley Field (Chicago; but not at night), Murphy's Tavern (Seattle), the Gold Coin Saloon (Central City, Colorado), anywhere on Lake Pontchartrain (Louisiana), the Peculier Pub (New York City), Hotel DeHaro (San Juan Islands), Berghoff (Chicago).

After reviewing all the results, the conclusion of Beer Trek '90 is that this was a dumb question, dumber than the others. One of the true joys of beer drinking is the continual quest for new environments and new company. Is that not what a Beer Trek is about?

A few references on great places to find great beer:

Pat Baker's Beer and Bar Atlas, *Baker and Owens Books, 999 Main Road, Westport, MA 02790*

Good Beer Guide, *c/o Vince Cottone, P.O. Box 30156, Seattle, WA 98103*

Beer Drinking in Madison, Wisconsin, *Warsaw Strohs, P.O. Box 695, Madison, WI 53701*

A Beer Drinker's Guide to the Bars of Reading, *P.O. Box 405, Temple, PA 18105*

Beer Drinker's Guide to Central Florida, *c/o Will Nally, 4 South Main St., Gainesville, FL 32601*

Enjoy these books, but better yet, write your own.

Stegmaier's new home is just down the road at the Lion, a physical plant with none of Steg's original grace and charm. This is a place to work. Brewmaster Don Mudrick and assistant Ed Siers greeted us in a crowded office on the fourth floor of the brewhouse. Like the beers brewed at the Lion, the office was unpretentious, a study in functionalism. Both men seemed glad to have us drop in to spice up what otherwise might have been just another day on the job. They were cordial, frank, and, with the wealth of experience between them, damn interesting.

Ed Siers graduated from the Siebel Institute and officially became a brewmaster in 1933, but clearly he had learned his craft during Prohibition. He told tales of brewing in toilet bowls where incriminating evidence could disappear faster than you could say "Elliott Ness." An Elks Club he knew created a particularly effective deterrent—poisonous snakes on the floor surrounding the brew kettle. Don explained the two-way spigots—pull them toward you and you get near beer, push them the other way and you got "high test."

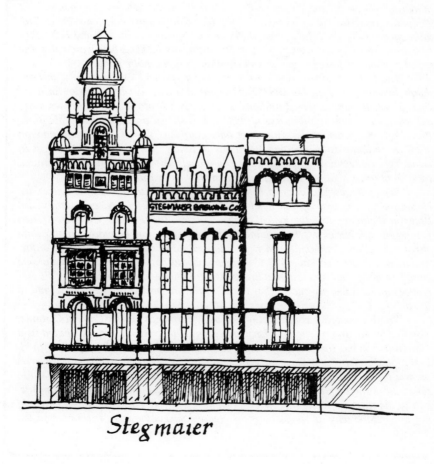

Stegmaier

Defiant Ale

"Contract brewing" describes a recent beer industry phenomenon whereby a regional brewer or microbrewery produces beer to be marketed by an independent company. Increasingly prominent brands like Sam Adams and New Amsterdam have successfully used the kettles of Pittsburgh Brewing Company and F. X. Matt to gain entry to the beer business. Sometimes, as the incident below indicates, the world of contract brewing can extend right out to the lunatic fringe.

The last Defiant wood stove was made by Vermont Castings, Inc., of Randolph, Vermont, on June 30, 1988. The Defiant, a sturdy cast-iron warrior for more than a decade, had delivered millions of usable BTUs into American homes in an era when the skyrocketing prices of fuel oil had shown us all our vulnerability to the whims of Mideast sheiks. But times have changed. We feel comfortable enough with fuel supplies to devote our attentions to issues like air quality. Advances in wood-burning technology have made early models like the Defiant into dinosaurs, capable of great heat but at too great a cost to the environment.

Vermont Castings decided to retire the Defiant with suitable festivities, including a custom-brewed and labeled beer. Vermont's microbrewery, Catamount Brewing Company, was the logical choice to create the libation. The brewery was willing enough but patiently explained that the effort would be more complex than stirring together some malt, yeast, and hops. First there was the question of formulation and then packaging. The company would have to guarantee sale of one complete batch, an amount that translated to 800 cases. Even counting all employees in for a few six-packs, that left a significant amount of beer to be sold to the public.

There were other considerations as well. Vermont's Liquor Control Commission needed assurance that the beer would be neither resold nor distributed as a premium, leaving the company confused as to what it could legally do with it. Catamount's distributor was concerned that it was being denied potential profits on any product distributed by the company at no charge but eventually agreed to take half of the batch. The Bureau of Alcohol, Firearms and Tobacco, meanwhile, had to approve the name and label. Vermont Castings's advertising agency could not understand why its suggestions for creative packaging were encountering the realities of Catamount's bottling equipment. Suddenly, getting into the beer business, a venture that had its origins in the desire to do something interesting and fun, did not seem like a very wise idea.

Sixteen thousand dollars, a few hundred telephone calls, and at least ten nervous breakdowns later, officials at Vermont Castings (and likely a few at Catamount too) were wondering how stove makers had come to make this foray into beerdom. With hundreds of dignitaries invited for the Defiant's retirement party, bureaucratic hassles were the last thing that anyone had time for.

Luckily the hurdles evaporated as quickly as the head on a light beer, and by the day of the party, everyone was toasting the longtime service of a great wood stove with a unique brew. The beverage itself, a brew as black as its namesake, was tart and quenching, a unique summer tonic.

The beer sold out, and the retirement of the Defiant drew the attention of media from coast to coast, making it a no-cost publicity venture for Vermont Castings. The intrusions faded into oblivion, leaving the tang of malt and hops and the glow of fellowship and eloquent toasts—a pretty damn good idea after all.

Contract brewing may be serious business for the Sam Adamses, F. X. Matts, and even Nude Beers of the world. For a certain wood stove company in Vermont, however, the beer business is best left to professionals.

The Lion is a collecting point for some great beers whose breweries could not survive—Gibbons, Stegmaier, Bartels, Liebotschaner. Clearly its present existence is tenuous and depends on low overhead. Ed Siers recounted the breweries for which he had worked. None of them exists any more, yet none had expired because the beer wasn't good. A moment of silence is observed for the dearly departed; then the indomitable spirit overtakes Ed: "Hey, why don't you come to the Master Brewer's Crabfest in Baltimore?"

"Sure," says Don, his voice alive with animation. "If you want good stories, that's the place."

"Or fancy beer drinking," adds Ed, "but I tell you, no matter how much beer a brewer drinks, you'll never see one get out of line. Not that we don't like to have a good time."

The phone rings. A minor emergency requires Don's attention, and he leaves. Ed continued, "Sure, you should come to the Crabfest. Lots of food, lots of beer." He clouded suddenly. "But it's not like it used to be. The meetings used to be even more fun. But with Horlacher going out, and Erie, and who knows what's happening with Carling and Schaefer, this might be the last one. I don't know, there just aren't that many brewmasters any more. I guess this is the last of the romantic industries."

Research created for us a strong sense of beer's formative role in America's history, and yet our travels yielded scant evidence of even vestigial remnants of our English beer tradition. Just as Sherlock Holmes needed the pacification of several pipesful of shag tobacco from his Persian slipper to ruminate on a particularly vexing problem, a Beer Trek needs the sustenance provided by experiencing the best that a local area can offer. Thus, we arrived in Baltimore determined to let actions speak louder than words. We are happy to report that good beer drinking is not hard to find in Baltimore.

First stop for the van was the Lexington Street market, where a bustling array of shops provided a suitably chaotic backdrop for Chesapeake Bay oysters to be washed down by National Premium. This inoffensive beer will never rank high on any connoisseur's list of favorites, but its blandness seems just right to allow the taste of seafood to bleed through. National is now owned by Heileman and brewed at the former Carling plant out by the Beltway. The original downtown plant stands fully equipped and idle, another red brick relic.

After the oyster bars of Lexington Street, we repaired to the restored harbor district of Fells Point for soft-shell crab sandwiches and more beer. Then it was out to the Bromwell Inn in Fullerton for seafood chowder and crabcakes. Bromwell's is the type of place that has the "Star-Spangled Banner" on the jukebox and where patrons drink National Premium just because it is brewed in Baltimore. The evening was still young, but we found ourselves too satiated to consider moving very far. The Bromwell seemed as good a place as any to contemplate what had happened to the English beer drinking tradition. Someone put on the national anthem. It had been written right here in Baltimore, hadn't it? And the tune was derived from an English tavern tune, right? We opted for another National Premium to help us consider the question.

The previous week had been brewery intensive as we drove from New York to the western boundary of Pennsylvania and back again. We uncovered no evidence of the English beer tradition that comprises our sudsy national roots, but we did find abundant examples of the Bavarian tradition that replaced it.

We finish the pitcher, finish recounting our recent escapades in Pennsylvania, and head for home, in this case the apartment of Bob, my college friend who had brought National Premium and boiled crabs to the Fourth of July festivity that spawned The Great Beer Trek. This was the first really steamy evening of the summer, and most of the town was out settin' on the stoop. Young and old, black and white, male and female—everyone in Baltimore sets on the stoop when the summer humidity sets in. All it takes is a transistor radio and a six-pack. The music changes by the block—rock, disco, schmaltz, soul. So does the beer. Pabst is very popular here, as is Miller, especially among blacks. No one seems to know why. National Premium holds its own in what is now a final stronghold.

Of course, none of the radios blare music if the Orioles are playing.

So this night we sat on a stoop in Baltimore, watching the cars stop at the traffic light. Da Boids were playing Boston, and there was a classic match-up, Palmer versus Eckersley. Around the eighth, Earl Weaver took exception to one of the ump's decisions and got himself tossed. Then in the ninth,

Murray belts a home run and da Boids win. On stoops throughout Baltimore, the crowd went crazy.

Trekker's Guide to the Colonies

The good news is that F. X. Matt is now the twelfth largest brewer in the United States. The bad news is that he is still struggling against the same market forces that have overcome many other fine regional brewers and forced them to sell out or give up. As others have disappeared, Matt's moved up in the rankings. Bud is still safe. Let's hope that F. X. is around for the Next Trek.

The regionals have participated in the beer renaissance as contract brewers, making fine specialty brews that, as brewers, they always wanted to make, but, as marketers, they never dared. Their customers are entrepreneurs who have everything to become brewers except the hardware. The beer drinker benefits, and the regionals get to strut their stuff.

So many great names are gone. John Koch gave up (although Genesee picked up his brands). So did Rudy Schaefer. Even his flagship brewery in the Lehigh Valley now flies the Stroh flag. Ortlieb, National Premium, Horlacher, Schmidt—gone. Rolling Rock is owned by Canadians.

Some diehards fight the good fight. The Lion in Wilkes-Barre is like a tough rodent that can't be killed, and at Straub's, they still close for deer season, then reopen immediately after to brew up the sulfurous concoction that cuts perfectly through coal dust.

Baltimore still has its great ethnic neighborhoods, but creeping yuppyism is everywhere, and without the glue of a true local beer, the social fabric will continue to decay. There is lots of good beer to be had—imports, contracts, and micros. And there is lots of exposed brick. Some call it prosperity. But there is no Boh, no mo'.

DELAWARE

KINDRED SPIRITS
Delaware Blue Hen Chapter (BCCA), 104 Edjil Dr., Newark, DE 19713

MARYLAND

★ G. Heileman Brewing Co., 4501 Hollins Ferry Rd., Baltimore, MD 21227
Type: Branch plant of G. Heileman, La Crosse, WI

★ British Brewing Co., 6759 Baymeadow Dr., Glen Burnie, MD 21061

KINDRED SPIRITS
Chesapeake Bay Chapter (BCCA), c/o Ron Holden, 1603 Odell Ave., Baltimore, MD 21237

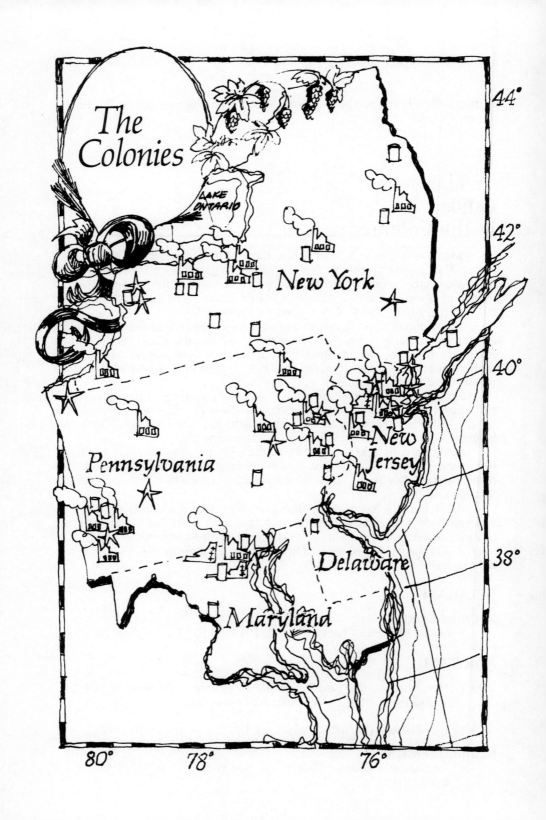

OF NOTE

Brewing Supplies
Flying Barrel, 111 South Carrol St., Frederick, MD 21701
Brew Masters LTD, Reuben Rudd, 12266 Wilkins Ave., Rockville, MD 20748
The Breweriana Collector, the classy publication of the National Association of Breweriana Advertising. George Hilton, editor, 9886 Postwick Rd., Ellicott City, MD 21043
Mead-Anderings, publication of Phoenix Imports, 2925 Montclair Dr., Ellicott City, MD 21043 ($5 per year).

GREAT PLACES

Baltimore: Haussner's, Bertha's, the Bromwell Inn . . . With great seafood and discreet ethnic neighborhoods, Baltimore remains one of the nation's great beer drinking locales. Now if it only had the beers of Seattle. Maybe by 2000.
(RIP) American Brewing Co., one of the nation's remaining treasures of brewery architecture.

NEW JERSEY

★ Eastern Brewing Corp., 334 North Washington St., Hammonton, NJ 08037
Type: Independent regional
Brands: Canadian Ace, Milwaukee Premium, Old Bohemian, Old German, and a slew of obscure brands, mostly from defunct eastern breweries

★ Anheuser-Busch, Inc., 200 U.S. Highway 1, Newark, NJ 07101
Type: Branch plant of Anheuser-Busch, St. Louis, MO

★ Pabst Brewing Co., 400 Grove St., Newark, NJ 07106
Type: Branch plant of Pabst Brewing Co., Milwaukee, WI

★ Vernon Valley Brewery, P.O. Box 1100, Rt. 94, Vernon, NJ 07462
Type: Microbrewery
Brands: Old World Classic, Pilsner, Winter Bock, Dark, Blond Double Bock, Vernon Lite
Tours: By appointment only. Call (201) 827-0034.
Breweriana: T-shirts
Slogan: "Have a Real Beer"

KINDRED SPIRITS

Mid Atlantic Sudsers and Hoppers (MASH) Homebrewers Club, c/o Mark Bernick, P.O. Box 105, Flagtown, NJ 08821
Garden State Chapter (BCCA), Jay Dertinger, 837 Seymour Ave., Linden, NJ 07036
Jersey Shore Chapter (BCCA), Joe Radman, 4 Maple Dr., Colts Neck, NJ 07722
Laphraoig Chapter (BCCA), Bill Christensen, P.O. Box 1732, Madison, NJ 07940

GREAT PLACES

There must be great places to drink beer in New Jersey, but The Great Beer Trek never found them. Maybe they can be found in the newsletter published by the Bar Tourists of America, c/o Jack McDougall, 12 Sylvester St., Cranford, NJ 07016 ($6 per year).

NEW YORK

* Anheuser-Busch, Inc., 2885 Belgium Rd., P.O. Box 200, Baldwinsville, NY 13027
  Type: Branch plant of Anheuser-Busch, St. Louis, MO

* Brooklyn Brewery, 230 4th Ave., Brooklyn, NY 11215
  Type: Contract
  Brands: Brooklyn Lager (contract brewed by F. X. Matt, Utica, NY)

* Miller Brewing Co., P.O. Box 200, Fulton, NY 13069
  Type: Branch plant for Miller Brewing Co., Milwaukee, WI

* Rochester Brewpub, 800 Jefferson Rd., Henrietta, NY 14623
  Type: Pub brewery
  Brands: Amber Ale, Oatmeal Stout, Oktoberfest Lager, Red Ale, Buffalo Bitter, Nickel City Dark

* Manhattan Brewing Co., Inc., 40-42 Thompson St., New York, NY 10013
  Type: Microbrewery
  Brands: Manhattan Gold Lager Beer, Manhattan Amber Ale, Manhattan Special Porter, Manhattan Royal Amber, Manhattan Sports Ale
  Tours: Call for times: (212) 219-9250. Brewery recently closed for renovation.
  Breweriana: T-shirts, sweatshirts, caps, glassware, pins, posters, etc.
  Slogan: Mascot and logo is horses and brewery wagon.

* Old New York Brewing Co., Inc., 610 West 26th St., New York, NY 10001
  Type: Microbrewery/contract. Originally a contract brewer, this company opened its own brewery, only to return to the contract route.
  Brands: New Amsterdam Amber Beer, New Amsterdam Ale (now defunct, brands sold to F. X. Matt)

* Flour City Brewing Co., Inc., 972 South Plymouth Ave., Rochester, NY 14608
  Type: Microbrewery

* Genesee Brewing Co., Inc., 445 Saint Paul St., Rochester, NY 14603
  Type: Independent regional
  Brands: Genesee Beer, Genesee Cream Ale, Genesee Light Beer, Genesee 12 Horse Ale, Genesee Cream Light, Kochs Black Horse, Kochs Golden Anniversary

Slogans: Genesee Beer and Genesee Light: "Boy, Could I Go for a Genny Now"; Genesee Cream Ale: "It's Not the Same Old Brewskie"

★ F. X. Matt Brewing Co., 811 Edward St., Utica, NY 13502
Type: Independent regional
Brands: Matt's Premium, Matt's Light, Saranac 1888 All Malt Lager, Utica Club Light and Ale, Maximus Super, plus contract brews (New Amsterdam, Dock Street Amber, Brooklyn Lager, Portland Lager, Boston Amber Export, Newman's Albany Amber)
Tours: June–August: Mon.–Fri., 10:00 A.M.–5:00 P.M.; Sept.–May: Mon.–Fri. Also by reservation (315) 732-3181.
Breweriana: Varied. On sale at brewery gift shop.

★ Buffalo Brewpub, 6861 Main St., Williamsville, NY 14221
Type: Pub brewery
Brands: Amber Ale, Oatmeal Stout, Roo Brew, Oktoberfest Lager, Red Ale

KINDRED SPIRITS

Simon Pure Chapter (BCCA), Bob Terray, 60 Wilkshire Pl., Lancaster, NY 14086

Long Island Chapter (BCCA), Ed Nichols, P.O. Box 513, Valley Stream, NY 11586

Knickerbocker Chapter (BCCA), Ed Nichols, P.O. Box 513, Valley Stream, NY 11580

Congress Chapter (BCCA), Steve Adydan, 2846 Rt. 174, Marietta, NY 13110

Officer Suds Chapter (BCCA), Wayne Ford, 424 Larchmont Ave., Utica, NY 13502

Schultz and Dooley Chapter (BCCA), Dennis Heffner, 17 Inverness Lane, Clifton Park, NY 12065

Southern Tier Chapter (BCCA), Don Holden, R.D. 5, Box 304A, Binghamton, NY 13905

Amateur Brewers of Central New York, Dick Goyer, 301 Wellington Rd., Dewitt, NY 13214

Broome County Fermenters Association, c/o Brice Feal, 2601 Grandview Place, Endicott, NY 13760

GREAT PLACES

Albany: Washington Tavern
Dewitt (near Syracuse): R. J. O'Toole's
Inlet: Red Dog Tavern
New York City: Manhattan Brewing Co., McSorley's Ale House, Cheyene Social Club
Rochester: California Brew House

OF NOTE

Beer Marketer's, 51 Virginia Ave., West Nyack, NY 10994. Industry newsletter.

Brewing Supplies
Hennessy Homebrew Inc., Dan Hennessy, R.D. 3, Box 470, Rensselaer, NY 12144

(RIP) William S. Newman Brewing Co., 32 Leonard St., Albany. Another testament to the American beer drinker's steadfast refusal to accept English-style ales.

Buffalo chicken wings. Get 'em mild, medium, hot, or blast furnace, served with celery sticks and bleu cheese dressing. This is the original nouvelle Americaine cuisine. Created by Frank and Teressa at the Anchor Lounge, 1047 Main St., Buffalo, NY 14209.

Great Fermentations
Chapter House Brewery, Ithaca, NY (new Pub brewery)

PENNSYLVANIA

★ Stoudt Brewing Co., Rt. 272, Adamstown, PA 19501
  Type: Microbrewery
  Brands: Stroudt's Golden Lager, Stroudt's Pilsner, Stroudt's Adamstown Amber, Stroudt's Seasonal Dark such as Oktoberfest, Christmas Beer, Mardi Gras, Spring Bock, Summer Bock
  Tours: Sat., 3:00 P.M.; Sun., 1:00 P.M. Group tours by appointment. During the summer: Fri., 8:00 P.M.; Sat., 3:00 P.M. and 7:00 P.M.; Sun., 1:00 P.M. and 5:00 P.M. (215) 484-4387
  Breweriana: Baseball caps, pins, T-shirts, polo shirts, glasses, mugs, barbeque aprons, banners, coasters, sweatshirts
  Slogan: Logo is taken from 1820 Pennsylvania Dutch coverlet made in Lancaster, PA

★ Stroh Brewery Co., S.W. Rt. 22 and Hwy. 100, Allentown, PA 18001
  Type: Branch plant of the Stroh Brewery Co., Detroit, MI
  Tours: Mon.–Fri., 12:00–3:00 P.M.

★ Braumeister Inc., 453 Easton Rd., Drexel Hill, PA 19026
  Type: Contract
  Brand: Trupert

★ Saint Michael's Brewing Co., 3002 Hempland Co., Lancaster, PA 17601
  Type: Contract
  Brand: Saint Michael's Non-Alcoholic Malt Beverage

★ The William Penn Brewing Co., 680 Middletown Blvd., P.O. Box L-565, Langhorne, PA 19047
  Type: Contract
  Brand: William Penn Colonial Lager

★ Latrobe Brewing Co., Box 350, Latrobe, PA 15650
  Type: Regional owned by LaBatt Importers, Darien, CT
  Brands: Rolling Rock Premium Beer, Rolling Rock Light Beer, Rolling Rock Light-n-Low

★ Dock Street Brewing Co., P.O. Box 30255, Philadelphia, PA 19103
Type: Contract
Brands: Dock Street Amber Beer (contract brewed by F. X. Matt, Utica, NY)
Tours: Brewery currently under construction.
Breweriana: Hats, T-shirts

★ Pennsylvania Brewing Co., The Bourse, Suite 900 West, Independence Mall
East, Philadelphia, PA 19106
Type: Contract
Brand: Pennsylvania Pilsner (contract brewed by Pittsburgh Brewing Co.,
Pittsburgh, PA)

★ Saint Michael's Non-Alcoholic Malt Beverage Corp., 230 South Broad St.,
2d Floor, Philadelphia, PA 19102
Type: Contract
Brand: Saint Michael's Non-Alcoholic Malt Beverage

★ Pittsburgh Brewing Co., 3340 Liberty Ave., Pittsburgh, PA 15201
Type: Independent regional
Brands: Iron City, Iron City Light, Iron City Golden Lager, Old German, Old
Dutch, American, Iron City Dark, Iron City Cooler

★ D. G. Yuengling and Son, Inc., 5th and Manhantongo Sts., Pottsville, PA
17901
Type: Independent regional
Brands: Yuengling Premium Brewed, Porter, Chesterfield Ale, Yuengling
Light, Amber Lager
Tours: Mon.–Fri., 10:00 A.M. and 1:30 P.M.
Breweriana: Hats, T-shirts, sweatshirts, mugs, posters, ashtrays, mirrors
Slogan: "American Eagle, America's Oldest Brewery"

★ Straub Brewery, 303 Sorg St., St. Mary's, PA 15857
Type: Independent regional
Brands: Straub Beer, Straub Light
Tours: Mon.–Fri., 9:00 A.M.–noon. No children under 12.
Breweriana: Yes
Slogans: "Have a Greenie," "Hi-Test"

★ Keystone Brewery of Western Pennsylvania, 110 Connelly Blvd., Sharon, PA
16146
Type: Pub brewery
Brands: Lager and ale

★ Jones Brewing Co., Smithton, PA 15479
Type: Independent regional
Brands: Stoney's Gold Crown, Esquire, Fort Pitt, Old Shay, Old Shay Golden
Ale, Stoney's Light

★ The Lion Inc., Gibbons/Stegmaier Brewery, 700 North Pennsylvania Ave., P.O. Box GS, Wilkes-Barre, PA 18703
Type: Independent regional
Brands: Gibbons, Bartels, Stegmaier, Esslinger, Liebotschaner, Steg Light, Lionshead

KINDRED SPIRITS

Homebrewers of Philadelphia and Suburbs (HOPS), c/o Richard Gleeson, 344 South Taylor Ave., Crum Lynn, PA 19022

Olde Frothingslosh Chapter (BCCA), Walt Wimer, Jr., 130 Germain Rd., Butler, PA 16001

Horlacher Chapter (BCCA), Alan Williams III, 1070 Brentwood Ave., Bethlehem, PA 18017

Greater Delaware Valley Chapter (BCCA), Jim Cartin, 532 Oak Dr., Harleysville, PA 19438

Fort Pitt Chapter (BCCA), Will Hartlep, 1304 Pinewood Dr., Pittsburgh, PA 15243

GREAT PLACES

Lancaster: House of Pasta
Philadelphia: Dickens Inn, McGillin's Old Ale House

OF NOTE

Brewing Supplies

Hayes' Homebrewing Supply, 311 South Allen St., State College, PA 16801

Home Sweet Homebrew, Kurt Denke, 2007 Sansom St., Philadelphia, PA 19103

Barnesville Oktoberfest, July. Unlimited beer and oom-pah bands.

Pittsburgh, any Sunday prior to a Steelers' game. Pregame tailgate parties and postgame trips to the local. One of the few towns left where they know how to drink beer.

A Beer Drinker's Guide to the Bars of Reading. Available from D. Wardrop, Box 405, R.D. 1, Temple, PA 19560 ($2 plus postage). Reading's 132 bars are described and rated. A local beer trekker's classic.

Beer can be purchased for takeout in taverns or by the case from designated beer outlets, an archaic distribution system that has worked to the advantage of Pennsylvania's small brewers.

BUY 'EM IF YOU CAN FIND 'EM

Genesee Cream Ale (Genesee). An ultimate American ale, slightly more body than a pilsner but utterly devoid of either taste or aftertaste. Exceptional in its inoffensiveness. To tell the truth, this is your average brewski.

Straub (Straub's). The aroma carries across the room. This beer's character comes not from imported malts and fancy hops but from the practiced hands that work the sulfurous water bubbling up from the coal-veined hills surrounding St. Mary's, PA.

Milwaukee Premium (Eastern). One of the least pretentious beers in America—and one of the worst. Still it is drinkable, cheap, cheap, cheap, and for most palates the equal of Bud.

Ballantine India Pale Ale (Falstaff/General). At the time of the original Beer Trek, one of the most unusual beers in America, supposedly approximating a highly attenuated brew aged in wood for the length of time it takes a clipper ship to sail from Southampton to Calcutta. Puts hair on your chest. But the microbrewers have now shown us what this beer is really supposed to taste like.

Matt's Premium (F. X. Matt), Utica's finest. Distinct fruity flavor and sparkling liveliness that you take for granted if you are from Utica but appreciate if you are from out of town.

Rolling Rock (Rolling Rock). A top-quality product from a regional brewer. Rolling Rock is light and bland but distinctive enough to have attracted a minor cult following.

Stegmaier (The Lion). An archetypal Pennsylvania beer once voted the state's worst by an incompetent panel from *Philadelphia* magazine. Steg's biggest sin is a total lack of pretension. For the price, you can't beat it.

Yuengling Porter (Yuengling). "It's getting darker all the time," claims Dick Yuengling. Not as exotic as when no other brewer in America still brewed a porter but fun to drink as much for nostalgia value as flavor.

Chesterfield Ale (Yuengling). Another great hoppy brew from Pennsylvania's only Chinese brewer ("Ying-ling," get it?).

New Amsterdam Amber (Old New York). Matthew Reich has been a tireless ambassador of the renaissance. Brand now owned by F. X. Matt.

4
THE
WASTELAND

WILLIAMSBURG, VIRGINIA, TO COVINGTON, KENTUCKY
28 DAYS, 6,930 MILES ON THE ROAD

GIVE ME LIBERTY OR GIVE
ME BEER
Washington, D.C.

It was worth a try. After all, we were in Washington, D.C., and would not have a better opportunity to call the White House. This was a task for Laura, fair maiden of The Great Beer Trek and first lady of the van:

Ring . . . Ring . . . Ring.

"Hello, The White House."

"Hello, this is The Great Beer Trek, and I would like to get some information on what beers are served at the White House, either informally or at state functions."

"Beer . . . OK, one moment."

Ring . . . Ring . . . Ring.

"Hello, Press Office. May I help you?"

"Yes. I'd like to know what beers are served at the White House, either informally or at state functions."

"What beer is served?

"Umm (snicker). Just a moment. (aside) Bob . . . I have someone here who wants to know about beer at the White House (chuckle). No . . . what kinds are served. Who could I connect her to? Grace (chuckle), there's a person calling who wants to know what kind of beer is served at the White House . . . I think so. Ask Charlie, does he know?"

(Back into the receiver.) "One moment please, we're working on it."

"Thank you."

(Aside) "Can we connect her to the kitchen? OK, then, how about the First Lady's press secretary?" (Back into the receiver.) "Hello, I'll connect you to the First Lady's press secretary. Sorry to keep you waiting."

"That's OK. Thank you."

Ring . . . Ring . . . Ring.

"Hello, First Lady's press secretary's office."

"Hello, I'm doing some research on beer in America. I'd like to find out what beers are served at the White House."

"You mean to the family?" (Snicker)

"Either to the family or at official state functions."

"Oh . . . (chuckle), I really wouldn't know."

"Could you connect me to someone who might know?"

"Umm . . . one moment."

Ring . . . Ring . . . Ring.

"Hello, Press Office." (A different voice.)

"Hello, I think I've been here. I'm doing research on American beer, and I would like to find out what beers are served at the White House either informally or at official functions."

"Beer?"

"Yes."

"Well . . . (sigh) Let me think who'd be able to help you. May I ask what organization you are representing?"

"This is The Great Beer Trek."

"The . . . Great . . . Beer . . . Trek."

"Yes."

"OK, one moment." (put on hold.)

"Hello? I really can't get you that information."

"Well, could you have someone check the refrigerator?"

"Hm-m-m. That would be the easiest route. What's your number? I'll call you back."

But they never did call back, a fact that demonstrates both a lack of follow-through on the part of national government and a disorientation of priorities. Oh, well.

Having not been invited to the White House to share a cold one, The Great Beer Trek visited the United States Brewers Association, the industry's biggest lobbying group. The association was founded in 1862 to help the

Union cause at a time when the Confederacy was threatening to dominate the conflict. Exactly what the USBA accomplished for the war effort has long since been forgotten, but the diehard beer drinker cannot help but notice the date of the organization's inception coincides exactly with the time the tide began to turn favorably for the Union.

The people we met at the USBA were polite and helpful, but they made it entirely clear that they were concerned with the Big Issues, those factors that can affect the nation's overall consumption. The Big Issues include topics such as litter, teenage alcoholism, and drunk driving, not beer treks. Beneath the apparent altruism of the trade organization is the very calculated desire to keep the trading environment as open as possible for its membership. The industry must keep a small step ahead of its critics if it hopes to avoid restrictive regulation that will make operating a brewery less profitable. The brewing industry lobbies hard, for instance, against bottle bills, which increase the price of goods and the nuisance factor of doing business. As an alternative, the USBA developed an educational anti-litter campaign called "Pitch-In," which encourages proper disposal of nonreturnable containers. The question remains as to whether the brewers can mount an effective campaign before being subjected to a bewildering variety of state-passed bottle bills. Probably not.

Positive Litter Reduction
FROM THE U.S.B.A.

Lurking in the deep recesses of the association's mind is the fact that for thirteen years their membership was subjected to the most rigorous restrictions imaginable in the form of Prohibition. The brewers of the time, who were aware of beer's historical reputation as the beverage of moderation, never anticipated that their product would be caught in the tangled net of temperance along with hard spirits. It could happen again, the USBA reminds us, but for their constant diligence. Let us hope they are wrong.

As for the Big Issues from the perspective of The Great Beer Trek, the USBA's explanations followed predictable party lines. Beer in the United States is not bland or faceless, they say. There is no lack of choice. The brewers give beer drinkers what they want and they want what they get. Otherwise they

Prohibition 1919 ~ 1933
COULD THIS HAPPEN AGAIN?

would not buy it, and the brewers would go out of business, but instead beer consumption has been on the rise over the past decade. American consumers get what they want.

The industry position is inarguable and equally irrelevant to the beer drinker. Consumption may be rising, but it is still low compared to other countries, notably England and Germany, where a wider range of malted products is available. Behind their professional smiles and expressions of encouragement, the industry association was stonewalling our efforts to learn about beer drinking in America. It was time to take the case back to the people. Luckily we found a proper place to do so, not far from the USBA, on 22d Street, NW.

The Brickskeller is a mecca for the homesick, the curious, the jaded, the can collector, or the beer trekker. The bar is downstairs in a brownstone. The walls are lined with all manner and description of beer cans, a display that can entertain for hours. A not uncommon sight at the Brickskeller is people drifting sideways, face to the wall, mesmerized by the variety of design and color. I began to whimper as I surveyed the beer list. By the time I had reached the end, tears were streaming down my cheeks, and I was throwing money at the bartender, a redoubtable lad named Jack Blush. The Brickskeller stocks over three hundred American beers and an almost equal number of imports. They were all there. I could complete our itinerary without moving from this one bar. From Billy to Blitz, from Lucky to Leinenkugel. I had found a home.

The Brickskeller's own truck travels the nation to acquire local brews, which in Washington become the exotic. The business is supported by can collectors and pure beer drinkers. On any given night 90 percent of the sane people of Washington can be found in the Brickskeller trying to undo the effects of trying to run the country for another day. The establishment is an umbilical attaching an entire city to reality. I asked Jack Blush, who is as honest as he is knowledgeable about beer, why such a haven had no draft beer available.

"Because draft beer doesn't come in cans."

Selling beer is just a single facet of the Brickskeller business. Cans are bottom opened. Those not kept by customers are sold via mail order to collectors nationwide. A private-label beer, Brickskeller Saloon Style, brewed by Pittsburgh Brewing Co., is sold across the bar, as are Brickskeller T-shirts. Jack introduced us to his boss, Maurice Coja, the mastermind behind this frothy empire. He has been a publican most of his life and has owned the present operation since 1957. The burgeoning interest in beer cans gave him the idea of creating a place where a collector could personally supervise the expansion of his collection.

There was more empire to see. The upstairs of the Brickskeller is a cavernous room bedecked with breweriana and a battery of dart boards. This is the dart capital of the nation's capital. The Brickskeller sponsors not one dart team but twenty-six. As a setting for darts, it is inspirational. Combined with a beer selection that borders on the infinite, this is a place where a beer drinker could spend the rest of his days. I pinched myself to be sure I had not died and gone to heaven.

And still the empire stretched on. There is a dart pro shop to satisfy the whimsy of even the most serious chucker. Then there is the import business. Mr. Coja is the sole importer of Le Gueuze, a weiss beer (brewed with wheat, not barley malt) from the Payottenland district of Belgium. This is one of the famous lambic beers, fermented without the addition of yeast, but rather by the controlled contamination of wild microorganisms, an unthinkable procedure for the antiseptic-minded modern brewer. [An excellent description of lambic beers appears in Michael Jackson's *The World Guide to Beer* (Running Press, 1982).] We were treated to a taste. The beer is fresh, winey, alive, and unlike anything made in this country.

Although the sun almost never sets on Maurice Coja's beer conglomerate, he is still gazing out toward the horizon. He would not be insulted to hear himself described as a wheeler-dealer. He has hustled a business from beer; now there appears to be no limit to what can be done. The secret is not to think small. Shortly after Miller began to brew Löwenbräu domestically, he began making inquiries into acquiring import rights to the real Löwenbräu. After a healthy does of bureaucratic shuffling, the government turned down his application, giving the reason for their denial that importing the real Löwenbräu would tend to confuse the public.

Maurice Coja shook his head slowly as he told the story. Taking no for an answer is not one of his strong suits. Some night while sitting in his throne at the Brickskeller he would figure out a way . . .

He asked about the Beer Trek, and we told him how we had encountered great interest in beer but a hopeless outlook for all but the largest breweries.

THE REAL
Löwenbräu..?

The consensus listed the remaining breweries by 1990 at fewer than ten.

"Don't be too sure," he said with the confidence of someone who knows that his four-of-a-kind beats your straight. "I think there will be *more* breweries in 1990 than there are now."

He deliberately left the bait dangling, and I willingly swallowed. "How do you figure that?"

"Look around," he said with an expanse of the hand. "People are willing to pay good money for good beer. Now grain is cheap, water is cheap, hops are cheap, and you don't have to be a genius to brew a barrel of beer."

I pressed him for details, wondering if future batches of Brickskeller might originate from the house brewery.

"Like I said," Maurice Coja shrugged and made eye contact to lend emphasis to the enigma, "grain is cheap, water is cheap, and you don't have to be a genius to brew a barrel of beer."

BLOOD, SWEAT, AND BEERS   Williamsburg, Virginia

In 1766 Josiah Chowning heralded the opening of his business by advertising an establishment "where all who please to favor me with their custom may depend upon the best of entertainment for themselves, servants and horses." His tavern was an "ordinary," a notch below the Kings Arms, Wetherburn's, and the Raleigh Tavern in appointments and service. It was, very likely, the liveliest place in Williamsburg. It still is.

Today Chowning's Tavern, as with all the other restorations of Williamsburg, achieves the proper balance of historical authenticity and twentieth-century functionalism. The tavern is crowded every night, just as it might have been during "Publick Times," a twice yearly event in the colonies when General Court was in session and the local populace flocked to the capital to join in the general merriment that accompanied horse races and fairs.

Josiah Chowning

FROM THE SIGN OUTSIDE HIS TAVERN.

Today costumed waitresses wedge tourists into rough-hewn tables where they munch peanuts and sip on bland approximations of colonial drinks while a troubadour serenades with period folk songs. Period games of skill and chance (mostly the latter) are distributed to the willing, and tourists participate with an enthusiasm that supersedes formal introduction. It is perhaps the closest approximation of the colonial tavern experience available to the denizen of the twentieth century, and yet not the least pretension is made of preserving the historical accuracy of the beverages.

At Chowning's they serve, albeit in a stoneware mug, a dark lager made by Miller and light lager made by Schmidt's. Although this choice is to be commended in terms of its variety compared to the average contemporary hostelry, the blandness becomes obvious when compared to the creative concoctions that might have been offered in the same tavern several hundred years ago.

History graces us with rose-colored glasses that make the world look blurrily cheerful as if viewed through the bottom of an empty mug. We forget Thomas Jefferson's pimples, George Washington's wooden teeth, and Daniel Boone's body odor. We correctly remember colonial taverns as being lively social centers where the pillars of society met, over beer, to discuss the principles that were to become the foundation of America.

With such properly motivated founding fathers, is it any surprise that these United States have gone on to become the mightiest nation on the face of the earth and, not coincidentally, its largest beer producer? And yet is it not an indication of the country's current predicament that our leaders no

Raleigh Tavern
COLONIAL WILLIAMSBURG

longer gather at the tavern for a fraternal tankard? The alcohol-tinged portrait of the current political leader is likely to be closer to the vodka-swilling senator in the arms of his floozie at the Silver Slipper or the lonely, depressed First Lady washing down her valium with gin.

That this nation was founded on the blood, sweat, and beers of great men is immediately apparent upon visiting Williamsburg. The Raleigh Tavern became the capital of Virginia when in 1774 the House of Burgesses met in its Apollo Room to unify support for blockaded Boston. Yes, it all happened over beer, and, in some respects, because of beer.

Until the 1760s the colonies had accepted a role as a part of the empire. The movement toward independence gathered momentum in the mid-1760s. Not surprisingly, from the beer's-eye view of a besotted historian, this coincides with the imposition of a British tax on imported beer. Hitherto the colonists had consumed the readily available English beers and ales. Suddenly, they faced being shut off without a domestic product to fill the void. A revolution was inevitable.

The Williamsburg guidebook tells us about the Raleigh:

The Raleigh was a center of social activity . . . planters and merchants gathered at the bar. Sturdy tavern tables were scarred by dice-boxes. Tobacco smoke from long clay pipes filled the air, together with heated political discussions. Good fellowship was sealed by a toast of Madeira or a hot rum punch, or by a pint of ale drunk from a pewter tankard.

But what about the beers? Were they as quenching to the thirst as the image of the Raleigh is to the memory? Or were those brews as appealing as George Washington's wooden smile?

The eighteenth-century American sought the same things at his local tavern as we do today: comfort, camaraderie, and booze. Although coffee and tea were popular beverages in the colonies, they did not appear as features on the tavern bill of fare. Principal liquors sold were domestic and imported wines, fortified wines (brandy, claret, and Madeira), rum, gin, hard cider, and, of course, beer. Exotic punches involving combinations of the aforementioned spirits carried colorful names such as Kill Divil, Ockuby, Rumbullion, Stonewall, Blackstrap, Tiff, Sillibub, Sampson, Hotch Potch, Caudel, Arrack, Athol Brose, and Swinglingtow and undoubtedly packed the same impact as the modern day depth charge or stump-lifter. Later in this chapter it will be shown how creatively beer was used as a base for the colonial punch.

An average tavern offered small beer, domestic ale, imported strong beers and ales, and porter. As opposed to today's selection of brews where

The Conceptualist's View of Beer History

(Prehistory–1640) North American native beverage pulque (fermented juice of maguey cactus) is augmented by the brewing of Spaniards (1544) and English (1607). Pilgrims, especially, bring with them an affinity for malted beverages. Home brewing becomes a way of life.

(1640–1760—Precolonial) Advances in mercantile trade make imported beers more readily available. Domestic industry lags, except in mid-Atlantic states where William Penn helps establish Philadelphia as the nation's brewing center, building the region's first commercial brewery in 1683.

(1760–1800—Revolutionary) War effort demonstrates vulnerability of beer supply. Founding fathers (Washington, Jefferson, Adams, Madison) promote legislation to encourage domestic brewing industry.

(1800–1840—English Tradition) Rooted in the traditions of our English forebears, commercial brewing industry attains regional viability. D. G. Yuengling Co., founded in 1829, is oldest U.S. brewer still in operation.

(1840–1880—The Bavarian Influx) Our greatest contemporary breweries date from this era. The United States Brewers Association forms during the Civil War. If there was a Golden Age of Brewing in the United States, this was it.

(1880–1920—The Precipice) Technological advances in the late nineteenth century barely overshadow the growing racial and social backlash to the burgeoning Germanic communities. World War I gives the "dry" contingent the outside stimulus needed to pass Prohibition.

(1920–1960—The Martini Era) The nation finally returns to its senses long enough to repeal Prohibition, but the sudsy recovery is hindered by yet another world war. Beer languishes during the fatuous fifties, a decade most notable for its staggering number of brewery closings.

(1960–2000—The Renaissance) The raising of consciousness in the sixties opens people's eyes to the bleakness of their sudsy surroundings. The Coors Mystique returns beer to respectability and paves the way for the enlightenment of the Beer Drinker. The direction for the balance of the century appears assured.

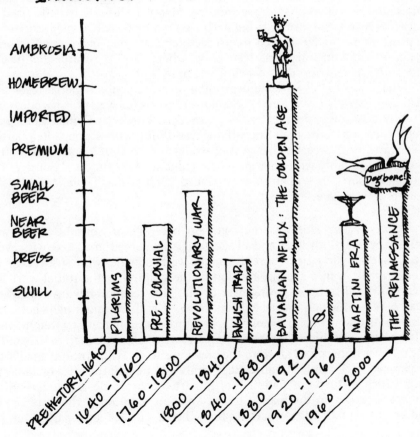

National Beerworthiness Indicator

differentiation is achieved more through packaging than taste, beers at the colonial tavern had distinct characteristics:

Strong Beer and Ale. Imported brews, then as now, were more respected than domestic products. Commercial brewing did not thrive in the New World until the 1760s when the British increased the tax on beer as part of the Stamp Act. Although barley was abundant in America, there were few commercial malt houses, and existing breweries depended on imported malt. Even worse, there was no bottle manufacturing industry. Until the 1800s most beer and ale was brewed in the tavern or home. Legislative acts initiated by Thomas Jefferson and James Madison encouraged brewing and established the fledgling industry.

The distinction between ale and beer was as unclear in colonial times as it is today. Some sources (and some early recipes) are consistent with sixteenth-century English custom defining ale to be a drink made without hops. Other sources differentiated beer and ale along the lines currently used in British brewing, the former being darker and more heavily bodied, the result of using more highly roasted malts. Neither definition bears much resemblance to contemporary American usage where "ale" is regarded as having double the macho quotient of a similarly branded beer.

Taste was highly variable depending on ingredients, regional taste, and local water supply (even New World brewers corrected water for hardness but could not remove minerals as does a modern brewery). Comparisons with present-day, top-fermented English imports (Whitbread, Watney's Red Barrel, MacEwan's or Newcastle Brown Ale) would not be unreasonable, although clarity and stability were inferior to the contemporary product. Some of the popular imports in Williamsburg included London Ale, Scotch Ale, Bristol Beer, and Welsh Ale.

Small Beer. This was the common beverage of working classes and country people. Both sexes and all age groups consumed small beer with every meal, especially in cities where the public water supplies were suspect. Small beer is made from a second infusion of the grain after the initial wort has been drawn off to make strong beer or ale. This second brewing produces a weak beverage, which must be drunk fresh. It is the original light beer. Because of its low alcoholic strength (approximately 2.5 percent by weight, variable by brewer), which gave it a low preservative value and high perishability, it was never transported far from the brewing site. In Williamsburg small beer was known as "Virginia Middling Beer" and cost one-half the price of domestic beer, which in turn cost one-half of imported beer or ale. No equivalent of small beer exists on the market today. An approximation of the taste can be had by mixing Bass Ale, or perhaps home brew, with an equal part water.

Porter. Some versions of this beer are highly hopped, while others tend toward sweetness; some are both. Porter is brewed from dark, highly caramelized malts that give it a mahogany color similar to bock. The name derives from the popularity of this beverage with the porters in the London markets where it originated.

HMM... EYE OF BAT, WING OF NEWT, 2 KEGS ALE...

A Colonial Sampler

In addition to the various beers and ales available, the frequenter of the colonial tavern might have had colorful and exotic sudsy concoctions prepared, and perhaps invented, by his friendly purveyor of spirits. Many recipes survive that provide insight to the good-humored wit of the creators, as well as the capacity of the imbibers. What would you call a mixture of half old and half bitter ale? Why, "Mother-In-Law," of course. Rum plus beer was "Calibogus," while "Lamb's Wool," "Rumfustian," "Bellowstop," and "Colonel Byrd's Nightcap" describe unique colonial beer-based cocktails. To read through these recipes is to appreciate the versatility of beer for the adventuresome palate. Not only were many brews served hot instead of cold, but they featured ingredients ranging from ground ginger, to egg yolks, to spiced toast, to a cucumber garnish. In honor of our visit to Williamsburg we created our ale punch, guaranteed to slake the thirst of any traveler. Ask for it the next time you stay at a Holiday Inn. If the bartender gives you a blank stare, you can tell him how to make it:

Beer Trekker's Bellyache—Pour 2 quarts strong ale into a cast-iron caldron. Warm gently with lemon peel and enough crumbled brown bread to make a pudding-like consistency. With a mortar and pestle crush ¼ ounce ginger together with 12 cloves, and 1 large pinch bruised cinnamon and grated nutmeg. Into a separate bowl crack a dozen eggs. Add spices along with 1 gill brandy, 1 gill gin and bitters, and 1 bottle of sherry. Mix contents; add to caldron. Stir vigorously with a glowing poker until the mixture starts frothing over. Strain through a tammy. Garnish with a slice of cucumber. Go to bed.

Varietal beers. These domestically brewed beers were limited in variety only by the imagination of the brewers making them. Each recipe combined regionally available items according to the whim of an individual. Varietal types included spruce beer, maple beer, lemon beer, hop beer, nettle beer, ginger beer, and corn beer. These beers live only in the memories of the contemporary home brewers whose imaginations know no restraints.

But were the colonial beverages any good? The modern American commercial brewer would say emphatically, "No!" Without the advantages of mechanical refrigeration and modern methods of achieving sanitation and quality control, these beverages must have seemed neanderthal compared to the clean, crisp, consistently sparkling product available today. On the other hand, the more adventurous home brewer, whose quest for gustatorial adventure will tolerate the flat cloudiness of occasional contamination, would counter with an equally resounding "Yes!" Particularly when drunk fresh, there is no reason these beverages could not slake the thirst as well as homemade bread satisfies the palate.

But after all, it's a free country where we can worship the brew of our choice. That is what the Revolution was all about.

WHERE HAVE YOU GONE, BILLY BOY, BILLY BOY
Plains, Georgia

All good Yankees have been conditioned to fear the South. Its residents have been portrayed as bombers of innocent black children, blasters of defenseless hippies, and aboriginal rapists of defenseless canoeists. Thus, it was with some trepidation that The Great Beer Trek hitched up its pants and plunged into a land that, in terms of its sudsy offerings, was as hospitable as a moonscape.

We were spoiled by this time. The initial shock of the recent carnage of independent breweries was now behind us. Any disappointment had been long since overcome by our positive reception at the remaining breweries and by meeting such a wide variety of likable and well-informed beer drinkers. The original hypothesis of the Trek—that almost any situation is improved through the addition of beer—had gained ample support. Despite some early setbacks we were clearly gaining momentum, momentum we would need to survive the Wasteland.

There are no independent breweries left in the Southeast. The regional beverages extend to the extremes—from Coke, Pepsi, and Dr. Pepper to sour mash, moonshine, and bourbon. The middle remains neglected. Beer prices are high, while liquor is relatively cheap. Dry counties dot the map, reviving the spectre of a beerless society.

Why?

From Williamsburg the van plunged South as far as Auburndale, Florida, site of the nondescript Duncan Brewing Co., makers of Dunk's Beer, a former

independent now operating under the Heileman corporate umbrella. This is the closest the Wasteland comes to having a native brewery. The nationals all have strategic outposts in the South, manufacturing dreadnoughts of minimal interest to us. Decent taverns are few and far between. In fact, the most popular watering hole in most southern towns is likely as not to be associated with a national chain, and we did not pack up in our van to drink beer in the Macon, Georgia, Pizza Hut.

And yet, if the brewers have plants here, obviously beer is consumed, but where and by whom? Not until we visited Plains, Georgia, did we learn about the southern beer drinking subculture.

Plains is as southern a town as exists. It has neither the mystery of the Piedmont, the allure of the Okefenokee, nor the lonely desolation of the Georgia coast; but it is a nice place where people tend to business and strive in their quiet ways for the comforts of twentieth-century life—a new pickup, a bass boat, a modern kitchen, and enough money for beer. At least, it *was* a nice place until one of its sons became president, catapulting the town into the national limelight.

On Route 280 is a huge parking lot asleep in a dusty field where the Welcome Center was built to handle the flood of tourists who never came. We went in and had forced upon us an unwanted armful of brochures touting the tourist attractions of Plains. The pamphlets were dutifully transported several hundred feet to a trash barrel half-filled with the things. Someone, in fact many people, had overestimated the appeal of Plains. Our goals were simple. When Jimmy Carter was elected president in 1976, a key factor in his victory was his appeal to the common man. Plains played a part in the image, as did his colorful family, especially brother Billy. Billy was a jewel whom the media discovered, polished, and eventually discarded.

Billy Carter ran for mayor of Plains on a noncommercial platform, vowing, if elected, to do everything in his power to keep Plains the simple, friendly town it has always been. He lost, and soon town residents were falling all over each other to make a buck off the expected tourist bonanza. The town dressed in the gaudy clothes of an amusement park to suit equally tasteless tourists who wandered about the simple town to break up the drive from Bayonne to

Disneyworld. Tours of Plains were initiated to show visitors points of interest such as the softball field where Jimmy played, Billy's wife's old home, Amy's school, and Jimmy's Uncle Alton's home.

If indeed it was inevitable that tourists would be coming to Plains and throwing money in the streets, then Billy, who more than anyone was in a position to pick up the money, was not too proud to bend. He formed his own tour to leave from his already famous gas station. If people wanted to pay $2.50 to look foolish sitting in a wagon pulled by a little choo-choo past the simple church, ranch homes, and softball fields of a backwoods Georgia town, Billy would oblige them.

We pulled into Billy Carter's gas station, swallowed an obligatory beer, and watched dust settle on Main Street, Plains. It was the kind of afternoon when Huck Finn would play hooky or Stanley Kowalski would come home drinking. There was nary a tourist in sight. We sat on the hard bench, swatted flies, and discussed what to do next. Plains was apparently a blind alley; time to move our lazy bones back into the van.

As we were pulling out of Billy's station, a young man with dark hair flagged us: "What's The Great Beer Trek?" (One does not drive around in a van with "The Great Beer Trek" plastered all over it unless one expects a few questions like this.) I explained our quest and about our loosely defined mission in Plains: to add another brush stroke to the national beer drinking portrait.

"Y'all looking for Billy?" The young man shielded his eyes from the late afternoon sun.

My reply carried at least a tinge of sarcasm. "I'm willing to bet he hasn't been here since the election."

The man replied slowly, without reacting to the sarcasm. "He was just here a few minutes ago. He's probably still around, or maybe up at the Country Club. Told me he had to get home because he has to go to Nashville tomorrow. You're interested in beer? You been up to the Country Club? It's the best place to drink beer in these parts. Maybe I'll meet you there later." He gave us directions. We decided it was worth the risk; our travels wouldn't be bringing us to Plains again.

The "Country Club" is a misnomer. This modest roadhouse, located on Route 280 a mile west of Plains, is described on its menu as "old and rustic." It is neither, although it is made of wood and has no furnishings more elaborate than a napkin dispenser. No one else had seen fit to grace the Country Club with their presence this day, not even any dumb tourists. We sat at the counter in awkward silence and sipped on another beer waiting for something to happen. The beers (Pabst, Schlitz, or Billy) were served ice cold and in the can. We asked the bartender, our voices again oozing with Yankee sarcasm, if Billy had been seen recently.

"Y'all just missed him. He couldn't have left more'n ten minutes ago. Y'all musta passed him on your way out of town," came the laconic reply. I

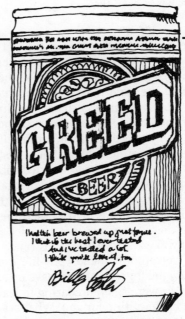

The Sad Saga of Billy

Billy Carter died in 1988, a victim of cancer, alcoholism, and fame. More than any other single person, his story is a testament to the changing nature of beer and how the beverage reflects the national spirit.

America in 1978 was a land of the defiant. The nation had been pummeled by inflation, mother nature, and Arab nations of all size and demeanor. The commander in chief, Jimmy Carter, returned decency to the head office but did so amid an environment of naiveté and incompetence. Beer was still a beverage of the common man.

Onto the national scene stepped Billy Carter, the president's brother and alter ego, a man as irreverent as Jimmy was pious. Beer was Billy's medium, and he rode its sudsy swell to national prominence. An elaborate plan was hatched to formulate a beer to be brewed and distributed by regional breweries and then marketed nationally. Advertising proved unnecessary; an avalanche of publicity launched the brand like a starship. After an initial blaze of glory, it came crashing back to earth.

Billy giggled and sipped his way through it all, raking in cash along the way. If people wanted to pay money to put his name on a beer, and if people wanted to pay money to ride on a little tourist train through Plains, and if people wanted to pay money to see him enter a bellyflopping contest, well, Billy would sure oblige them. "Greed?" Billy once told Newsweek *(November 14, 1977). "I know him. He's a good ol' sonovabitch."*

The refreshing good ol' boyness of Billy became old and less savory. The novelty faded, his brother was defeated, and the beer was bad. Billy stayed in the news, ironically, as a neoprohibitionist's symbol of the evils of alcohol. The business deals went sour, and the good-hearted, beery wisecracks did not sound so good coming from a man being treated for alcoholism. When Billy died, he was a shadow of the hard-living, suds-swilling man who showed many Americans that there was a common man within those Carter genes. The story deserved a happier ending.

began to get the feeling that this was the official party-line response around Plains to inquiries as to Billy's whereabouts.

The bartender and the cook at the Country Club, Gene Bacon, serves a mean, cold beer and makes a more-than-passable barbecue. He likes people but will not speak unless spoken to. Initially we thought him taciturn with strangers but later understood his silence as a form of acceptance. Had he not liked us, he would have busied himself in the kitchen. We asked, but Gene had no strong opinions about the transformation of Plains or the celebrity of Billy. Everyone else in town worried about such things. Gene concerned himself with barbecue, where his expertise could be documented by taste, not words. His barbecue sauce, containing 1,001 ingredients, is his legacy. A man needs something of his own, something of his own creation, that will live on when he dies. Gene may not be slick or glib, but neither is he gullible or dumb. If you want to recreate his sauce, he will give you the ingredients, and you are welcome to spend your life experimenting as he has. We started to copy down the ingredients but gave up somewhere between the grapefruit and Tabasco. We were again preparing to leave when our friend from town showed up. "I've been waiting for you. What are you doing up here?" Our puzzlement showed in our lack of response, so he continued. "This front part is for tourists. The good beer drinking's out back."

The entrance to the back section of the Plains Country Club is through a slightly askew door with a scrawled sign "Good Ol' Boys." The inside is rough and spare, proudly so. By comparison, the back makes the front seem as plush as any lounge in Atlanta's Peachtree Plaza. There is a jukebox and a pinball machine, both of which operate constantly, lending the scene a veneer of reality. Out here in the sticks, miles from the nearest Cuisinart or St. Pauli Girl, it is fitting that one should be able to listen to the ties that bind hillbillies nationwide—Willie Nelson, Ol' Waylon, Jerry Jeff Walker, and Dolly. Beyond the noise there is a rough wood floor, rough wood tables, and rough wood chairs. As in all the finest beer drinking places, there is nothing to distract one from the other people.

Introductions were accomplished easily. The people we met were Sam, Walter, Ed . . . all good 'uns who accepted us immediately since we were guests of one of their own. The lack of amenities was a patch worn on every sleeve, as if the Good Ol' Boys were clinging to a rough hewn ethic that changing times and the community's notoriety threatened to strip them of. These were rednecks in a small world where the redneck was king. We were flattered that they welcomed us into their temple.

They liked the idea of a Beer Trek and pumped us with suggestions, opinions, and questions. Their own sense of style was unique. Bartenders and customers were one. Proper etiquette was to get a beer in the most expeditious way—usually to walk back to the cooler and grab one. At the end of the night everyone pushed through beer-fuzzed brains to reconstruct tabs. We were treated to a house specialty, a deep-fat-fried porkskin. This delicacy appears on the menu whenever so-and-so feels like cooking and what's-his-name

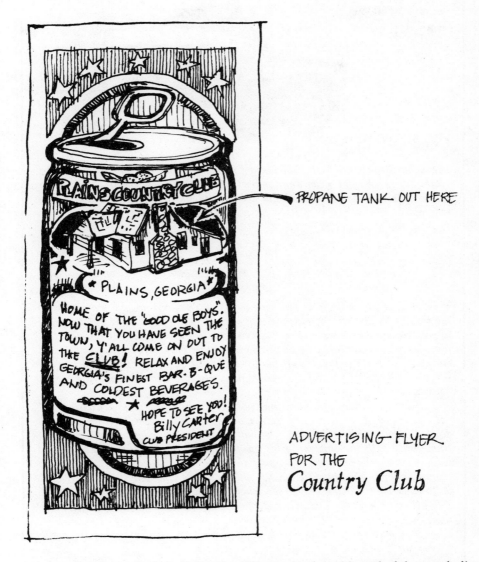

PROPANE TANK OUT HERE

ADVERTISING FLYER
FOR THE
Country Club

has just slaughtered a hog. Pabst is widely the preferred brand of the good ol' boys, with Schlitz a close second. Everyone agreed that Billy Beer tasted all right, but a hillbilly is too independent to identify with any man's beer, even Billy's. Quality is synonymous with temperature: the colder the better.

A favorite pastime of the Good Ol' Boys of Plains is to make fools of tourists. We were challenged to several raucous pinball games that accomplished just that. Tall tales began coming out by the third or fourth beer. Billy's celebrity was regarded as a perfect example of cracker cunning. They giggled hilariously at some of the famous and pretentious people he had dragged into the back room. Reporters, country singers, politicians—many

- ROLL BAR
- CIBIE SUPER OSCAR
- LIGHTRO BURNERS
- GUN RACK
- HAT RACK

Good Ol' Style

The Good Ol' Boy can be a Gulf Coast cowboy or a Georgia hillbilly. There are subtle differences, but, even more important, striking similarities. A pickup, for instance, is required, although style, color, and make are left to choice. Also required:

1. *A pretty girl who knows what she is getting into.*

2. *A cooler.*

3. *Tapes of Waylon, Willie, and "The Killer" (don't ask, or you'll show your ignorance).*

And, of course, beer. In favor are the 7- and 8-ounce midgies introduced by the brewers for diet-conscious women but appreciated by Good 'Uns for their ability to preserve the maximum chill and carbonation of the brew. (The mania for coldness was best demonstrated for us at a Florida oyster bar where the waitress floated a glass of ice in our unfinished pitcher to keep it frosty.) The floor of the pickup cab is properly a clanking sea of these containers, which fall out whenever the door is opened.

Hats are required, although the choice is a personal affair. Gulf Coasters will opt for lacquered, straw cowboy hats, which rise a foot above the head and then dip precipitously below the chin. The hillbilly prefers the adjustable baseball cap emblazoned with the emblem of his favorite macho product. Cowboy boots and jeans complete the uniform.

The final requirement is the CB radio, and the language that accompanies it. To make your twang suitably indecipherable, practice such phrases as:

"Eyowjow rahjah thassa beeg tenfoah yar yar whass yer twenny? Kamoann-n-n."

Your vocabulary will need to be expanded. For instance, the word for beer in CB'ese can be selected from among the following:

Bevo	*Rocky Mountain Kool Aid (Coors)*	*Super cola*
Barley pop	*Honey*	*Little pony*
Brown bottle	*Red, White & Blue (Pabst)*	*8-0-7*
Buttermilk	*7-0-8's*	*Forty-eight*
Cold coffee	*Spring Water*	

Now train yourself to live on a diet of Slim Jims, biscuits and gravy, and barbecue. You're almost there.

had faced the acid test of the Country Club regulars, and many had failed. Typically they would endure the coarse surroundings and even coarser language for only so long before bolting to the Holiday Inn from which they came. "Good riddance," sniggered the good 'uns, another unworthy stranger driven from their midst.

"Used to be," a wild-eyed, bearded man at the pinball machine told Laura, "this room was where the nigguhs drank. But when the tourists came, us old 'ol boys got pushed back here." He watched her reactions carefully, hoping she would blanch. She held fast. "Don't know where the nigguhs drink anymore. Most go up to the motel in Americus." The test finished, our points scored, the pinball game merrily continued. Like most of the other regulars, he had come directly from work in the fields, just hopped in the truck or on the cycle and come down to the club for a few cold ones, the chance to guffaw with the guys, and, tonight, to gawk at a few strange Yankees. I obligingly provided the biggest laugh of the night when I asked for directions to the men's room.

"Hell, we got the biggest men's room in the whole wide world," said the bearded man. With that I was directed to a propane tank in back of the Country Club. I pissed long and hard into the Georgia dusk, experiencing a sense of freedom along with bladder relief. To my right, sharing the planet of a men's room, was a tall man with dark hair flecked with gray.

"Like our men's room?" he asked.

"I feel honored. I mean, I'm really pissing where Billy Carter has pissed."

"Billy, hell. You'd be surprised who's pissed out here. You think we build a men's room when Jimmy comes?"

"You mean the president has pissed here?"

"Sure," the man said over his shoulder as he headed back to fill his bladder again. The import overwhelmed me. I looked around for some kind of confirmation, a historic plaque on the propane tank, something. The machinations of the cosmos had me reeling. When the Beer Trek left Massachusetts, it was beyond my wildest dreams to think I would urinate on the same patch of real estate as a president. Ironically, there was no way to document the historic occasion. A picture would be fruitless, and a handful of soil would not impress anyone who had not shared the experience. I would have nothing to show my grandchildren.

The Country Club closes around 9:00 P.M., mercifully. At the accelerated rate of beer consumption, by midnight there would have been one large pile of drunk hillbillies and Beer Trekkers. Gene Bacon had long since abandoned his post in the tourist part of the Country Club and quietly joined in the clamor. Every so often he would shake his head slowly and complain how his wife would kill him when he came home to their trailer, but for now he was having a good ol' time. And all the while Willie, Waylon, and Dolly played on.

At nine everyone piled out into the parking lot for a final farewell. These people truly believed in the nobility of our odyssey and were proud to have participated. On our part we had met enough good beers drinkers to have made meeting Billy superfluous. The vehicles—motorcycles, pickups, and even a pink 1969 Lincoln Continental—peeled onto the two-lane blacktop into Plains, roaring engines punctuated by rebel whoops. The Great Beer Trek, slightly rougher at the edges but happy to have pierced the armor of the Wasteland, made a quick trip back to the propane tanks before heading north.

WHEN YOU'RE OUT OF SCHLITZ
Southern Roads

The Good Ol' Boys of Plains, enthusiastic as they were regarding beer consumption, were inarticulate on the subject. Beer was, to them, a yellow, highly carbonated beverage meant to be drunk at near-freezing temperatures. End of discussion. Choice meant beer in 7-, 12-, 16- or 32-ounce containers.

These were the limits of their sudsy horizons. Through no fault of their own they had not been exposed to the vagueries of home brew, the spectrum of imported beers, or even the regional subtleties of local breweries à la Pennsylvania. In a way we envied their innocence. They have so much to look forward to.

Ironically, it is the unsophisticated tastes of the Good Ol' Boys that are the targets of the marketing efforts of the major brewers, and rightly so. The big national brewers brew 99 percent of the beer in the United States, and the Good Ol' Boys drink 99 percent of that. It is natural they should get together.

When we visited the United States Brewers Association in Washington, we asked if they had any suggestions for future stops. "Yes," came the reply. "St. Petersburg, Florida. There is more brewing experience collected there than anywhere else in the country." Although the van never made it to St. Pete's, several days before our visit to Plains we encountered a man on tiny Captiva Island just off Fort Myers who raised our IQs substantially regarding what it takes to bring buyer and seller together in the world of big brewing.

DeWitt Jones had for many years been in charge of the Schlitz account while a vice-president of the Leo Burnett Advertising Agency in Chicago. During his tenure, Schlitz maintained the number two position in the national volume sweepstakes, riding the backs of such memorable lines as, "Real Gusto in a Great, Light Beer" and "When You're Out of Schlitz, You're Out of Beer." Now they have fallen substantially and have even lost their status as an independent concern, having been acquired by Stroh of Detroit. The Great Beer Trek hoped to find out, from the perspective of someone whose orientation was product identity and media strategy rather than malt and hops, why Schlitz's fortunes changed.

DeWitt Jones spends more time these days fighting condominium developments and photographing roseate spoonbills than wondering about the ebbs and flows of the beer wars. He broke from these pursuits long enough to educate us. He serves Schlitz to his guests, and we shared one as we talked:

Beer Trek: Did everyone at Leo Burnett know immediately that "Real gusto in a great, light beer" was a great line?

DeWitt Jones: We knew it was a good line. It felt good. It had all the right strengths and none of the negatives. It wasn't hard to understand. It was executable. You could do something with it.

Beer Trek: Did the line have a secret ingredient?

DeWitt Jones: It was simple, and simplicity is the soul of good advertising. Also we discovered that there were absolutely no negative connotations to the word *gusto*.

Beer Trek: Who were the gusto ads directed toward?

DeWitt Jones: Everyone. The beer people always want to reach the heavy beer drinker, the guy who drinks twenty-seven six-packs a minute. Problem is, there aren't that many heavy beer drinkers, and they are hard to identify, so it is hard to target your advertising toward this group. We worked on the theory that if we could get more people to drink a little bit, we'd be better off. At the same time, we felt it important that we not turn off the heavy beer drinker.

Beer Trek: Other ad campaigns, such as Schaefer's "One beer to have when you're having more than one," have been successful because they reached the heavy beer drinker. What is the difference?

DeWitt Jones: With Schaefer you are dealing with a regional product where you can reach your entire market. With a national product like Schlitz, this is impossible. You can't afford to fractionate your advertising or your appeal.

Beer Trek: That the "gusto" campaign had unprecedented success was proved by increased sales. Why was it changed?

DeWitt Jones: Most good ad campaigns are changed long before they outlive their usefulness.

Beer Trek: Why?

DeWitt Jones: Because the client lives with the advertising more than the customer. The customer sees an ad maybe once a week, but the client sees it every day. He gets sick of it.

Beer Trek: How does an agency keep a client from changing a campaign they know to be doing a good job?

DeWitt Jones: You have to keep good advertising fresh—change the picture, change the scenery—just don't change the message, if it's good.

Beer Trek: What has happened with the most recent "gusto" advertising?

DeWitt Jones: In an attempt to keep the advertising fresh, the simplicity was covered up by foolishness and frippery.

Beer Trek: Are the changes in the advertising the cause of Schlitz's current problems?

DeWitt Jones: Advertising alone can't be held responsible for that, nor can it take sole credit for Schlitz's success in the sixties. Advertising is one part of a total effort. It is more than one magical phrase like the "gusto" line. It's the execution of the line, the execution of the marketing plan, the enthusiasm of the sales force, the enthusiasm of the management. You can't get by with just good advertising. You need good beer.

DeWitt related a story about how the line, "When You're Out of Schlitz, You're Out of Beer," came to be. An agency person was having a beer in his favorite tavern when the man next to him ordered a Budweiser. When informed by the bartender that their supply was exhausted and offered a second choice, the customer shook his head and stood to leave. "Nope," he said. "When you're out of Bud, you're out of beer."

The executives at the advertising agency were so taken by the musical simplicity that they used it for their own beer, lest it fall into enemy hands, a purely defensive maneuver.

When you're out of beer, you're out of beer.

Later, when I related the story to a Good Ol' Boy at a local roadhouse, he put another perspective to the situation: "Shee-it! That ain't the way the line should go. It's "When you're out of beer, you're out of beer!" The logic was inarguable.

The Schlitz fall from grace has an important factor that DeWitt Jones did not discuss. At the height of their popularity, Schlitz management changed their manufacturing to achieve greater efficiency, reasoning that the indiscriminate beer drinker would never notice or care. He did notice, and he did care. As Jones said, you need good beer, and Schlitz did not have it. As important as good advertising is, it is worthless without the beer.

Northward, and northward still. Despite the interlude in Plains, the beeriness of the northern climes attracted us. We pushed harder and drove longer. We stopped in Nashville, hoping to experience the associations between beer and life so frequently celebrated in country songs. No such luck. Nashville is simply the place where the experiences of elsewhere are recorded. We did find the Gerst House, however, which made up for any disappointment.

The Gerst House is the former lunchroom for the workers at the William

Gerst Brewing Co. The brewery is no more, but the restaurant provides the best glimpse of Bavariana this side of the Mason-Dixon line. The pace is frantic, the beer plentiful (they feature Andeker, Pabst's superb premium brand served in bowllike goblets), and mittwurst. It is the service, however, that sets the Gerst House apart from the Ground Rounds and Bonanza Steak Houses, which sprout like weeds along southern roadways, for the service is, in a word, abusive. The waitresses, chefs, and kitchen help are one at this establishment, and while the food is unquestionably excellent, the moods of the staff cover the range of human emotions. In a world where scrub-faced, beaming faces of uniformed (and uninformed) help in the fast-food chain now proliferate, it is a relief to encounter real humanity. At the Gerst House the surliness of the help is definitely made tolerable by the excellence of the fare.

And northward still. By now one could sense Bavaria in the air. Louisville even had the warm corpse of a brewery, Falls City, creators of the renowned Billy Beer. (Alas, the concern ceased operation soon after we passed through.) We found a friendly neighborhood tavern, Chek's Cafe, on Burnett Street, which served a splendid array of regional delicacies, both solid and liquid. The gentlemanly owner, Joe Munroe, gave us beers on the house simply because we were new faces and he wanted us to remember him kindly. He made us promise to send postcards and whenever we did, he always replied with a polite note. At lunchtime, Chek's runs on the honor system. Eat as much as you want, then settle up as you leave. The crowds are so heavy he often spreads tablecloths on the pinball machines to accommodate them; yet no one would dare cheat someone with as much class as Joe Munroe. He claims that no one has. We believed him.

That evening we spent in Covington, Kentucky. By now the stirrings were unmistakable, and Covington confirmed it. This town is so sudsy that it is hard to believe one is still south of the Ohio River. The crowded streets are dotted with tiny locals where the entire block gathers, kids and all, to share

Return to Bavaria

MICK NOLL'S
COVINGTON HAUS.

the latest gossip while sipping a local beer, either Wiedemann's from nearby Newport or Burger, brewed by Hudepohl just across the river in Cincinnati. After visiting five or six friendly joints we found a comfortable roosting place on the roof of Mick Noll's converted firehouse. The muffled grunt and moan of an oom-pah band could be heard beneath us. The locals were clearly going crazy, as it was a Saturday night. For once, however, we did not join in. We sipped at our Christian Moerlein, a super-premium made by Hudepohl, and gazed through the budding trees beyond to the Ohio River, which separated us from Cincinnati and the heart of Bavaria. Lewis and Clark must have felt the same when they gazed onto the Pacific.

"We made it," said Laura, her sigh of relief superfluous. The maltiness of the Christian Moerlein, which has a characteristic husky taste of grain, was now imprinting itself on my brain, making the statement seem profound. A lot of miles, many of them beerless, were now fading peacefully away, leaving the highlights of good ol' boys and mittwurst. She offered a toast.

"To the Wasteland, and to survival." We drank. And the beer tasted very good.

Trekker's Guide to the Wasteland _____

In the Next Trek, the name of this region will have to be changed; the southern beer drinker is rushing headlong into the twentieth century. Beer is assuming its rightful place as a noble and healthy beverage, as opposed to the tactile, frigid oral assault favored by Good Ol' Boys with their coolers on the front seat of the pickup.

Not that the Good 'Un is completely dead, but he is more sensitive now than a decade ago. Maybe it was the sad end to Billy Carter, maybe the fact that drunk driving is no longer something that generates a wink and a nudge. Maybe it's all those Yankees moving into Georgia, and Charlotte, and Asheville, and Jacksonville, and Huntsville. There is less outlaw in the South these days and more good beer.

The nationals still have the region checkmated, with A-B, Miller, Heileman, Stroh, and now Coors competing for logistical dominance with modern megaplants. Enough room has been left for concerns like Chesbay and the Weeping Radish in Manteo, North Carolina, to promise of a new southern beer drinking tradition just over the horizon. Grass-roots brewers are like the creeping kudzu that lines the Georgia highways. Once a foothold has been gained, ground will be held as tenaciously as the front lines at Manassas. The South has risen, and the launch has just begun.

ALABAMA

KINDRED SPIRITS

Birmingham Brewmasters, c/o Ben Meister, P.O. Box 19728, Birmingham, AL 35219

'Bama Canna's Chapter (BCCA), Ray Kynard, 26 Rosemary Rd., Montgomery, AL 36109

DISTRICT OF COLUMBIA

★ Olde Heurich Brewing Co., 1111 34th St., NW, Washington, DC 20007
Type: Contract
Brand: Olde Heurich Amber Lager (contract brewed by Pittsburgh Brewing Co., Pittsburgh, PA)

KINDRED SPIRITS

Capitol City Chapter (BCCA), Dee Lander, 13892 Grey Colt Dr., Gaithersburg, MD 20878

GREAT PLACES

Washington: Brickskeller, Dubliner

FLORIDA

★ Florida Brewery, Inc., 202 Gandy Rd., Auburndale, FL 33823
Type: Independent regional
Brands: Fischer's Beer, Fischer's Ale, Master's Choice, ABC

★ Anheuser-Busch, Inc., 111 Busch Dr., P.O. Box 18017, AMF, Jacksonville, FL 32229
Type: Branch plant of Anheuser-Busch, St. Louis, MO

★ Miami River Brewing Co., 90 Southwest 6th St., Miami, FL 33130
Type: Pub brewery
Brands: Lager, Pilsner, Stout
Slogan: "A Sandwich in Every Glass." The mascot is Suds Manatee.

★ Anheuser-Busch, Inc., 3000 Busch Blvd., P.O. Box 9245, Tampa, FL 33674
Type: Branch plant of Anheuser-Busch, St. Louis, MO. Adjacent to Busch Gardens.

★ Stroh Brewery Co., 11111 30th St., Tampa, FL 33604
Type: Branch plant of Stroh Brewery Co., Detroit, MI

KINDRED SPIRITS

Escambia Bay Brewers, c/o Steven J. Fried, 4544 Monpellier Dr., Pensacola, FL 32506

Gator Traders Chapter (BCCA), Marcella Schinski, 2632 Spyglass Dr., Clearwater, FL 34621

GREAT PLACES
Coral Gables: Duffy's Tavern
Hallandale: Billabong South
Key West: Captain Tony's
Miami: Tobacco Road
New Port Richey: Dog and Gun

OF NOTE

Brewing Supplies
Continental Brewing Supply, Ken Sills and Elizabeth Bosek, P.O. Box
1227, Daytona Beach, FL 32017
The Brewster, Ed and Carl Cooper, 720 West University, Gainesville, FL
32601
Homebrew International, Box 4547, Fort Lauderdale, FL 33338
Wine and Brew by You, 5760 Bord Rd., Miami, FL 33155
Home Wine and Beer Trade Association, c/o Dee Roberson, 604 North Miller
Rd., Vairico, FL 33594
Daytona 500, Daytona Beach, spring break. The motorheads come here,
while the preppy types hit the beach at Fort Lauderdale.

Great Fermentations
New Pub breweries: Zum alten Fritz, Miami
Winter Park Brewing Co., Winter Park
JV's Cafe & Brewery, Palm Beach
Mill Bakery, Eatery, and Brewery, Gainesville
Mill Bakery, Eatery, and Brewery, Tallahassee
Maguire's Irish Pub, Pensacola
Lee Nicholson's Tampa Brewpub, Tampa

GEORGIA

★ Miller Brewing Co., 405 Cordele Rd., Albany, GA 31708-6601
Type: Branch plant of Miller Brewing Co., Milwaukee, WI

★ Friends Brewing Co., P.O. Box 29464, Atlanta, GA 30359
Type: Microbrewery
Brand: Helen Oktoberfest Beer

★ G. Heileman Brewing Co., Inc., Georgia Hwy. 247 Spur, Perry, GA 31069
Type: Branch plant of G. Heileman Brewing Co., La Crosse, WI
Tours: Mon.–Sat., 10:00 A.M., 11:00 A.M., 2:00 P.M., 3:00 P.M.

★ Savannah Beer Co., 126 West Bay St., Savannah, GA 31401
Type: Contract
Brand: XIII Colony Amber Beer (contract brewed by Pittsburgh Brewing
Co., Pittsburgh, PA)

OF NOTE
> (RIP) A historical plaque marks the remnants of Georgia's first brewery, built on Sea Island by James Oglethorpe to quench the thirst of his soldiers.

KENTUCKY

★ Oldenberg Brewing Co., I-75 at Buttermilk Pike, Fort Mitchell, KY 41017
Type: Microbrewery and pub brewery
Brands: Oldenberg Premium Verum sold outside brewery, plus Oldenberg Schenk and a brewmaster's special such as Bock, Wheat, or Doppelbock for sale at the brewery
Tours: Available daily during pub operation hours—both guided and unguided. Video presentation area plus walking tour of breweriana collection.
Breweriana: "Anything you could want"
Slogan: "A Classic German Tradition Brewed in America"

NORTH CAROLINA

★ Dilworth Brewing Co., 1301 East Blvd., Charlotte, NC 28203
Type: Pub brewery
Brands: Reeds Gold, Albernerie Ale, Dilworth Porter

★ Miller Brewing Co., 863 East Meadow Rd., P.O. Box 3327, Eden, NC 27288-22099
Type: Branch plant of Miller Brewing Co., Milwaukee, WI

★ Weeping Radish—Bavarian Restaurant and Brewery, P.O. Box 1471, Manteo, NC 27054
Type: Pub brewery
Brand: Hopfen Beer
Tours: Daily
Breweriana: Beer glasses and 5-liter minikegs

★ Stroh Brewery Co., 4791 Schlitz Ave., P.O. Drawer T, Salem Station, Winston-Salem, NC 27108
Type: Branch plant of Stroh Brewery Co., Detroit, MI
Tours: Mon.–Fri., 11:00 A.M.–4:30 P.M.

KINDRED SPIRITS
Alternative Brewers, c/o Gary Ackerman, 627-A Minuet Lane, Charlotte, NC 28217
Triangle Homebrewers' League, c/o Mike Barrett, 4104 Toroella St., Durham, NC 27705
Atlantic Chapter (BCCA), c/o Bruce Dann, 1148 Robinhood Circle, Charlotte, NC 28212

GREAT PLACES
    Asheville: Bill Stanley's BBQ

OF NOTE
    Brewing Supplies
    Alternative Beverages, 827 Minuet Lane, Charlotte, NC 28210
    New World Enterprise, 308 Chapel Hills, Boone, NC 28607

    Great Fermentations
    Greenshields Brewing Co., Raleigh. New Pub brewery.

SOUTH CAROLINA

KINDRED SPIRITS
    Hopportunists, c/o Tom King, P.O. Box 71, Clemson, SC 29633

OF NOTE
    World Beer Review, P.O. Box 71, Clemson, SC 29633. Newsletter rating the
    world's great beers.

TENNESSEE

    ★ Stroh Brewery Co., 5151 East Raines Rd., Memphis, TN 38118
    Type: Branch plant of Stroh Brewery Co., Detroit, MI
    Tours: Mon.–Fri., 10:30 A.M.–3:30 P.M.

    ★ Bohannon Brewing Co., 134 Second Ave., N., Nashville, TN 37201
    Type: Microbrewery (brewery under construction)
    Brands: Market Street Pilsner Draft, Bock, Wheat Beer, Oktoberfest, Holi-
        day Ale

KINDRED SPIRITS
    Hillbilly Hoppers Homebrew Club, c/o Brewhaus, 4955 Ball Camp Pike,
        Knoxville, TN 37921
    Goldcrest 51 Chapter (BCCA), P.O. Box 1364, Lavergne, TN 37086

OF NOTE
    Soda Mart/Can World, Ridgecrest Dr., Goodlettsville, TN 37072. Great se-
        lection of beer books for sale.

VIRGINIA

    ★ Blue Ridge Brewing Co., 709 West Main, Charlottesville, VA 22901
    Type: Pub brewery
    Brands: Hawks Bill Lager, Piney River Lager, Afton Ale, Humpback Stout,
        and White Oak Weizen (seasonal)
    Breweriana: T-shirts, coasters, matches

★ Adolph Coors Co., Rt. 340 S., P.O. Box 25, Elkton, VA 22827
Type: Branch plant of Adolph Coors Co., Golden, CO

★ Virginia Brewing Co., 1373 London Bridge Rd., Virginia Beach, VA 23456
Type: Microbrewery
Brands: Doppelbock, Chesapeake Gold Cup Pilsner, Peoples Choice, Virginia
Native, Occidental Chesapeake Lager
Tours: By appointment only (804) 427-5230
Breweriana: T-shirts, glassware

★ Anheuser-Busch, Inc., P.O. Drawer U, 2000 Pocahontas Trail, Williamsburg,
VA 23185
Type: Branch plant of Anheuser-Busch, Inc., St. Louis, MO. Brewery adja-
cent to Busch Gardens theme park.

KINDRED SPIRITS
Hampton Roads Brewing and Tasting Club, c/o Lyle C. Brown, 1916 East-
over Ct., Virginia Beach, VA 23464
Brewers United for Real Potables (BURP), c/o John Gardiner, 7915 Charles
Thomson Lane, Annandale, VA 22003
Richbrau Chapter (BCCA), c/o James Street, Rt. 2, Box 357-1, Woodford, VA
22580
Tidewater Chapter (BCCA), c/o Hugh Griffin, P.O. Box 1492, Portsmouth,
VA 23705

GREAT PLACES
Alexandria: Union Street Public House

WEST VIRGINIA

KINDRED SPIRITS
West Virginia Maltaineers, c/o Jim Plitt, Stone's Throw, 171 Walnut St.,
Morgantown, WV 26505

OF NOTE
Brewing Supplies
Turkey Hollow Farm, Robert Kent, P.O. Box 304, Charleston, WV 25301

BUY 'EM IF YOU CAN FIND 'EM

Fischer's (Florida Brewing Co.). Slightly dark, slightly sour. Maybe it is an
accident, but this beer is better than one would expect from a brewery
whose forte is brewing generic beer for supermarkets.
Country Club Malt Liquor (General/Pearl). Originates in Texas but as southern as Dr. Pepper. Could have been named "First Date Malt Liquor."
Rarely consumed by anyone of legal drinking age.

5
THE
BEER
BELLY

CINCINNATI, OHIO, TO LA CROSSE, WISCONSIN
40 DAYS, 8,120 MILES ON THE ROAD

THE GHOST OF GEYER Frankenmuth, Michigan

Cincinnati is populated with stout Bavarian stock for which the brewing tradition is cherished. Two independent breweries survive, even prosper, while a third (Wiedemann's across the river in Newport, Kentucky) turns out, at least for the present, a solid workingman's brew for an affordable price.

On Friday we spent the morning at the Schoenling Brewery, a company started in 1937 by two fellows so aggravated by the long wait for their weekend's quarter-keg that they decided the town needed another brewery. Now a second generation of Schoenlings is finding success by carving a niche among brewing giants, not so much through the taste of their beer as by packaging in ways that the major brewers would not find economical. Little King's Ale, a full-flavored cream ale, is available only in eight-packs of distinctive 7-ounce bottles, while Schoenling Lager can be had in giant 64-ounce party-size bottles known affectionately as Big Jugs. Dick Schoenling plays a tape of a radio commercial that advises us to "snuggle up to a couple of big jugs." Budweiser could never get away with that, he snickers. Even more important, the "old man" said it would never work. The original brewing Schoenlings built a successful business, watched it wither, and now, thanks in part to the infusion of new blood, are weathering the storm waters just fine, thank you.

The brewery that kept the Schoenling brothers waiting for their quarter-keg in 1937 was Hudepohl, for years the undisputed kingpin of the Cincinnati brewing scene. In recent years this company has appeared destined for the statistical graveyard, another victim of antiquated equipment and the economics of scale. The inevitable, however, has apparently been postponed by the strategy of specializing in whatever the big breweries cannot. The most recent success has been the introduction of Christian Moerlein, a beer named for the most famous brewer in Cincinnati's sudsy history. Here is a beer designed not for the casual beer drinker but for the quaffer who values personality, not blandness, in his mug.

After visiting both breweries The Great Beer Trek, infused with enthusiasm and with the huskiness of Christian Moerlein at the back of our throats, set out for a weekend of visiting places our brewing hosts had suggested as personifying the quintessential Cincinnati beer drinking experience. As always with trekkers, blind alleys outnumbered good leads. The "great, raunchy, little bar" in Newport turned out to be only raunchy and little. The Oar House and Sleep Out Louis's had potential but did not fulfill it during our visit. At the University of Cincinnati we watched a chugging contest where contestants sucked brew from baby bottles. Sacrilege! And a waste of good beer to boot. Total satisfaction came finally by accident when we stopped in one of Cincinnati's myriad chili parlors. The first fiery spoonful had hardly been doused by a slug of Hudepohl when we realized we had been trying too hard. The unique delights of the Queen City of the Ohio were now literally within our grasp. (One mystery we were never able to answer: Why is chili more popular here than in any other city north of Laredo?)

On Sunday afternoon it was back to work. We pushed hard and north, flogging the van along Interstate 75. For once we eschewed the back roads, because the next day would feature a rare triple-header—visits to all three of Michigan's remaining breweries: Stroh, Carling, and Geyer Brothers.

The Stroh Brewing company is conveniently located within sight of the interstate that bypasses the downtown area. Rubble-filled lots offer unimpaired vistas of highway overpasses, distant tenements, and the mammoth brewery. The neighborhood causes one instinctively to roll up the windows and lock the doors. Against the horizon, skyscrapers of Motor City rise like the Grand Tetons against a sky streaked with industrial excess, as unlikely and as unappetizing a location for ambrosial suds as could be imagined.

Stroh, as a company and as a beer, is universally well thought of—everywhere, ironically, but its home town. Detroiters mouth the same mumbo-jumbo as beer drinkers everywhere to describe their prejudices against the local product: "Taste doesn't hold up . . . taste is still with you the next day . . . they're not making it the way they used to . . . gives you diarrhea . . . has a bad head . . . company hires too many blacks . . . company doesn't hire enough blacks." Rarely is there truth to any of the claims, certainly not in this case. Stroh stands for Detroit, and most Detroiters want to be associated with anything and anywhere but Detroit. When one lives in the Motor City, where there is not much of anything green, the grass is greener in the Rockies, the desert, wherever there are jobs. Stroh's cannot claim the magic of mountain spring water or even an association with God's Country. An exotic image is farfetched when your plant is in the middle of a Detroit ghetto.

Stroh is a clean beer, free of warts, moles, and beauty marks, undeserving of either extravagant praise or condemnation. A good beer for most of the time, it provides the beer drinker with no hooks on which to hang his hat. Stroh's is "fire-brewed," a process where the brew kettle is heated directly by oil flame rather than via a steam coil within the kettle. The higher heat reportedly precipitates unwanted solids, resulting in longer shelf life and more durable taste. As Stroh's literature points out, the other famous brewery in the world to employ this technique is the renowned Pilsner Urquell plant in Czechoslovakia, a fact of inconclusive coincidence.

The personnel of Stroh were uniformly courteous and professional in their treatment of The Great Beer Trek. Survival for this company, unlike Schoenling or Hudepohl, will not be dependent upon carving a niche in beerdom so much as surviving as an equal among the combatants in the Beer Wars. As a family and a company the Strohs are determined to survive. Their recent acquisitions of Schaefer and Schlitz show that Stroh's posture will be active and aggressive.

Following a tour of the brewery, beer was sampled in the Stroh hospitality room. Maybe it was the early hour or perhaps the Bavarian-plastique surroundings, more akin to McDonald's than a true rathskeller, but it was time to move on. One down, two to go.

North of Detroit giant factories flatten, first into endless parking lots, then into endless suburbs. Unions, churches, and fraternal groups add three more influences to an already overgoverned life. Television, tempered by beer, provides narcotic relief. It is a way of life seemingly mired in despair yet defended with such vigor that one must assume its beauty to be hidden from the passing van.

Frankenmuth is centered on the most fertile farmland in Michigan. Founded in 1845 by Lutheran missionaries who hoped to Christianize the Chippewa Indians, the German settlers until recently still spoke a unique form of pidgin German called Bi-rish. Now the ethnic heritage has been converted into Old World quaint, and Frankenmuth is Michigan's largest tourist attraction.

There are two breweries along Main Street. The more prominent, and the first visited by The Great Beer Trek, is a Carling-National plant, now owned by Heileman. It is known locally as the Frankenmuth "Dog" Brewery, a description applying not to the beer but to the mascot—a dachshund. The company in its heyday maintained a kennel for public relations purposes. Now

"I find holding the shot glass between first and middle fingers affords greater control."

— DOGBONE BROWN

Boilermakers

The boilermaker is the Friday afternoon drink. It's payday, you've just cashed your check, the weekend stretches endlessly before you, and a little celebration seems in order. If you order a boilermaker, however, what you get and how it is served will depend on where you are.

Wisconsin wins the award for the most creative combinations. In Milwaukee there are no questions asked. You are served a glass of beer with a shot of brandy, probably Coronet. Farther north in Stevens Point we observed beer accompanied by a 4-ounce glass of chablis. In Monroe, where there is a strong Swiss population, a "schnitt" of beer is accompanied by a shot of Appenzell, a bitter, herb liqueur from the homeland. When we inquired about this unusual combination, we were informed that the Appenzell is correctly accompanied by a schnitt of Huber Bock beer, which is only available seasonally. (Of course the establishment where we observed this, called The Depot, has as its motto the epitaph of a famous engineer genius named—appropriately enough—George Train:

> Here lies George Train . . .
> The mind of twenty men
> Pulling in different directions.

George, it seems, had a little too much Appenzell and Huber.)

In Buffalo a boilermaker will get you beer and peppermint schnapps. In Boston beer and scotch, unless in South Boston where Irish whiskey will be substituted for the scotch. Elsewhere, the consensus choice is beer and blended whiskey from the bottom shelf.

The style of consumption varies. Generally the shot is served separately without ice. In some places you sip it; in others you belt it back in a single gulp using the beer as a chaser. A "depth charge" is where the shot glass is dropped, whiskey and all, into the beer vessel, gently settling to the bottom and mixing its contents with each sip. The trick is to finish the drink without having the shot glass chip your teeth.

The Great Beer Trek award for creative drinking style goes to the fraternity crowd in Ann Arbor, Michigan, where both the shot glass and pilsner tumbler are held in the same hand. As the beer glass is tipped toward the mouth, the contents of the shot, held between the first and middle fingers, dribble into the beer below. Practice, if you must, this technique with something other than whiskey because the first few attempts are guaranteed to result in a snootful of 86 proof.

the brewery, the original home of Mel-O-Dry beer, produces a range of Heileman products—including Tuborg, Black Label, and Colt 45. Altes Golden Lager, a long-standing Michigan brand, is also made here. This brew is supposedly reminiscent of Fassbier, an archaic type of German draft beer. Since no one has tasted real Fassbier for several hundred years, the claim is safe. Beer, remember, is a fluid subject. With such a diverse roster of products, it is unrealistic to think that any difference among the brews goes deeper than the packaging. Although Heileman is to be commended for maintaining some of the diversity once available to the beer drinker, it is questionable how meaningful the differences are. After a forgettable tour, we passed up the hospitality room in favor of continuing on, our throats growing increasingly parched.

Thus far the day had produced fascinating insight to the plight and dilemma facing the contemporary brewer but precious little in the way of good beer drinking. What was this, we mused, a Beer Trek or field study for an MBA program?

It was just past 5:00 P.M. when we arrived at the brick Geyer Brothers plant. As opposed to our two previous stops, there was no clearly marked visitors' entrance, and the office was locked. Fearful of having missed our chance to see the brewery, we poked our heads in an open door hoping to see a sign of humanity. There was one fellow visible, a swarthy guy with a two-day stubble and a sweat-drenched T-shirt. We introduced ourselves and apologized for the late arrival. He countered with a simple "Hi, want a beer?"

He gestured to a single spigot protruding from the brick wall. Only a simple sign reading "Free beer today, free peanuts tomorrow" designated this as the brewery hospitality room. He drew three glasses of Frankenmuth Dark—a tart, husky brew that instantly compensated for the overdose of blandness that had characterized the day thus far. One could think of many words to describe this bierstube environment of painted brick, cement floor, and hissing pipes, but *pretentious* would not be one.

Our host drained his glass, drew another, and did the same for us, simultaneously motioning us to a wooden bench. We thanked him and made a polite inquiry as to his role at the brewery.

"Oh, me?" he said offhandedly. "I'm the janitor." We nodded politely as he continued: "and the bottler, and the accountant, and the public relations man, and the truck driver . . . " We marveled at his versatility but now realized that we were being set up—"and the maintenance man, and the president." He laughed at the punchline, a booming laugh that filled the empty brewery and instantly transformed an eerie setting into one of conviviality.

Dick Brozovic's belly attests to sharing a few too many beers with customers, tourists, and Beer Treks. The sweat and the grime are real. He is a workingman.

Brozovic and his wife, Jeannie, were thrust into the brewing business by the unexpected death of a brother who had been attempting to revive the tiny Frankenmuth brewery. His own experience with beer consisted of sampling brews at various enlisted-men's clubs as a career army man. Had he known what he does today, Brozovic asserts, he would never have undertaken the kamikaze mission of maintaining an antiquated brewery in a world of cutthroat giants. In his first year of operation the deficit stood at $50,000. The next year, thanks to long hours and drastic cost cutting, the amount was halved. In the third year, Dick and Jeannie broke even. The prospect of prosperity is remote, but at least the financial monkey is off Dick's back enough that he can have the fun of sharing a brew with the likes of us and tweaking the noses of the Miller and Budweiser juggernauts.

Our glasses are refilled without asking, and we are taken on an impromptu tour of the darkened brewery. In contrast to the programmed pap that is customary from the squeaky clean, uniformed tour guides at most large breweries, we are regaled with stories of ornery condensers with whom Dick has waged all-night combat and compressors salvaged from dairies. Each tale is punctuated by the characteristic booming laugh.

Inevitably we wind back to the tap, where Dick waxes philosophic, sharing with us some of his experiences in the early days when he spent entire nights in the brewery trying to keep alive refrigeration equipment that belonged in a museum but still maintained the brewery bloodstream. It was then that he met the legendary ghost of John Geyer, the man who founded the brewery on the Cass River in 1879. It was old John, claims Dick, who would appear to him at the point of despair to provide the courage, advice, and abandon to go on. He is deadly serious as he speaks. No one believes him, he knows, not even Walter Geyer who still oversees brewing operations, but maybe we will. In the semitwilight the surroundings recall an era when beer had more taste and brewing was still fun as opposed to the calculating profession witnessed earlier this day at Stroh. We nod. We believe.

There are more stories to tell, Dick insists. Why don't we follow him home where he can clean up, grab Jeannie, and take us around to some of the Frankenmuth taverns that do justice to his brew. He grabs his keys and hits the light switch, leaving us momentarily in a dark, malty world of hisses and clanks. There is a sudden noise from upstairs in the brewhouse. The ghost? Dick Brozovic lets the suspense continue for just the right length of time, then dispels the ghost with a booming laugh.

A QUESTION OF TASTE   Chicago, Illinois

In Mishawaka, Indiana, just east of South Bend, the brewing complex of the former Kamin & Schellinger Brewing Co. has been lovingly preserved and given new life as a home for trendy shops, restaurants, and offices. Although it is heartening to see such veneration of our Industrial Revolution, one cannot avoid the inevitable twinge of sadness at the disappearance of yet another regional brewing tradition. Nowhere is the loss more acute than in Chicago.

At one time Cincinnati made pretenses of becoming the Queen City of brewing, but the lack of a good natural ice supply dictated that the crown move farther north. Chicago, being the hub of midwestern commerce, was the obvious choice, and indeed the Windy City wore the brewing crown until the Great Fire incapacitated many of the city's breweries. Chicago's thirst was satisfied by Milwaukee's breweries. Although Chicago never recovered the crown, it regained status as a first-rate brewing center, feeding a burgeoning population of Slavic immigrants.

Chicago's minions are still thirsty, but their beer now comes from St. Louis, Milwaukee, and, especially, La Crosse, Wisconsin. Semis filled with Old Style stream down Interstate 90 from "God's Country" as daily reminders that Chicago no longer has a single brewery to call its own.

There is no shortage of good beer drinking here. Good taverns are a tradition, as any reader of Mike Royko or Studs Terkel knows. This is the "city that works," and beer is the drink of the upwardly mobile blue-collar stiff. Chicagoans brag about their sudsy heritage, then admit sheepishly that the tradition has neither a present nor a future.

For The Great Beer Trek, Chicago was a place to don the business suit and tie. While Chicago is no longer the heart of the brewing industry, it is the home of Siebel Institute, the industry's preeminent technological center.

Any doubts about what kind of reception an institution dedicated to the technological aspects would have for a venture whose priorities clearly lay on the softer side of the subject were quickly dispelled. Our host, Ron Siebel, made it clear that the nuances of beer manufacturing must never interfere with the basic goal of producing a beverage that is fun to drink and tastes good. The traditional side of beer drinking is not taken lightly by the technological side.

We were discussing the *Rheinheitsgebot,* a sixteenth-century German law affirming the beer drinker's right to pure beer when our conversation was interrupted by a bell, the kind that in many offices heralds the arrival of the coffee-and-Danish vendor. At Siebel, the bell signals time for taste testing. Ron is a member of the tasting panel and invited us along. We entered a plain room partitioned into separate booths, each occupied by a studious white-frocked gentleman completely absorbed in the task at hand, specifically sniffing, swishing, swizzling, and swigging samples from red glasses. After each sample a score sheet was filled out. Ron tasted his brews, then explained the process in more detail.

Breweries around the country use Siebel as an independent consultant to give impartial feedback on their products. Since many brewing problems are cumulative in nature, periodic tastings from an impartial source help keep a brewer honest by providing an independent quality-control checkpoint that might be impossible to achieve in-house where subtle alterations occur too gradually for the resident brewmaster to notice.

The beers to be tested are served under highly controlled conditions. The special red glasses prevent the testers from being influenced by visual

Taste testing at Siebel's

factors such as cloudiness. Flavor, body, and odor characteristics are broken down into nearly forty variable categories and then rated numerically according to the degree to which they are present. The results are fed into a computer, which generates a composite profile that is returned to the brewer. The tasters never know whose beers they are testing to avoid any possibility of prejudicial evaluation.

Tastings occur up to three times daily, with as many as seven beers in each. Despite the sophistication of the technology available today, no one has developed automated techniques that surpass the human palate for sensitivity. Man's greatest drawback is that he is fallible. Individual tasters have blind spots to certain flavor characteristics that have to be maneuvered around. One taster might be supersensitive to phenols, a very specific off-flavor, while completely taste blind to the presence of diacetyls. Man also tends to get tired, to have colds, and to have lapses of attention. The use of multiple tasters in combination with the computer-generated profiling technique should correct for human factors in the rating process.

The taste testers at the Siebel Institute are workmanlike while in progress, but once the evaluation forms have been turned in, the banter becomes lively, not unlike what one might encounter at the local pub. One of the testers, a kind, brewmasterly type with a heavy, appropriate Germanic accent, gave me a sample to taste.

"Vot do you think?" he asked.

I sipped cautiously, trying to imitate the techniques I had just observed and hoping desperately that I would not say something foolish. "Not too good," I ventured. "It has an unpleasant aftertaste that ruins the initial flavor."

My mentor nodded indulgently. "Skunky!" he practically spit the word out. "It's terrible! This beer has been exposed to light. Ve call it light struck. Beer is very fragile; that is vy it is packaged in brown bottles, to protect it from the light. Now try this one."

The second beer was sweeter. Even the red glass could not hide that it was a dark beer. "Nothing bad," I said. "But nothing special either. No distinctive flavor characteristics."

My mentor nodded. "The brewer calls this a 'bock' beer, but all he has done is add food coloring to his regular lager. To be true to the type, he should be getting his color and sweetness from the use of roasted malts. But at least," he sighed, "he has not made any other mistakes."

I realized that I was sweating profusely. I did not mind being exposed as a novice, but I did not want to say anything to make myself seem completely ignorant. The gentleman perceived my uneasiness and smiled, "You did very well." No comment could have sent my spirits soaring higher. In a very small way The Great Beer Trek had earned a stripe. We spent a few moments telling everyone about our trip to date. The world of professional brewing was apparently smaller than I realized. Who had I visited? How were they doing? Where were we heading next? "Be sure to visit old so-and-so and tell him I sent you. He's an ornery old cuss, but he knows brewing like no one else in the country." When the gossip and chitchat was finished, our notebooks were loaded with names and places enough to sustain the balance of the trip.

Ron showed us the rest of the operation, including the test brewery, the hospitality lounge, and the classrooms where would-be brewmasters from all over the world come for the eleven-week course that officially qualifies one as a brewmaster.

Ron answered all questions openly and thoroughly. He seemed interested in developments on the home-brewing front and grass-roots trends in beer consumption that we had observed in our travels. We swapped thoughts on the feasibility of opening a small brewery. He painted a bleak picture of the prospects of survival of such a venture, but he did so in such specific terms that he had obviously given the project a lot of thought. As a counterbalance, he painted a glorious portrait of Siebens, a famous Chicago brewery that served its own brews in their restaurant and gardens. Had Ron, I asked, investigated the possibility of opening up his own brewery?

"Oh, I don't think a small brewery makes a lot of sense in this day and age."

But, I persisted, had he at any point considered opening up his own plant?

"Listen," said Ron, glancing furtively about as if to make sure we weren't being overheard, "there is no one in the beer business who doesn't dream of opening up his own brewery someday."

I was glad to have my suspicions confirmed.

Following our visit to Siebel, a wiser Beer Trek entered onto Eden's Expressway, heading north toward Milwaukee, just in time for evening rush hour. Our spirits were soaring. Ever since the beginning of our trip there had been a sense that the big national brewers were the bad guys and the small brewers the good guys. Will Anderson and Tim Matson had contributed to this feeling, while DeWitt Jones and now Ron Siebel helped dispel it. Now, for the first time, I began to see the need to segregate the people, the businesses, and the beers. Nice people can make bad beer. Conversely, good beer can be made

There's <u>no one</u> in the beer business
who doesn't dream...

by bastards. In either case the business part is simply an impartial structure for the people and products. A business does not cast judgments about whether a given move—acquiring an ailing brewery, for instance, or cutting back on the hop content in a beer—is "good" or "bad." It follows the path of greatest profitability as determined by its decision makers.

As for the beer drinker, he really doesn't care. Like the tasters on the Siebel Institute panel, the proof is in the palate. What really matters is what is in the mug. A simple, but crucial, lesson had been learned.

HONEY, CHEESE, CHOCOLATE, AND BEER
On the road in Wisconsin

The drive from Milwaukee to La Crosse can be completed in four hours. For The Great Beer Trek, however, six days proved to be entirely too short a time.

Milwaukee is a town where, for once, all the taverns serve local beers. One need not feel guilty about ordering Miller, Pabst, or Schlitz. The same choices that are bland and unappealing elsewhere, in Milwaukee have character and snap. This is Pittsburgh, but a Pittsburgh scrubbed, detoxed, and sent for a permanent rest cure in the pristine north. The industrial machinery operates at the pace and schedule of a steroid-fed Black Forest hamlet.

Milwaukee rivals Covington, Kentucky, and Baltimore for watering holes per capita. The block is the unit of social organization, and each one has an establishment named for the owner who doubles as bartender and cook. No one argues the merit of Miller, Schlitz, or Pabst. So long as you are drinking Wisconsin, no one cares. Regional foods abound, most testifying to a slavic heritage—blood sausage, summer sausage, bauerwurst, beerwurst, and brats. Fridays are for fish fries. The good places feature native perch or walleye. The rest serve frozen cod. Pool is the favorite recreation, and many bars light the action with elaborate pseudo-Tiffany Schlitz lamps that will someday be collector's items. There is even a word to describe the collective spirit of beer drinking and hospitality—*gemütlicheit*. If a given brew or tavern passes muster, it can be said to have *gemütlicheit*.

Milwaukee has had its brewing casualties, although, surprisingly, fewer than other cities. At its busiest, sixteen companies brewed beer here, as compared to five times that number in Chicago. Signs for Gettleman's can still be seen, and the buildings of Blatz are owned and used by Pabst (which owned the company for eleven years during the fifties and sixties until forced to divest by the federal government).

Historic Milwaukee breweries include Jung ("Jung Beer Serves You Right"), John Graf ("The Best What Gives"), and Milwaukee-Waukesha ("The Imperial Health Beer"). Add to the list since the passage of our van, Schlitz, now owned by Stroh. Even venerable Pabst, whose name is synonymous with Milwaukee, is a radically altered version of its former self, having merged with Olympia and simultaneously selling large chunks of itself off to Heileman in a recent Beer Wars' confrontation. The Pabst plant is well worth visiting. Its Tudoresque beer garden puts a 350-year shield between the beer drinker and the twentieth century. Ivy and leaded glass create an environment in which the consumption of beer, particularly on a summer afternoon, is raised to the sublime. Statues of King Gambrinus and Frederick Pabst look on approvingly.

The Pabst brewhouse is the city's second best, the best (Schlitz's) having recently been closed. The copper and tile sanctuary that places man in proper perspective with the brewing gods, stands idle, a victim of the inexorable movement toward stainless steel and efficiency. The Brown Bottle, Schlitz's legendary hospitality room, is likewise lost to the public. Both the brewhouse and taproom are monuments to the bygone era that holds such great appeal for the nostalgic beer fanatic. The mighty have fallen. The truth is as sad as it is inevitable.

On the opposite side of Wisconsin there is a new challenger to the throne, and a most unlikely one. As majestic as Schlitz and Pabst are, Heile-

THE BREWHOUSE

The Milwaukee Dreadnaughts

THE SCHLITZ PALM GARDEN

When you're out of Point, you're out of town.

STEVEN'S POINT. WISCONSIN'S SMALLEST BREWERY

man is a plain Jane. No Gothic spires, no statues of the founder, no inspirational beer gardens. This plant has simply discovered ways to brew, to sell, and, especially, to distribute beer that make the company more adaptable to the contemporary brewing environment. Just as the battleship and dinosaur eventually reached an age where they could no longer survive, so have the brewing dreadnoughts. Meanwhile, Heileman thrives.

In between Milwaukee and La Crosse, there is no shortage of good beer drinking. Wisconsin's beer drinkers rank among the most enthusiastic in the nation on a per capita consumption basis, and they have been rewarded for their efforts by the best beer drinking environment of any other state. Choices are abundant, prices are moderate, and freshness is assured. Everyone we met seemed knowledgeable and appreciative of the advantages of living in the heart of America's Bavaria. They all have *gemütlicheit*.

Each brewer left us with something special, but collectively they left us with even more. Bill Leinenkugel let us participate in one of the blind taste tests he conducts regularly. At first he was embarrassed that he could not distinguish his own light beer from Miller Lite when we could, but then he rationalized that Leinie Light must be pretty good if even he could not distinguish it from the country's best-selling light beer.

When he heard that we had just come from Wisconsin's three other independent family brewers (Stevens Point, Huber, and Walters), he was filled with questions, specifically about their bock beers. Each of the Wisconsin brewers still produces a seasonal bock in which the firm takes justifiable pride. Bill Leinenkugel's questions were quite pointed, portraying a healthy dose of competitive curiosity. Had we tasted the other bocks? What did we think? Had the other brewers sold out their supplies?

There are too few independent brewers for anyone to wish anyone else ill. None of the small brewer's beers are sold in the other's market, so there is no real competition. Within a context of mutual support, however, each one wants to be the best. People have an innate need to strive for excellence, and the need finds its finest opportunity for expression in the field of brewing. We answered Bill Leinenkugel's questions as tactfully as possible. Yes, we had tried the bocks, yes, they were all excellent, and yes, it's quite possible that his was the best. He looked pleased at our enthusiasm. Nothing pleases a brewer as much as knowing people enjoy his beer. The statement is as true for the home brewer as for Augie Busch III.

OKTOBERFEST   La Crosse, Wisconsin

Heileman is the success story of the Wisconsin brewers. Not long ago they were the peers of the Walter's and Huber's. Now they own the remnants of Carling, Blatz, Sterling, Fall City, and even parts of Pabst. They have broken the rule that a company needs a flagship brand to be big. Old Style may be a household word in Chicago, but it is unknown in Atlanta and Los Angeles.

Old Style is a good beer, bland and malty in the style customary for the region. It is "fully krauesened," a carbonation process in which young, unfermented brew is added to the aged lager ready for bottling. Beers carbonated in this way claim to be naturally conditioned as opposed to beers where the effervescence is achieved through the injection of carbon dioxide. The term *fully krauesened* also finds use locally in La Crosse as a term to describe anyone who has had a few too many Old Styles.

It is the primary function of The Great Beer Trek, lest we forget, to interpret, whenever feasible, all events by examining related beer drinking phenomena. The quintessential Milwaukee beer drinking experience is, depending on one's orientation, either the Andeker sipped in the shadow of Fred Pabst on a sunny afternoon or the pitcher of Schlitz that accompanies the fried walleye at Ed and Charlene's on Friday night. There is no disputing the ultimate La Crosse beer drinking experience. It occurs on the first weekend of October, when the population of the Midwest funnels into this riverside town for the simple purpose of drinking beer with thousands of likeminded souls.

A Proper Beer Tasting

Cleanse the palate with a solution of baking soda and Perrier. Stimulate the tongue by massaging vigorously with steel wool. Put the blindfold in place, seal the ears with wax, and immerse yourself in a 7 percent saline solution of 98.6°F.

The taste test is a time-honored tradition that can be as elaborate as the procedure above or as simple as closing your eyes at the bar and trying to guess whether the first brew handed you is a Heineken or a Bud, knowing that the incorrect answer means you have to pay for the next round. Taste tests have only one thing in common—they prove nothing. Skeptics can review the promotional literature of virtually every brewing company in which a test by a panel of experts has rated their Swillbräu brand as second only to Pilsner Urquell in the taste derby. Unfortunately, an equally distinguished panel in a different tasting has rated Guzzleweiser as the planet's premium brew, while bringing up the rear is old friend Swillbräu. Perhaps the height of tasting absurdity was reached in The Great American Beer Book *(Warner Books, 1980) where a well-meaning panel religiously tasted a number of identically formulated beers from the same brewer and managed to find no two alike.*

Tasting takes great practice and concentration. Still there is significant room for error. Even at the Siebel Institute where tastings are held under ideal conditions by professionals, variation is unavoidable. The human palate, while the most sensitive instrument of measuring taste, is one of the most fallible. The experts acknowledge this; your buddy at the bar will not likely be so rational.

Some of the variables that must be controlled to achieve even the most remote approximation of accuracy are:

1. *Temperature of samples. A dark ale served at a lager temperature will not taste right, and vice-versa.*

2. *Age and handling of samples. If your beers come off the shelf, how do you know if one is brewery fresh, while a second has languished in a hot warehouse for the past year?*

3. *Abilities of tasters. Some people are genetically more sensitive to certain tastes—saltiness, for instance—while being oblivious to others.*

4. *Prejudices of tasters. If a taster has a predilection toward sweet beers, the first sample with a pronounced hop character is certain to get a low rating, whatever its merits.*

5. *Order of tasting. The ability to concentrate diminishes with each sample, and a judge's scoring will be altered accordingly. Whether this works to the advantage or disadvantage of beer #1 is completely arbitrary.*

6. *Reliability of the brewer. McSorley's Ale, as one example, is actually a series of brews under the same name. And who is to say that Pabst from the Georgia plant is identical to that produced in Milwaukee?*

And finally there is the simple fact that the conditions of a taste test are generally alien to the normal manner in which beer is drunk. A proper beer tasting would be to buy a six-pack, bring it to a friend's house, drink it, and say what you think. Next night, buy a different six-pack, go to a friend's house . . .

Taste tests, then, are completely biased and unreliable. Does this mean they are worthless? Absolutely not. Remember, any occasion that gives an excuse to drink beer is a worthwhile event. Just don't spit out the samples.

Our timing was off by several months, so Oktoberfest could not be an official part of The Great Beer Trek. We chanced to meet someone, however, who, for the price of an evening's beer drinking, provided a graphic tour of an event that deserves a place on every beer drinker's calendar.

Jeff is a carpenter who lives outside of Chicago, but where he really lives is La Crosse for one weekend each autumn and periodic vacations. He is a carpenter, but he does not actually work for anyone or even for himself. He gets by, he enjoys himself, and he makes for charming company on a night out in La Crosse. He has not yet bothered to settle down, but there will always be time for that. He is in his mid-thirties, going on seventeen, and he has attended the last eleven Oktoberfests.

To maximize the intensity of the Oktoberfest "high," Jeff transports himself from Chicago to La Crosse by riding the rails. Although the danger and discomfort of the two-day trip make this means of conveyance as illogical as it is romantic, he claims that the journey helps the end to justify the means. The festival grounds were dark and empty when we visited, but with the aid of Jeff's descriptions and enough Old Styles it became easy to imagine the real thing. After all, the only difference was the absence of a few thousand beer drinking revelers.

The foliage is at its peak, and for the sake of artistic perfection, make it a brilliantly sunny day, bright enough to turn the Mississippi the color of new blue jeans. There is a nip in the air, enough to let you know that winter is on the way, but it is offset by the warm sun, which reminds you that summer is not long past.

La Crosse is jammed with people, all of them fair-haired with clear blue eyes. Even the blacks and Hispanics fit the description. Their names are Jensen and Gundersen. Their speech is interrupted by "Jah's" and "Geez's" and they call their native state "Wis-skaaann-sin."

By eleven in the morning everyone has cracked that first beer. Old Style is popular, as are Blatz, Special Ex., Schmidt's, Grain Belt, and Hamm's. All are products of Heileman now. The hordes line the parade route watching an endless stream of local beauty queens and squeaky-clean high school bands. Young and old, male and female watch the spectacle and drink the beer, for this is Oktoberfest.

After the parade the crowd drifts toward the festival grounds—the younger and more raucous choosing the main pavillion downtown and the locals preferring the grounds slightly to the north. A button costing $2 gains one admittance, and many people wear their accumulated buttons from Oktoberfests as a good-humored status indicator. Lunch is a series of brats, knockwursts, corndogs, and assorted junk foods. It's OK. Oktoberfest comes just once a year.

At the main grounds the band is on an elevated platform in an open hall lined with pictures of the presidents. There are a couple of televisions but only if the Brewers are still in the pennant race. A cryptic sign beneath the band-

stand reads, "Please, for the Enjoyment of Others, No Beer Throwing . . . Thank You." You can ponder the meaning as you push to the massive bar staffed by local fraternal organizations peddling plastic cups of Old Style, Special Export, et al. Here is a situation where the logistics of volume beer drinking are well understood. Kegs on pallets are off-loaded by forklifts and delivered right to the bar. Someone has given careful consideration to the logistics of feeding beer to the masses. If your taste runs to wine, bourbon, or even bottled beer, go somewhere else. You won't find anything here but draft.

To save yourself an extra trip to the bar you get two beers, as does everyone else, using as exchange the tickets purchased at a booth by the entrance. Slowly a cry rises from the crowd—nothing sudden or shrill, just a random, animal opening of the vocal chords on a certain pitch that incites a deepseated species' need to join in. So you do, wondering where it will all lead. The volume grows as does the pitch, the band members run for cover, then you see the beer globules arching upward, a fluid chandelier. The magic is ended when the fluid chandelier lands in a malty splash. It's all in good fun, but now you understand the signs.

No one would dare throw beer at the North Fairgrounds, just 2 miles up the road. This is the preferred drinking spot of the locals who do not need the spontaneous exuberance of beer throwing to have a good time. The setting has none of the splendor of the Milwaukee breweries, its architectural style being best described as "basic roof." The beer drinker at Oktoberfest needs only to be protected from torrential rain to be happy.

The hall is packed, and progress to the beer lines is as hard won as the turf at Verdun. Between the area that you have staked out with your friends and the bar, you will meet no end of new friends, all of them smiling a beer drinker's grin and babbling a constant, "Hi, howya doin? Jah! Me too!" If you have to ask, "What's the point?" then you've missed the point, because this is what it's all about. For the likes of Jeff, this is when he is most alive. By nine o'clock the mass of humanity sways in unison, and each passing face greets you with a smile. This is the same state of mind following 2 pints of home brew that, in *Mountain Brew,* is described as "blissed." In La Crosse the feeling is the same, only the description is different. At Oktoberfest Jeff would describe everyone as "fully krausened."

Trekker's Guide to the Beer Belly

Leinenkugel's is now owned by Phillip Morris. No other development illustrates how this region has gone topsy-turvy more than the fact that a huge, international conglomerate bought Bill Leinenkugel's funky little brewery in Chippewa Falls, Wisconsin. Perhaps it has something to do with the fact that Miller built a megaplant in Trenton, Ohio, that was closed before it was ever open. That's it! So they bought Leinenkugel's. Makes sense? Huh?

Don't expect any of this to make sense. During the first Trek, John Walter (Walter's, Eau Claire, WI) and Dick Brozovic (Geyer Brothers, Frankenmuth, MI) were struggling to make no-nonsense farmers' beers. Now their plants have been taken over by city slickers who are making weizen beers, Oktoberfests, doppelbocks, and all other kinds of fancy stuff. Heileman, which for years moved in on failing regionals and took over their brands, has opened a state-of-the-art specialty plant (Val Blatz Brewing Co.) to compete with the micros. Stroh, which used to be in Detroit, is no longer there, while Siebens, which used to *not* be in Chicago, is now back there. Schoenling, the Cincinnati brewery that started to be free of Hudepohl, is now owned by them. And meanwhile Miller goes out and buys Leinenkugel's.

While the Beer Belly has turned upside down and inside out, it still provides a foundation for this beer drinking nation. Milwaukee may no longer brew more beer than other cities, but it is still a good point to launch a mini-Trek into the Bavarian heartland. This is still the land of fraternities, Turners' Clubs, VFWs, and softball diamonds. Beer is ubiquitous. Beer reigns supreme. Beer is consumed in great quantities, with gusto, at occasions ranging from catfish fries to weddings. And if the pedigree of the brewer has changed, then so be it. Beer reflects the changes in the nation, and the Beer Belly has been witness to some of the most profound changes in the past decade. This is a region that relates to its beer not with the eye, not with the heart, and not with the mind, but with the gut.

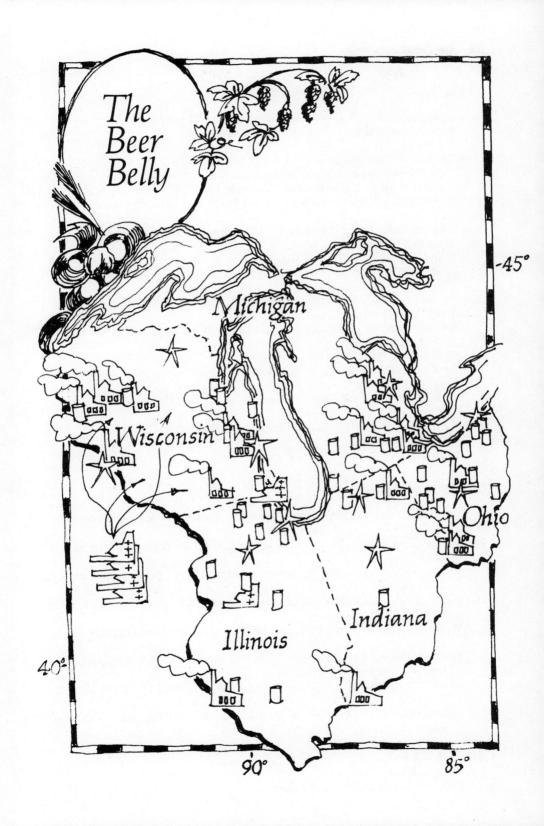

ILLINOIS

★ G. Heileman Brewing Co., 1201 West E St., Belleville, IL 62221
Type: Branch plant of G. Heileman, La Crosse, WI

★ Weinkeller Brewery, 6417 West Roosevelt Rd., Berwyn, IL 60402
Type: Microbrewery, restaurant, bar, and liquor store
Brands: Berwyn Brew Pilsner, Pickwick Pale Ale, Aberdeen Amber Ale,
Weinkeller Bavarian Weiss, Doublin Stout, Duesseldorfer Deppelbock

★ Sieben's River North Brewery, 436 West Ontario St., Chicago, IL 60610
Type: Pub brewery
Brands: Sieben Amber Ale, Golden Ale, Stout, Lager, Nut Brown Holiday Ale

★ Tap and Growler, 901 West Jackson Blvd., Chicago, IL 60607
Type: Pub brewery
Brands: Lair Dog Lager, Gruner Gold Lager, Ankner Best Bitter Ale, Eagan's
Irish Ale, Ambier

★ Goose Island Brewing Co., 1800 North Clybourn, Chicago, IL 60614
Type: Pub brewery
Brands: Lincoln Park Lager, Golden Goose Pilsner, Honkers Ale

★ Pavichevich Brewing Co., 383 Romans Rd., Elmhurst, IL 60126
Type: Microbrewery
Brand: Baderbrau

KINDRED SPIRITS

Bullfrog Chapter (BCCA), Augie Parochelli, 2304 Arrow St., Carpentersville,
IL 60110
Windy City Chapter (BCCA), George Rendl, 1921 West Warner, Chicago, IL
60613
Prison City Chapter (BCCA), Dorothy Hartog, 17911 Commercial, Lansing,
IL 60438
Heart of Illinois Chapter (BCCA), Bob Mutters, 432 South Montana, Morton, IL 61550
Westmont Stroh's Chapter (BCCA), Bill Rex, 367 Evergreen, Bensenville, IL
60106
Northern Illinois Better Brewers Association (NIBBA), c/o Jon Huettel, 2316
Oak St., Northbrook, IL 60062
Chicago Beer Society, c/o Steve Kamp, 6733 Edgewood Dr., Palos Heights,
IL 60463
Headhunters Brewing Club, c/o Greg and Lynne Lawrence, Rt. 1, Box 64W,
Sugar Grove, IL 60554

GREAT PLACES
Berwin: Weinkeller
Chicago: Berghoff, Resi's Bierstube

OF NOTE
>   *Brewer's Digest*, 4049 West Peterson Ave., Chicago, IL 60646. The industry's
>   trade publication. A must for beer fans, especially to follow the fortunes
>   of Otto.
>   Siebel Institute, 4049 West Peterson Ave., Chicago, IL 60646. Training fa-
>   cility and consulting service for the brewing industry.
>   Berghoff's, downtown Chicago. Famous for more than the halibut sand-
>   wiches served every Wednesday and Friday. There are four seasonal fes-
>   tivals—celebrating bock beer, May wine, Old Heidelberg, and Christmas.

INDIANA

>   ★ Evansville Brewing Co., 1301 Pennsylvania St., Evansville, IN 47707
>   Type: A onetime independent, swallowed by G. Heileman, La Crosse, WI,
>   that now has regained its independence, proving once again what a fluid
>   subject beer can be.
>   Brands: Sterling, Falls City, Drewry's, Wiedemann

>   ★ Falstaff Brewing Corp., P.O. Box 926, Fort Wayne, IN 46801
>   Type: Branch plant of Falstaff Brewing Corp., Vancouver, WA
>   Brands: Falstaff, Ballantine Beer, Ballantine Ale, Falstaff Light, Narragansett

>   ★ Nap Town Brewing Co., Inc., 3250 North Post Rd., Suite 285, Indianapolis,
>   IN 46226
>   Type: Microbrewery (brewery under construction)
>   Brand: Main Street Premium Lager

KINDRED SPIRITS
>   Hoosier Chapter (BCCA), c/o Robert Koch, 404 South Beech Rd., Osceola,
>   IN 46561
>   Three Rivers Chapter (BCCA), c/o Al Brand, 910 Milton, Fort Wayne, IN
>   46806

OF NOTE
>   Indy 500, Memorial Day, Indianapolis. Cars, beer, spring, beer, girls, more
>   beer. More action off the track than on.
>   Antique advertising show, Indiana State Fairgrounds, Indianapolis, March,
>   July, September. If you are a wheeler-dealer in breweriana, don't miss
>   this.
>   Town of Mishawaka. Former Kamm and Schellinger complex now houses
>   offices and restaurants. Hopelessly yuppified, but at least a piece of brew-
>   ery architecture is beautifully preserved.

MICHIGAN

>   ★ Stroh Brewery Co., 100 River Place, Detroit, MI 48207
>   Type: National
>   Brands: Stroh's, Stroh Light, Signature, Old Milwaukee, Old Milwaukee
>   Light, Schaefer, Schaefer Light, Schlitz, Schlitz Malt Liquor, Red Bull,
>   Piels, Piels Light, Goebel, Primo, White Mountain Cooler, Sundance Nat-
>   ural Juice Sparklers

Breweriana: Clothing, signs, towels, golf items, etc.
Slogans: Stroh's: "Stroh's Is Spoken Here" (Alex the dog is the mascot); Old Milwaukee: "It Doesn't Get Any Better Than This"; Goebel: "Great Taste—No Hype"; Mr. Joe Bell Piels: advertising characters Bert and Harry Piel, Jr.

★ Frankenmuth Brewery, Inc., 425 South Main St., Frankenmuth, MI 48734
Brands: Frankenmuth Old German Pilsner, Frankenmuth Old German Dark
Tours: Mon.–Fri., 10:00 A.M., 11:00 A.M., 2:00 P.M., 3:00 P.M.
Breweriana: Yes
Slogan: "Frankenmuth Old German Style Beer—You Deserve It"

★ G. Heileman Brewing Co., Inc., 926 South Main St., Frankenmuth, MI 48734
Type: Branch plant of G. Heileman Brewing Co., La Crosse, WI
Tours: Mon.–Fri., 10:00 A.M., 11:00 A.M., 2:00 P.M., 3:00 P.M.

★ Kalamazoo Brewing Co., Inc., 315 East Kalamazoo Ave., Kalamazoo, MI 49007
Brands: Bell's Beer, Third Coast Beer, Great Lakes Amber Ale, Great Lakes Porter, Kalamazoo Stout
Tours: Yes; call in advance (616) 382-2338
Breweriana: T-shirts, glasses, hats
Slogan: "The Beer Is Flowing"

KINDRED SPIRITS
Stroh's Fire Brewed (BCCA), Joseph Tomasak, 349 First, Northville, MI 48167
Silver Foam (BCCA), Bob Venners, 2505 Cobb Rd., Jackson, MI 49203
Mid-Michigan (BCCA), Jim Thompson, 336 Fourth St., Rt. 2, Breckenridge, MI 48615
Goebel Gang (BCCA), Leonard Wentland, 24780 Lancer Dr., South Bend, IN 46619
Giant Imperial Quart (BCCA), Dave Launt, 305 Gingham, Portage, MI 49002
Patrick Henry (BCCA), Don Hicks, 3595 Arbor St., St. Joseph, MI 49085

GREAT PLACES
Ann Arbor: Full Moon Cafe
Detroit: Ye Old Taproom

OF NOTE
Frankenmuth Bavaria Festival, 2d week of June, Frankenmuth. A celebration in the Bavarian tradition, held in a town that takes its roots seriously. Appropriately attended in a Winnebago. A smaller polka festival is held in late August.
Lindell A/C, corner of Michigan and Cass Aves., Detroit. Required attendance after Tiger games. You might even get a stool next to Billy Martin. Lots of beer.

OHIO

★ Hudepohl-Schoenling Brewing Co., Executive Offices and Plant, 1625 Central Parkway, Cincinnati, OH 45214
Brands: Little Kings Cream Ale, Hudy Delight, Christian Moerlein, Hudepohl 14-K, Burger
Breweriana: Limited items available for purchase
Slogan: "Cincinnati's Brewery." The logo features the Cincinnati skyline highlighted by the fountain, Riverfront stadium, and a riverboat paddle wheeler.

★ The Cleveland Brewing Co., 2456 Lakeside Ave., Cleveland, OH 44114
Type: Contract
Brand: Erin Brew

★ Anheuser-Busch, Inc., 700 East Schrock Rd., Columbus, OH 43229
Type: Branch plant of Anheuser-Busch, Inc., St. Louis, MO

KINDRED SPIRITS

Queen City (BCCA), Dave Gausepohl, 6439 Adahi Dr., Independence KY 41051
Pioneer City (BCCA), S. Roger Kirkpatrick, 927 Colegate Dr., Marietta, OH 45750
Miami Valley (BCCA), Bob Kates, 2474 Apricot Dr., Dayton, OH 45431
Old Dutch (BCCA), Don Johnson, 2227 Seneca Dr., Lima, OH 45806
Wooden Shoe (BCCA), Mel Olberding, 15211 Schmitmeyer-Baker Rd., Minster, OH 45865
Gambrinus (BCCA), Arthur W. Zerby III, 876 Minerva Ave., Columbus, OH 43229
Lake Erie (BCCA) Marcia Sticht, 23200 Hardwick Rd., Shaker Heights, OH 44122
Buckeye (BCCA), Mike Bocian, 3950 Shadylawn Dr., Toledo, OH 43614
Dayton Regional Amateur Fermentation Technologists, c/o Patrick Pickett, 109 Oakview Dr., Kettering, OH 45429

GREAT PLACES

Cincinnati: Arnold's
Columbus: The Distillery

OF NOTE

Germantown, Columbus, is a well-preserved example of a German-American neighborhood dating from the late nineteenth century.
(RIP) August Wagner's Gambrinus Brewery of Germantown.

Great Fermentations
New Pub breweries:
Growler's Brew Pub, Dayton
District Brewing Co., Columbus
Strongsville Brewing Co., Strongsville

WISCONSIN

★ Jacob Leinenkugel Brewing Co., 1-3 Jefferson Ave., Chippewa Falls, WI 54729
Brands: Leinenkugel's Regular, Leinenkugel's Light, Limited, Bock
Tours: June, July, August: Mon.–Fri., 10:00 A.M.–3:00 P.M. every half-hour. The hospitality center is open all year, 9:00 A.M.–4:00 P.M.
Breweriana: Extensive selection

★ Hibernia Brewing Ltd., 318 Elm St., Eau Claire, WI 54703
Type: Independent regional
Brands: Walter's, Eau Claire All Malt Lager Beer, Eau Claire All Malt Light Pilsner Beer, Hibernia Bock Beer, Hibernia Weizen, Hibernia Oktoberfest, Hibernia Winter Brau

★ Brewmaster's Pub Ltd., 4017 80th St., Kenosha, WI 53142
Type: Pub brewery
Brands: Harborside Light, Kenosha Gold, Amber Vienna Style, Royal Dark

★ G. Heileman Brewing Co., Inc., Executive Offices, 100 Harborview Plaza, La Crosse, WI 54601
Type: National
Brands: Old Style, Rainier, Lone Star, J. Schmidt, Henry Weinhard, Special Export, Colt 45, Champale, La Croix Sparkling Pure Mineral Water, Cold Spring Sparkling Pure Mineral Water, Mickey's Malt Liquor, Kingsbury Non-Alcoholic Malt Beverage, Iron City
Tours: La Crosse, WI: Mon.–Sat., 8:00 A.M.–4:00 P.M.
Breweriana: Gift shops located in La Crosse, WI; Frankenmuth, MI; Perry, GA: San Antonio, TX; and Seattle, WA

★ Capital Brewery, 7734 Terrace Ave., Middleton, WI 53562
Brands: Garten Brau Lager, Garten Brau Special, Garten Brau Dark
Tours: Mon.–Fri., 1:00 P.M. Group tours by special appointment (608) 836-7100

★ Ambier Brewing Co., 5325 West Burleigh St., Milwaukee, WI 53210
Type: Contract
Brand: Ambier Vienna Style Beer (contract brewed by Jos. Huber Co., Monroe, WI)
Tours: Possibly at Jos. Huber Brewing Co. Check first.
Breweriana: Glasses, apparel
Slogans: "A Head of the Imports"; "Portrait of a Fine Beer." The mascot is Emperor Franz Josef.

★ Century Brewing Co., 2340 North Farwell Ave., Milwaukee, WI 53211
Type: Pub brewery
Brands: Century Gold, Cream City Ale
Note: Brewery destroyed by fire in 1988; future uncertain.

★ Lakefront Brewery, Inc., 818A East Chambers St., Milwaukee, WI 53212
  Type: Microbrewery
  Brands: Riverwest Stein Beer, Klisch Lager Beer
  Tours: By appointment only (414) 372-8800
  Breweriana: T-shirts, table tents
  Slogan: "For Those Who Prefer a Finer Flavor" (Klisch Lager)

★ Miller Brewing Co., 3939 West Highland Blvd., Milwaukee, WI 53201
  Type: National
  Brands: Miller High Life, Miller Genuine Draft, Lite, Löwenbräu, Meister
    Brau, Milwaukee's Best, Magnum Malt Liquor, Matilda Bay Coolers
  Tours: Summer: 10:00 A.M.–3:30 P.M. except Sun. and holidays; winter:
    Tues.–Sat., 11:00 A.M.–2:00 P.M. Tour lasts approximately 90 minutes and
    includes sampling at restored turn-of-the-century Miller Inn, tours of
    lagering caves, museum, and gift shop
  Breweriana: Yes
  Slogan: "Quality—Uncompromising and Unchanging"

★ Pabst Brewing Co., 917 West Juneau, P.O. Box 766, Milwaukee, WI 53201
  Type: National
  Brands: Pabst Blue Ribbon, Hamm's Beer, Olympia, Olde English 800 Malt
    Liquor, Andecker Beer
  Tours: At the brewery in San Antonio, TX
  Slogans: Pabst: "What'll You Have?"; Olympia: "It's the Water." The Hamm's
  bear is the mascot for Hamm's.

★ Sprecher Brewing Co., Inc., 730 West Oregon St., Milwaukee, WI 53204
  Type: Microbrewery
  Brands: Black Bavarian, Sprecher Special Amber, Milwaukee Weiss, Winter
    Brew, Dunkle Weizen, Mai Bock, Milwaukee Pils, Oktoberfest

★ Val Blatz Brewing Co., 1515 North 10th, Milwaukee, WI 53205
  Type: Microbrewery owned by G. Heileman Brewing Co., La Crosse, WI
  Brands: Blatz Old Heidelberg, Culmbacher Imperial Dark, Ansbach Light,
    Edel Weiss

★ Water Street Brewery, 1101 North Water St., Milwaukee, WI 53202
  Type: Pub brewery
  Brands: Water Street Amber, Old World Oktoberfest, Sporten European
    Lager, Kilbourn's Bock, Callan's Irish Red
  Tours: Upon request (brewery equipment on display behind glass at all
    times)
  Breweriana: T-shirts, pilsner glasses, key jobs, coasters

★ Jos. Huber Brewing Co., 1208 14th Ave., Monroe, WI 53566
  Type: Independent regional. (The brewery was recently closed but has
    reopened.)
  Brands: Huber Premium, HiBrau, Wisconsin Club, Wisconsin Gold Label,
    Regal Brau, Bavarian Club, Rhinelander, Augsburger Golden, Dark, Bock

and Light, Dempsey's Irish Ale. (The Augsburger brands have been sold to Stroh and the company will focus on its Berghoff brands.)
Tours: May–Sept., weekdays, 10:00 A.M.–4:00 P.M.

★ Stevens Point Beverage Co., Stevens Point Brewery, 2617 Water St., Stevens Point, WI 54481
Type: Independent regional
Brands: Point Special Beer, Point Bock Beer, Point Light Beer, Special Edition (all malt, fall season), Eagle Premium Pilsner (special hopping, 120 calories)
Tours: Fri. at 1:15 P.M., or by appointment (715) 344-9310
Breweriana: Many items, free brochure available on request
Slogans: "Brewing Excellence since 1857," "Score a Few Points Tonight," "Wisconsin's Great Tasting Hometown Beers"

KINDRED SPIRITS

Badger Bunch (BCCA), Lou Capriotti, 3508 27th St., Kenosha, WI 53142
Lakeshore (BCCA), Robert Waskow, 2920 43d St., Two Rivers, WI 54241
Packer (BCCA), Ken Treml, 721 East Mission Rd., Green Bay, WI 54301
Central Wisconsin Amateur Winemaker's Club, c/o Tom Bauer, 112 West Fifth, Marshfield, WI 54449
Madison Homebrewers and Tasters Guild, c/o Steve Klafka, 141 North Hancock, Madison, WI 53703
Wisconsin Vintners' Assoc., c/o John Rauenbuehler, 6100 North Kent, Whitefish Bay, WI 53217

GREAT PLACES

Milwaukee: Fourth of July, Port of Hamburg, Gasthaus Zur Krone, Water Street Brewery
Middletown: Capital Brewery Beergarden
Madison: Ohio Tavern, Essen House
Kenosha: Brewmaster's Pub
Bay View: Kniesler's White House

OF NOTE

Basement Brewmaster, Mark May, 2342 West Acicia Rd., Milwaukee, WI 53209
Nort's Worts, David Norton, 7625 Sheridan Rd., Kenosha, WI 53140
Wine and Hop Shop, Cara Doyle, 434 State St., Madison, WI 53703 (Homebrew supplies)
La Crosse Oktoberfest, autumn. The granddaddy. Bavaria by the river. Jah!
Milwaukee Summerfest. The brewers do it up big every July. German America at its best.
Treaty Beer, produced by a Minoqua pizza parlor owner, is a contract brew that protests the hunting and fishing rights granted the Chippewa Indians. C'mon guys. Beer was never meant to serve political purposes. Belly up to the bar and talk this over.

Great Fermentations

Appleton Brewing Co., a new brew pub, is housed in the original Appleton Brewing Co. building.

BUY 'EM IF YOU CAN FIND 'EM

Andeker (Pabst). Perhaps the best of America's superpremiums. Smooth and well balanced. The first always makes you want a second, with just enough hops to peek through the maltiness. The best product from one of America's most traditional brewers, especially if sampled at the brewery.

Augsburger (Jos. Huber). The light is a terrific, import-style beer. There is a perceptible aroma of Hallertauer hops that the company says it flies in from Germany in refrigerated airplanes. The care shows. Even beer snobs like it.

Augsburger Dark (Jos. Huber). Augie Dark is sweeter but appropriately balanced. Small brewers shouldn't be able to make beers this good, but, thank God, they do.

Stroh (Stroh). A clean, inoffensive beer, entirely professional. Well regarded everywhere but Detroit.

Frankenmuth Old German Dark (Frankenmuth). The scientific brewmaster could rip this brew to shreds, but if you have a sense of adventure, it's worth a try.

Christian Moerlein (Hudepohl). A laudable attempt at a European-style premium beer that misses the mark but earns points for trying. Unfortunately one needs more than a foil top and hard-to-read graphics to create a superior beer.

Little Kings Cream Ale (Hudepohl/Schoenling). More notable for its packaging than its content. The 7-ounce miniexport bottles are ideal for those who want maximum flavor in minimum consumption.

Miller High Life (Miller). People like it or hate it based on their opinion of the company, but the brew itself can be faulted only for its total lack of personality. The former Champagne of Lager Beers is now a starlet—nice looking in a vacuous way. Currently on the skids as younger drinkers are turning to Miller Draft.

Löwenbräu Dark (Miller). Miller has taken a lot of flak from connoisseurs for their ripoff of the Löwenbräu name. Without casting judgment on that, their dark has an appealing winey aftertaste that stands up well to repeated drinking. Don't let your opinions of Miller interfere with your enjoyment of this fine brew. The Light Löwenbräu is less distinguished.

Old Milwaukee (Stroh). It doesn't get any better than this? Thank goodness, it does.

Point Special (Stevens Point). The beer is overrated, but the can is exceptional. Buy it to show you are glad to be in Stevens Point. Remember, "When you're out of Point, you're out of town."

Old Style (G. Heileman). The best-selling beer in Chicago. You can see the semis barreling down Interstate 90 to serve the thirsty masses. Bland and malty, it serves midwestern tastes well.

Special Export (G. Heileman). Supposedly the highest expression of G. Heileman's art, it spices its minimal body with a liberal dose of pretension. Stick to Old Style.

6
THE
GREAT
RIVER

COLD SPRING, MINNESOTA, TO NEW ORLEANS, LOUISIANA
55 DAYS, 11,920 MILES ON THE ROAD

HEADWATERS

The Great Beer Trek made its first crossing of the Mississippi at La Crosse, Wisconsin. It was another significant passage that provided an occasion to take stock. We had now been gone forty days and had traveled 8,120 miles. We had visited most of the nation's breweries and had stopped at countless taverns. The attrition of independent breweries that had begun as an abstract statistic was now a harsh reality, brought home by viewing too many riddled hulls of once-vital businesses. On the positive side, our ability to taste beer intelligently had improved significantly thanks to minilessons from the likes of Ron Siebel and Bill Leinenkugel. Our appreciation for the delicacy of a fragile foodstuff had grown enormously. Good beer can become bad very quickly if the packaging and handling are not equal to the brewing. Not all the pieces were in place, but a perceptible sense of progress could be sensed in the van. Despite some early disappointments, our trip to date was a smashing success and still continuing onward, upward, and beerward.

The Bavarian traditions in Wisconsin continued in Minnesota. Although in strictest racial terms Minnesotans include a variety of populations who migrated from all over northern Europe and Scandinavia, in terms of beer we are talking strictest pedigree. This became apparent after we visited Minnesota's two country breweries.

Cold Spring Brewing Co., in Cold Spring, is not a spectacular-looking affair. What made it special for us was the tour provided by brewmaster Jim Schorn who explained in detail the function of every valve and pipe in a Rube Goldberg maze. Cold Spring ships much of its product to the badlands to the west. "And there aren't many people between here and the West Coast," Jim reminded us. Marketing-wise the company can't afford to be too proud, so their beers run the gamut from little-known budget brand White Label to superpremium Cold Spring Premium Export. As for the difference between the brands, Schorn answered, "For the most part, the cans."

In addition to providing honest answers to simple questions, Schorn proved to have a sentimental side to counter his technical expertise. He grew misty-eyed when describing his previous employer, the Mankato Brewing Co.

"There were 110 different rooms, all on different levels, so you couldn't even use a forklift. She was built on the side of a hill, with lagering caves dug right into the hillside. I knew every pipe and switch. Once, after they turned off the electricity, they had to send me back in the pitch black to find a certain valve to turn off. In some places you couldn't even use a flashlight, and I had to do everything by feel, but I did it.

"There was no way for her to survive, but oh, she was pretty. To see her from the other side of the valley was a sight. I couldn't bear to be there when they finally tore her down."

Later that day, at the August Schell Brewery in New Ulm, Minnesota, we felt that we were reliving Jim Schorn's vision. The brewery is built on a lush hillside with lagering cellars that penetrate the rich earth. The brewery grounds are well maintained and feature a park with grazing deer and a Victorian mansion for the resident brewery owner. Man, the brewing gods, and the cosmos seem to be in harmony at August Schell.

As had become our custom, we asked at the brewery for the best place locally to sample the company's wares. We were directed to the local Turner Hall. August Schell arrived in New Ulm sponsored by the Turner Colonization Society (Turn Verein), a group that took upon itself the task of properly populating the New World. Its recruits were followers of Father Friedrich Ludwig Jahn who developed a patterned series of exercises for Germans to promote their strength of body, mind, and society. Its recruits were dispatched to remote American outposts where they were charged with starting the German-American equivalent of a Brave New World. Many Wisconsin and Minnesotan towns had as their first substantial structure a hall where the Turners could meet for exercise, followed—not surprisingly—by healthy doses of fraternal beer drinking. Beer was an integral part of the formula, demonstrating the

THE OWNER'S "BIG HOUSE" AT

Schell's

SURROUNDED BY THE PARK.

esteem in which the beverage was held by the society of the day. Beer was not a luxury beverage with connotations of wickedness and degeneracy; rather, it was a liquid foodstuff, brewed by a pillar of the community and consumed as a matter of course by its members. A demonstration of the brewers' community status occurred in 1862 when the Sioux of southern Minnesota rose up against the invading whites. New Ulm was pillaged, with great loss of life. The Schell family returned to their hillside expecting ashes and rubble. There were many signs of Indian occupation, but the brewery was intact, a fact the family could attribute only to the universally beneficial role of the brewer. Indians may have hated whites, but they knew good beer when they tasted it.

After our tours of the country breweries, we visited Minneapolis where we saw another glorious testament to the Bavarian heyday. Of the great meccas of beer consumption—Siebens in Chicago, Trommer's in New York, the Gerst House in Nashville—the Grain Belt Brewing Co. and its drinking garden was reputedly the granddaddy of them all. Now it stands as a champion out to stud—only this champion is sterile and will bear no offspring. At present the Grain Belt plant seems to be merely sleeping, awaiting the return of workers to start the juices flowing and of patrons to enliven the handsome gardens. Once the best families of Minneapolis gathered here to share steins of Grain Belt, good food, good music, and good company on Sunday afternoons.

The patrons would certainly come today if they could, but the owners would lose money with every glass of beer sold. Grain Belt is a monument to the Gothic excess of Bavarian fancy. Alas, this is an age that requires high-speed functionalism. The whole became worth less than the sum of its parts. A professional liquidator moved in, sold the brands to Heileman, the equipment to whichever South American breweries wanted it, and kept the rapidly increasing real estate, which appreciates just as fast whether or not the handsome complex continues to make beer. The magnificent structure and equally magnificent grounds lie fallow, stubbornly awaiting the inevitable wrecker's ball and hoping for a miracle. Only when she is gone will we realize we have lost a treasure.

Beer drinkers everywhere lament the loss of Grain Belt. To have it standing so magnificently, its brick and mortar outliving economic viability, rubs salt in the wound. Sentimentalities are heard amid elaborate plans for its revival and curses for the hard-hearted liquidator. We stare into our beers and understand the battleship captain whose mastery of the ocean's surface is now irrelevant in the light of the capabilities of the submarine and airplane. We

Grain Belt

try to keep a stiff upper lip, to remember not to cry over spilled beer. A tradition is now past; it is the function of The Great Beer Trek to understand why.

The explanation is deceptively simple. Grain Belt's downfall was as inevitable as Schaefer's, Ballantine's, and hundreds of other worthy brewers. When the country was growing by leaps and bounds, there was opportunity aplenty for any industrious firm. Brewers grew, expanded capacity, and built monuments such as Grain Belt where the aesthetic considerations superseded the practical. Once the combined industry capacity created more than was necessary to slake the national thirst, the brewers could achieve growth only by taking a portion of a neighbor's market share. Add to the mathematics Prohibition and several decades of war-related anti-German sentiment to affect negatively total national beer consumption, and the stage was set for the attrition and consolidation, which, in fact, is still occurring. The excesses of a Grain Belt could no longer be obscured by a burgeoning marketplace. Just as survival of Cold Spring and Schell is remarkable, the downfall of Grain Belt, however lamentable, could not have been prevented.

THE GREAT RIVER ROAD   Dubuque, Iowa

The Great River Road rides the bluffs on either side of the Mississippi. At the foot of the steep embankments run the railroad tracks, a conduit for the nation's commerce. Between the bluffs, filled with barges, tugs, and water, runs the greatest conduit of all, the mighty Mississippi. We caulked the seams of our van and followed the current, our senses peeled for telltale signs of beer.

By the time we crossed the river at Prairie du Chien, we had already lost count of the number of times the river had passed beneath us. Thunderstorms had been rolling down the valley with us, buffeting us with hail and violent winds. Had we somehow incurred God's wrath?

In Dubuque we stopped to visit the Picketts, family brewers since 1977. Beer runs as thick in the veins of the Picketts as in the Strohs, Coors, and Busches in the country. The Picketts' problem is that their family never owned their own brewery until they purchased the bankrupt Dubuque Star plant in the early seventies. Joe, Sr., claims the title of senior brewmaster in the country, having graduated from the first brewmaster class of the Siebel Institute following Prohibition. (Note: One other member of that class is still alive and brewing, Ed Siers of the Lion in Wilkes-Barre, Pennsylvania. Mr. Pickett earns the senior brewmaster award, according to Mr. Siers, on the basis of meritorious service during Prohibition.)

The Picketts' plant is located in a turn-of-the-century industrial park within sight of the river. The area is strangely silent, its best days—in fact, Dubuque's best days—forty years past. On the day The Great Beer Trek arrived, the scene was painted with violence. A thunderstorm meeting its first

It's the Water

The river that flows past the Rolling Rock brewery had a shopping cart in it when we peeked over the bridge. The river by Genesee foams with multicolored effluents from decades of industrial use. In "God's Country" where Heileman's Old Style is brewed, the Mississippi lives up to its name of the Big Muddy. Clearly, if water has the importance in brewing that some brewers would have us believe, we are in trouble.

How important is water to the brewing process? After asking the question a hundred times of a hundred people, The Great Beer Trek has settled on the answer: "Water is as important to the finished beer as the brewery's marketing department would like us to believe it is." Thus, while the people at Coors have us imagine their cans to be filled with rivulets of melted mountain snow, the city brewers freely admit to obtaining their water from the municipal supply. Because all commercial brewing water must be brought to a chemically neutral point before the brewing process can begin, claim the latter, all waters are created equal in the eyes of the modern scientific brewer.

For the home brewer, however, the character of the original "liquor" (as brewing water is correctly called) is a crucial element in the finished product. The same recipe made from a treated municipal source and an artesian well may vary so much as to be unrecognizable. Ironically, the chemically adulterated one may well be the better tasting. Brewers long ago discovered that certain beer types taste best when brewed from a chalky, oxygenated source. The river Trent in England, wherein comes the liquor that becomes Bass Ale, has long been renowned as the archetypal brewing source. The hardness of these waters is estimated at 1800 ppm (parts per million). The modern brewer scoffs and claims that with the right filters and additives, he can create water indistinguishable from that plucked from the Trent.

In fact municipal water supplies average about 100 ppm hardness. U.S. brewers adjust their water to 400 ppm, while German brewers go 50 percent further to 600 ppm.

The hardness can come in many forms, including such delicious items as calcium sulfate, magnesium sulfate, and good old sodium chloride. "It's the water" may be the claim of the marketing department, but the truthful brewer will tell you, "It's the chemist."

resistance after a thousand miles of prairie turned the sky black, then rent it asunder with lightning and thunder. The hail came in rhythmic waves, an army of tap dancers on the van roof, interrupted by eerie interludes of silence.

In between downpours we dashed from the van to the second-story office of the Pickett Brewing Co., pausing just long enough to ask directions of a

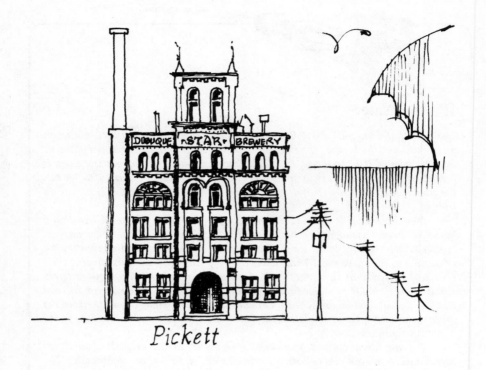

Pickett

man walking his dog, an exotic Hungarian vizsla. Inside we asked the receptionist if Mr. Pickett was available. "Which one?" she asked. Joe, Sr., it turned out, was the nice man with the vizsla who had just disappeared into the thunderstorm. Val Pickett was on vacation, but if we did not mind waiting, she was sure that Joe, Jr., could be talked into taking some time with us.

The Pickett offices are plain—a few functional desks and straight wooden chairs. The look is neither ugly nor unfriendly but gives the accurate impression of having been designed by people who have neither time nor money to spend on appearance. They are too busy making beer.

When Joe, Jr., finally came out, he was sweaty and tired but not too tired—never too tired—to take a moment to tell anyone interested about the beer his family makes. We talked in the deserted hospitality room, a quaint taproom on the ground floor of the brewery that bears testament to the working-class roots of Dubuque and its home-town beer. Joe drew us a beer, and we toasted a hospitality room that glorifies a different side of beer drinking than the Bavarian plastique we had encountered in so many other breweries. Subsequently we toasted to thunderstorms, to catfish, to vizslas, to Dubuque, to Chevy Beauville vans, to Picketts, and to The Great Beer Trek. The beer, brewed exclusively with two-rowed barley, has a roundness that seems to lubricate the throat as it goes down. This beer is as good as any other yet encountered in our travels.

Joe Pickett, Jr., was well on his way to a promising career in the beer business before his crazy father went and bought this rundown, debt-ridden riverside plant. He worked as a technical service representative for the Siebel Institute, wore a jacket and tie, traveled the United States, drew a good salary, and did not have to get his fingernails dirty. Now his twelve-hour days are followed by evenings of backslapping and flesh pressing as he and other family members strive to convince Dubuque that just because a beer comes from the home town does not mean it cannot be good. He earns half of what he could elsewhere in the industry, and his future is as unsure as the outcome of the Beer Wars. As for the fingernails . . . well, no one cares much about that in Dubuque. Tonight when he leaves the plant, Joe will load a quarter-barrel in his car to deliver to some Good Ol' Boys having a catfish fry. There will be all the fish anyone can eat, cooked over an open fire in an ostrich egg skillet with a 6-foot handle, and homemade onion rings—the thick kind—and lots of beer. He is just supposed to drop off the beer but will probably wind up setting up the tap, eating some fish, and sharing a few brews. It is a night when he might rather be home with the family, but a brewer has responsibilities. Besides, if Joe, his father, and his brother are not out there selling the beer, who will?

Joe Pickett is his own boss. He treats us to definitive explanations on every complex beery situation we can throw at him. The explanations are bold, comprehensive, and unique, the pronouncements of someone who does not have to worry about displeasing superiors. "You wanna know about the Coors' mystique? It all goes back to World War II. Light beers? I'll tell you something about light beers. The whole problem with beer comes down to one thing: drinkability."

We take it all in, and too quickly it is time to move on. Joe locks up Zigi's, as the hospitality room is called, and gives us tips for fishing in Iowa if we get the chance. He swears there are trout spots in this maligned state that have to be seen to be believed. Before Laura and I leave Dubuque, we stop at a take-out joint that advertises fried catfish. Our appetites have been whetted by the Pickett hyperbole. The thunderstorm has passed, we've all survived, and there is even a poststorm sunset to grace Dubuque.

I drop off Laura to order food and leave to gas up the van for the miles still to be covered. The attendant asks in what could only be described as a Dubuquan drawl, "What's The Great Beer Trek?"

"My wife and I are making a trip around the country, learning everything we can about beer."

"Oh, yeah? Well, have you tried our local beer?"

"Sure have."

"And what did you think about it?"

"I think it's great. You can't beat it."

He looked genuinely surprised. "You think it's good?"

"Yup, and I've tasted almost all of them."

And it is true, Picketts has won widespread praise among beer aficiona-dos. Yet in their own home town, they have to constantly combat the blank stare of the gas station attendant. I flashed back to our meeting with Will Anderson when the Beer Trek was barely wet behind the ears. He had predicted we would find beer drinkers thoroughly ignorant of the virtues of their local breweries. "When's the last time you tried some?" I asked.

"Oh, I haven't had any in years," replied the attendant. He paused, his answer sounding a bit flat in the light of my enthusiasm. He decided to check again, in case his ears had deceived him the first time, "And you think it's good?"

PRETTY LITTLE THINGS
St. Louis, Missouri

St. Louis greeted The Great Beer Trek with temperatures approaching 100 degrees and humidity to match, a climate more commonly associated with primeval rain forests than the Midwest. The natives took it in stride, having perfected life-styles in which they hop with great facility from air-conditioned car to air-conditioned office, exposing themselves to the elements for only minimal periods. The day was best suited for floating down the river à la Huck Finn, but Huck did not have a Beer Trek to make.

Our attitude toward Budweiser had by this time made a dramatic turnabout. No longer were the people of Anheuser-Busch villains who had mercilessly driven hundreds of colorful local breweries into obsolescence. Instead they had become the most prominent survivors of an era, the success story, that through luck, skill, and fate have been in a position to turn the misfortune of others to advantage. And do not for a moment think there is another brewer in the history of America who would not change places with Anheuser-Busch. Their St. Louis brewery alone has an annual capacity of over 12 million barrels of beer, well more than the combined capacity of all the breweries in Pennsylvania. Along with the Pabst plant in Milwaukee, this plant is one of the remaining citadels of beerdom, a Gothic masterpiece, a Notre Dame. Someday the scions of Anheuser-Busch will have to cope with the fact that strategically located plants of half the size make the St. Louis plant a dinosaur, but for now they need all the capacity they can get, thus ensuring the vitality of this fulfillment of an Industrial Revolution dream.

The self-proclaimed King of Beers has been crowned only recently, but it wears the crown so easily one would think that Budweiser had been a fixture for generations in America's refrigerators. Prior to the 1950s, lest we forget, there was no such thing as a national beer. Thus, brewers all over America could, and did, refer to themselves as the "King of Beers." Nor was the brand "Budweiser" (derived from the renowned Budvar brewery in Czechoslovakia) unique. Versions of Budweiser have been served up from concerns as varied as the DuBois Brewing Co. in DuBois, Pennsylvania, Budweiser Brewing Co. in Brooklyn, New York, and even Joseph Schlitz of Milwaukee. Why did the St. Louis Budweiser succeed where so many others slipped into obscurity?

Anheuser-Busch   1893

The contemporary King displays its royal gowns willingly to all who care to see. The first-rate tour features a glimpse of the Clydesdale stables and a view of a brewhouse that, with the closing of Schlitz's Milwaukee plant, is unrivaled as a cathedral for the worship of the brewing gods. Compared to many other tours offered by major brewers, the Budweiser story features a healthy dose of hard information, the technical story being one the company is proud to tell. Within the brewing industry, no one faults Anheuser-Busch for what goes into their beer (more barley and malt and hops per barrel than any other national brewer), for their brewing methods (partial kraeusening and beechwood aging), or even for what they return to the beer drinker (tours and widespread support of related interest events ranging from NASCAR races to offshore powerboat racing). The Budweiser approach is slick, intelligent, and professional. Moreover, the beer is good. If one prefers the type of beer that Budweiser, Michelob, and Busch represent, the argument can be made that no finer or fresher beer can consistently be found in America.

AA/Fuel Funny Car, 1981

We met with a variety of Anheuser-Busch personnel, ranging from the company historian to their head of publicity, and including more than a couple of guys off the line. No dramatic secret of success was uncovered, beyond a dedication to the basics: make good beer and run a good business. The formula is revolutionary only in its simplicity. So long as Anheuser-Busch resists the tendency to overcomplicate their business, Budweiser will remain the King of Beers.

On this steamy summer day, a tour of Anheuser-Busch's refrigerated lagering cellars followed by a free sampling is a refreshing prospect for the tourist on a Beer Trek. We happily joined the minions, well satisfied at how far we had come since our early acquaintance with Budweiser at their Merrimack, New Hampshire, plant. No longer the adversary, we now felt like members of the same team.

From a pay phone at Anheuser-Busch we called the first of several local beery leads collected along the way—Bill Henderson, vice-president of the Beer Can Collectors of America (BCCA). After we explained the purpose of our trip, we never got to the second call. He instructed, nay commanded, us to:

1. Proceed directly to his house.
2. Cancel any plans for dinner.
3. Plan to spend whatever time we had in St. Louis with the can collectors.

Later we discovered this to be not atypical of the hospitality of can collectors.

Here's the story.

You collect toothpaste tubes. Damned if you know how this whole thing started. As a kid you thought the colorful tubes attractive, and once in a while when an unusual tube design was found you threw it in a drawer. Before long the drawer was filled. One ambitious night the tubes were glued to strips of wood and hung prominently around the rec room. Your friends thought you unusual, and you had to agree.

The more tubes collected, the more they were sought. You began writing to toothpaste manufacturers to obtain mint condition tubes that had never been filled. Old dumps were searched for obsolete brands, painstaking hours spent restoring rusty tubes. One day a reporter from the local paper came by to do a small article ridiculing the town nut who collects toothpaste tubes. Then, surprise of surprises, you receive a letter from a man in a nearby state who says that he thought he was the only toothpaste tube collector in the world. He wants to come and see your collection this weekend. The letter is like a salve to your abused subconscious. You are not alone! Someone else appreciates the beauty of an empty tube. There are more calls and letters, and soon there are enough of you to form an organization!

Beer can collectors no longer need to feel alone. To their credit they have maintained the giddy enthusiasm they had on the evening of April 15, 1970, when a group of six met at Denver Wright's house in St. Louis for the purpose of organizing to further the cause of can collecting. Now, more than 24,000 members later, with 93 chapters in the United States and 24 more spread across the globe, whenever they get together, they still have a good time.

At the early meetings, members brought duplicate cans that they placed on the table for the others to take. Soon the inevitable occurred, and one member swapped his duplicates for a particularly desirable can from someone else's collection. A tradition was born. The BCCA's by-laws reflect the desire on the part of the founders to keep the fun in their hobby. One of the hottest issues currently among can collectors is how to keep the hobby free of creeping commercialism. The damn things have gone and gotten valuable!

Dinner at the Henderson's consisted of pot roast and nonstop beer can stories, no offense intended to Bill's wife Kathy, who is long accustomed to unannounced visitors and Beer Trekkers.

Bill Henderson once worked in the keg racking room of the Pabst Brewery in Milwaukee, his home town. This is where the biggest and burliest men were assigned. Bill looks as if he has lifted a few kegs in his day. With red hair, blue eyes, and the build of a defensive end, he looks potentially menacing until he tempers his appearance with a smile. Without a sense of humor, this man could be dangerous.

The dinnertime stories invariably have as their butt Bill himself. This is the man who tips over a hand cart of 300 beer cans in the middle of a busy street, risking life and limb to save his empties. This is the man who removes his spare tire to fit more traders in the car for a 1,500-mile convention trip, the man who spends a week accumulating cans in Canada only to find out that they will not let him back through customs. Can collectors delight in ignominy. Bill returns to pick up a previously purchased piece of breweriana from a liquor store only to be subjected to the humiliation of hearing the counterman yell to the back room, "Hey, Hymie, where's the sign we got for the fat boy?" Bill roars with laughter at the punchline. In every one of the stories, someone is made a fool of. Sometimes it's Bill, sometimes another collector, sometimes the person on the other end of the transaction. No matter; it's all in good fun.

Henderson's
VEST OF MANY COLORS

The downstairs of the Henderson's has been surrendered to Bill's treasures. The walls are lined with cans and festooned with colorful electric signs. In the center of the room is a tangled mess of breweriana collected at recent flea markets. In contrast to Will Anderson's, where each item is handsomely mounted and displayed, with Bill Henderson the collection clearly rules the man.

As he showed us his collection, Bill Henderson donned his togs, the outfit he wears on the trading floor at the national convention. His costume consists of a blue denim vest dappled with the patches of different beers and can-collecting chapters. The effect is not unlike that produced by a Hell's Angel wearing full colors. The spectre is imposing in its frivolity.

Soon after the Hendersons moved to St. Louis, they began receiving calls where the caller hung up as soon as the phone was answered. Bill, knowing the experience of some other collectors, made a difficult decision. He took each can in his collection worth more than $20 and sold it, making sure that everyone in the local can world knew what he had done. The phone calls ceased almost immediately. His collection is now worth less, but the fun is back. He collects obscure groups of cans—cans with bottles pictured on them, cans with a history on the back, bock beers. As he leads us through the metal maze, arranged in an order that has meaning only to him, Bill revels in past dealings with other collectors, of being both a BCCA honcho and somewhat of a nut, and in the tall tales and practical jokes that seem to be a part of every gathering of the clan. In his vest of many colors, he is a changed man.

Unintentionally I do something very stupid and cruel: I ask what he does for a living in the real world. He brushes the question aside with a curt, "Oh, I'm just a salesman." What he really is is a beer can collector. And what he really does is collect cans. In an instant the twinkle has returned to his eye.

"You know," he giggles, "one of the guys was showing his collection to his mother-in-law, and the only thing she could do was keep saying, 'You poor thing, you must not have had any toys when you were young.'"

We continue our slow tour, learning the random circumstances that formed this gathering of cans. An old flat top, blighted by rust, is taken from the shelf to show us the Internal Revenue stamp that once appeared on all cans. We are told the history of the particular brewery, the whys and where-fores of revenue stamps, and the conditions surrounding the acquisition of this can. Bill lectures on the can for ten minutes, stopping not because the topic is exhausted but because there is so much more to see. He gives the can a last, loving look before returning it to its resting place.

"It's not worth much. It might be if it was in perfect condition, but really none of them are worth anything. You're supposed to use them and throw them away. They're not supposed to be worth anything. It's just . . . they're such pretty little things."

The second Beer Trek day in St. Louis was, like the first, hot and steamy. Also, like the first, it was commandeered by the BCCA, as we returned to the Henderson household where some of St. Louis's finest were assembled. Any illusions that we had of being beer authorities were quickly shattered, as each new topic brought our appalling ignorance to the light. Everyone had a spe-cialty: beer in movies, beer in song, brewery suicides and kidnappings.

A typical interchange:

BCCA'er: Did you see *Deliverance*? [the movie starring Burt Reynolds]
GBT: Yes.
BCCA'er: What did you notice?
GBT: What do you mean?
BCCA'er: (expressing disbelief) You know . . . the Lucky Lager scene.
GBT: (completely befuddled) The Lucky Lager scene?
BCCA'er: Yeah, when Burt Reynolds cracks open a beer while they're canoeing.
GBT: What about it?
BCCA'er: Well, it was a Lucky Lager.
GBT: (utter bafflement; incapable of further response)
BCCA'er: (speaking slowly, as if explaining something elemental to a child): The river was supposed to be in Georgia, but Lucky Lager is only sold on the West Coast. Get it? Someone really screwed up.

Dumping

The fall issue of Beer Can Collectors News Report *was very late. Between arranging conventions, holding full-time jobs, and leading normal lives, the editors had simply not met their deadlines. When the issue finally appeared, chockful as usual with indispensable information for the collector or general beer enthusiast, the normal cover photo had been eliminated in favor of a stark, self-deprecating, typically honest BCCA statement in 72-point type:*

"Yes, This Issue is Very *Late."*

The good humor that permeates the BCCA, its conventions and publications, has its roots in the fact that what its members are doing is absurd. That established, any degree of fanaticism is accepted, yea, encouraged. No pursuit captures the passion and frivolity of this group so perfectly as dumping—the practice of exhuming abandoned dumps in search of old beer cans. For the serious collector who wants to earn his or her stripes, here are some pearls of wisdom gleaned from recent issues of the News Report:

- *Wear your worst clothes. Your pursuit of the perfect can will bring you in connection with the most foul oozes and excrements known to humanity. Waders, work gloves, and a fishnet helmet are advisable apparel.*

- *Hazards to be encountered while dumping include hornets, wasps, poison ivy, snakes, irate landowners, and the law. If you are nabbed, do not bother to explain what you are doing; it's likely to make things worse.*

- *Places to look for cans include old homesites, railway crossings, abandoned cars, drained lakes, hollow logs, and any place you see a "No Dumping" sign. People to ask about prospective sites include police, firefighters, and anybody old.*

- *Items to bring dumping include spades, machetes, pitchforks, cardboard boxes, plastic bags, and a cooler of beer.*

- *Dented cans can be undented by dropping a firecracker inside. Lemon juice, oxalic acid, and Naval Jelly are useful in removing rust. A soft-bristled toothbrush is your best cleaning implement. Cleaned cans can be protected with car wax, Clear Rustoleum, or Krylon Workable Fixit. If you don't trust yourself, send it to a professional beer can restorer.*

If you are not yet discouraged, you might have the right stuff to collect beer cans. For the acid test, pack your gear, pack your beer, pick up your buddies, and begin the four-hour drive to a reputedly good dumping site. If, at the end of a long day of driving, tramping around, digging, and drinking, you can truly say you've had fun, you have found your calling.

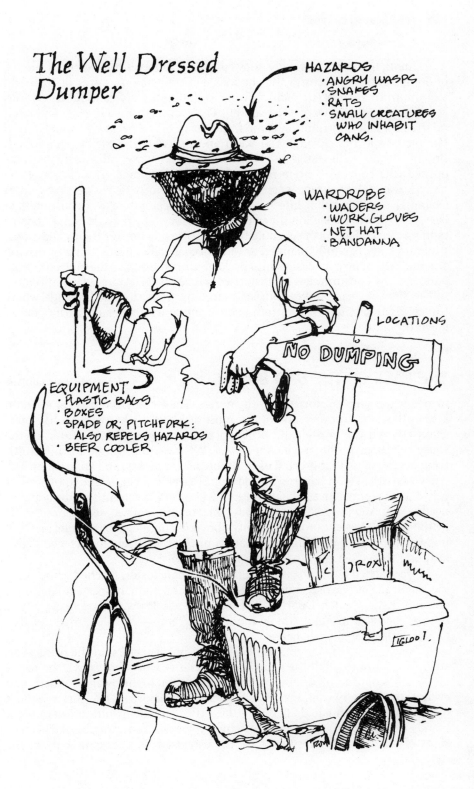

The Well Dressed Dumper

HAZARDS
- ANGRY WASPS
- SNAKES
- RATS
- SMALL CREATURES WHO INHABIT CANS.

WARDROBE
- WADERS
- WORK GLOVES
- NET HAT
- BANDANNA

LOCATIONS

NO DUMPING

EQUIPMENT
- PLASTIC BAGS
- BOXES
- SPADE OR PITCHFORK: ALSO REPELS HAZARDS
- BEER COOLER

IGLOO

Another member proudly showed off a scrapbook that featured photos of dumps and liquor stores that had yielded tremendous stores of steel and aluminum treasures. The pictures were as dull as a rusty can, but the stories accompanying them were entertaining. The evening passed quickly and often hilariously. Our contribution came in the form of the beers we brought from our recent journey through the Bavarian northwoods. Schell's Deer Brand, Bosch's (from Leinenkugel), and Point Special were religiously bottom-opened (the collector's preferred method) and consumed. The choice of the natives was eclectic. One person brought Buckhorn (a budget brew from Olympia), another Miller Lite. Although can collectors are avid consumers of beer, it is clearly packaging they prefer. One story tells it all. It is not uncommon for can collectors to schedule trips to Europe to bolster their collections. Itineraries are carefully planned around needed cans. Long hours of driving are punctuated by mad dashes into package stores. Because the collecting rate outstrips the consumption rate, startled natives have frequently been treated to the sight of mad Yankee tourists marching from store to curbside where the contents of the cans (bottom-opened, of course) are summarily poured down the gutter.

THE CASE OF THE BAD BATCH   New Orleans, Louisiana

Armed with trinkets, stories, and memories, The Great Beer Trek set forth on a span that was to prove one of the most arduous of the trip. We had once again entered the Wasteland, although this time we entered drunk on the sudsy successes of the previous few days. We were unprepared for the stultifying beerlessness that greeted us in Tennessee, Arkansas, and Mississippi. The trip was marked with hazards. In addition to heat and beerlessness, tiny mites called no-see-ums invaded our sleeping quarters, keeping us from much-needed rest. And for the first, and only, time on our trip, we were apprehended by the law. We were thoroughly guilty of making an illegal left-hand turn, but midway through a babbling explanation of the Beer Trek and its nobility of purpose, the officer good-naturedly waved us on.

We reached Louisiana on the upswing, a conclusion reached while sucking the heads of crayfish and sipping on Dixie as a suitably spectacular sunset enveloped the French Quarter. The morrow, we knew, would bring better things, even if it brought simply more of the same—the gustatorial delights of New Orleans and Dixie beer.

New Orleans is not yet a no-beer town, but it teeters on the brink. Falstaff owns a brewery but the plant was inoperative when we visited, the result of a work stoppage by union workers striking for higher wages. When, and even if, the brewery would refill its kettles was unknown. The other riverboat beer whose renown equals Dixie's is Jax. The attractive white brewery commands the French Quarter as if watching for Napoleon's warships. The only signs of life at the brewery now are the exhaust fans that spin lazily in the wrong direction whenever struck by a puff of wind. Jax is another casualty, another good beer that could not go on. The brand is still available, made by Pearl in San Antonio, but if the present product matches the old Jax, perhaps the demise was just. The beer was one of the most forgettable we had yet encountered.

"There's nothing as New Orleans as Dixie," the saying goes, and only the Mardi Gras Committee or Preservation Hall Jazz Band would quibble. The Great Beer Trek, however, did not receive a rousing welcome at Dixie because the day of our arrival coincided with the appearance of a bill before the state legislature that would give a tax break to Louisiana's small brewers, i.e., Dixie. The passage of such a bill had important ramifications for the survival of the business, and we willingly took a back seat. This beer, for many years a city fixture, was now struggling to stay afloat, a victim of obsolete equipment, discriminatory competition, and a bad batch of beer that in a span of several days destroyed a reputation decades in the making.

The timing could not have been worse—Fourth of July weekend, 1975. All through Louisiana and the adjacent states, beer drinkers were stocked up with local favorite Dixie, primed for a weekend of softball, picnics, and fishing. But something was wrong, drastically wrong, as thousands of Dixie drinkers simultaneously found out as the sun crossed the yardarm on that fateful day.

The trouble was apparent from the first "psscht." The beer was terrible. It was worse than terrible. It had a medicinal taste more akin to Vicks NyQuil than a decent lager. For legions of loyal Dixie drinkers, a nightmare had become a reality. It was the ultimate affront: their brew had let them down. For Dixie, a company of limited resources already trying to stave off the onslaught of the nationals, the blow was nearly fatal. In the modern brewing wars, the odds were stacked against the little guy to begin with. His only ace in the hole is the loyalty of his longtime consumers.

It did not matter that the cause of the bad taste was discovered—the beer had picked up flavors from phenol fumes given off by a floor sealant used near the brewhouse—and quickly rectified. The problem now was how could the faith be restored in the consumers who had abandoned Dixie in droves? Word-of-mouth reputation among beer drinkers spreads fastest when the news is bad, and in Dixie's case the news was catastrophic. How could the brewery convince people that good ol' Dixie was back?

Necessity is, indeed, the mother of invention, and the situation was desperate enough to make Ben Franklins of the dullest of us. The officers of Dixie came up with a suitable plan. They decided to put their money where their mouths were. They would give their beer away, gambling that a taste of the real Dixie would convince the beer drinkers of Louisiana to let bygones be bygones.

The plan worked! Sixty thousand free six-packs convinced the residents of New Orleans that the South, and Dixie, had risen again. Dixie still walks the fine line between prosperity and extinction, but the Disaster of the Bad Batch has been survived.

Trivial Beer

If one attends the annual BCCA or the summertime gathering of the NABA (National Association of Breweriana Advertising) clan, one best be prepared to make proper small talk. Certainly the beer will flow like water, and the predominant spirit will be one of conviviality, but what will separate this group from a mere fraternal gathering will be the topics of conversation. These are informal scholars who have directed considerable energy into their pursuits. Individually each one likes nothing better than to strut his stuff verbally in front of the other experts. Below are twenty trivia questions and answers that will help you tread water when the big guns start swapping shots. 1–5 correct means you should stick to diet soda. 6–10 means you will win at least an occasional free beer. 11–15 denotes a certifiable beer nut, and 16–20 means you should have written this book. A true Jedi Master will know all the answers but will quibble with each one so as to show off the full extent of his knowledge.

1. The name of Schlitz's Milwaukee hospitality room?

2. Who is the oldest brewer of lager beer in the United States?

3. Who were the four brewers of Billy Beer?

4. Prior to the opening of New Albion in 1978, who was America's youngest brewer?

5. What brewer used the slogan "The Best What Gives"?

6. How many additives has the FDA approved for use in beer?

7. "MFR" stands for?

8. Two beers referred to as "The Green Death"?

9. The name of Rudy Schaefer's famous yacht?

10. The only female sole owner of a brewery in history?

11. The animal traditionally associated with Lone Star Beer?

12. How many brew kettles are in the brewhouse of America's largest brewery?

13. Who was John Jenny?

14. Which is the only American brewery known to close for deer season?

15. The first American microbrewery to open east of the Mississippi?

16. Which city in the United States currently produces the most beer?

17. What brewery currently "gives its soul for rock 'n roll"?

18. What brand of beer compares itself to German Fassbier?

19. Who is the creator of New Amsterdam beer?

20. The name of the "diet beer" brewed by Rheingold?

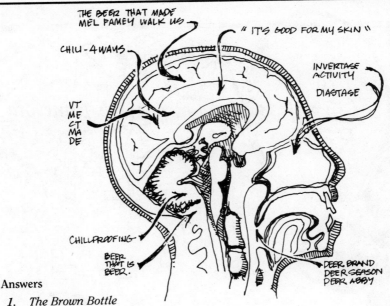

THE BEER THAT MADE
MEL FAMEY WALK US

"IT'S GOOD FOR MY SKIN"

CHILI - 4 WAYS

INVERTASE
ACTIVITY

DIASTASE

VT
ME
CT
MA
DE

CHILLPROOFING

BEER
THAT IS
BEER.

DEER BRAND
DEER SEASON
PEER ABBY

Answers

1. *The Brown Bottle*

2. *Schaefer*

3. *Fall City, F. X. Matt, Cold Spring, Pearl*

4. *Schoenling Brewing Co., Cincinnati (1937)*

5. *John Graf, Milwaukee*

6. *59*

7. *Mountain Fresh Rainier*

8. *Haffenreffer Malt Liquor, Rainier Ale*

9. *America*

10. *Cecelie "Miss Celie" Spoetzl, Shiner Brewing Co.*

11. *The armadillo*

12. *38 (Coors)*

13. *The first known professional brewmaster to arrive in the New World (1623)*

14. *Straub Brewery, St. Mary's, PA*

15. *William S. Newman Brewing Co., Albany, NY*

16. *Los Angeles*

17. *Dixie*

18. *Altes Golden Lager (Carling/Heileman)*

19. *Dr. Joseph Owades*

20. *Gablinger's*

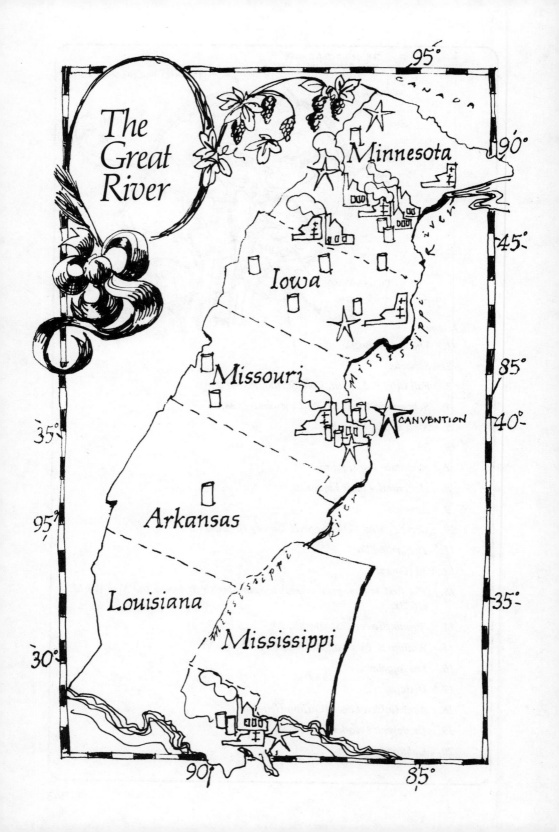

Trekker's Guide to the Great River ────────────────

During the drought of 1988, barge traffic on the Great River slowed to a halt. Is it a sign? And if it is, how is it reflected in the beer? Great Beer Treks are filled with tales of the obscure and exotic brews that enrich the nation's liquid tapestry. The truth of the decade, however, is that while micros and pub breweries have been popping up like dandelions on a green lawn, the real growth story has been Budweiser. The total volume of specialty beers is less than a million barrels. In the same span of time Anheuser-Busch has grown three times annually what the small brewers have managed for the entire decade. If there is a great river of beer, then it flows from St. Louis, and its name is Budweiser, and it is in no danger of drying up.

Both upstream and downstream of St. Louis, there have been flashes of malty brilliance. Dubuque Star, a.k.a. Rhomberg, a.k.a. Pickett's, has survived seemingly annual changes in management. In a life-imitates-art scenario, it served as the setting for a movie about a brewer's struggle to remain independent in an era of big, bad, evil, greedy, all-consuming business. The film *Take This Job and Shove It* did little for either Hollywood or the beer business.

Farther north, toward the headwaters, the story is a familiar one of consolidation and renaissance. The demise of Hamm's and Schmidt's is buffered by the tenacity of Cold Spring and August Schell and the emergence of Summit and James Page brewing companies. Anyone who feels that Minneapolis has the upscale, quality-conscious consumership to appreciate fresh, locally made beers is right.

At the other end of the stream, Dixie hangs tough, giving all those who think that life's ultimate experience revolves around pinching tails and sucking heads by the Pontchartrain something to look forward to. We're talking crawdads, darlin'. For the more adventurous, newcomer Abita Beer, brewed 40 miles north of New Orleans, gives the southern beer drinker a fresh and bold alternative in a region that has been without them too long.

The Mississippi draws together Oktoberfest and Mardi Gras. It borders the Beer Belly, the Wasteland, and passes by the gateway to the West. The river is a ribbon of transition, and, drought notwithstanding, it continues to flow as lustily as the golden fluid from the tanks of Anheuser-Busch.

ARKANSAS

KINDRED SPIRITS
AR-CAN-SAS Chapter (BCCA), c/o Kenn Flemmons, 2707 Peachtree Dr., Little Rock, AR 72211

IOWA

★ Millstream Brewing Co., P.O. Box 284, Lower Brewery Rd., Amana, IA 52203
Type: Microbrewery
Brands: Millstream Lager, Schild Brau Amber, Millstream Wheat

Tours: Self-guided or by appointment for groups (319) 622-3672
Breweriana: Labels, glasses, caps, shirts, jackets, crowns, thermometers, etc.
Logo: Mill on stream

★ Dubuque Star Brewing Co., East 4th St. Ext., P.O. Box 1248, Dubuque, IA 52001
Type: Independent regional
Brands: Dubuque Star Beer, Erlanger Marzen Bier, Rhomberg All Malt Beer
Tours: May 1–Labor Day, 7 days a week, 11:00 A.M.–6:00 P.M.

KINDRED SPIRITS
Hawkeye Chapter (BCCA), Don Villers, 805 7th Ave., Belle Plaine, IA 52208

LOUISIANA

★ Abita Brewing Co., Inc., P.O. Box 762, Abita Springs, LA 70420
Type: Microbrewery
Brands: Abita Golden Lager, Abita Amber Lager
Tours: By appointment only (504) 893-3143
Breweriana: T-shirts, posters, coasters, labels—by mail or at the brewery
Slogan: "The New Louisiana Lager"

★ Dixie Brewing Co., Inc., 2401 Tulane Ave., New Orleans, LA 70119
Type: Independent regional
Brands: Dixie Beer, Dixie Amber Light, New Orleans Best, New Orleans Best Light, Coy Beer, Coy Marathon

KINDRED SPIRITS
Crescent City Homebrewers, c/o Mike Biggs, 1928 Metairie Heights, Metairie, LA 70001
Mardi Gras Chapter (BCCA), Lew Burritt, 125 Vogt Dr., Belle Chase, LA 70037

GREAT PLACES
Any takeout on the Pontchartrain
New Orleans: Cooter Brown's

OF NOTE
(RIP) Jackson Brewing Co., New Orleans. Originator of Jax Beer now produced by Pearl in San Antonio, TX. Inspirational riverfront plant stands idle, as does Falstaff plant several blocks away.
Mardi Gras. Grand celebration anointed with beer. Starting date varies according to Lent, but celebrations get a bit longer each year. Bring a costume and leave your breakables and valuables at home.

MINNESOTA

★ Cold Spring Brewing Co., Inc., 219 North Red River Ave., Cold Spring, MN 56320

Type: Independent regional
Brands: Cold Spring, Cold Spring Export, Fox Deluxe, North Star, Kegle Brau, White Label, North Star Sparkling Mineral Water

★ James Page Brewing Co., 1300 Quincy St., NE, Minneapolis, MN 55413
Type: Microbrewery
Brands: James Page Private Stock, Boundary Waters Harvest Beer
Tours: Mon.–Thurs., 5:00–6:00 P.M.
Breweriana: T-shirts, labels
Slogan: Logo is a scenic picture of the Saint Anthony Falls on the Mississippi River in Minneapolis and the old Stone Arch Railroad Bridge

★ August Schell Brewing Co., Inc., Schell's Park, New Ulm, MN 56073
Type: Independent regional
Brands: Schell's Deer Brand, August Schell Pilsner, August Schell Weiss, Ulmer Lager, Ulmer Braun, Schell's Bock, Schell's Export, Schell's Light, Steinhaus, Twins Lager, plus Kristian Swedish Regale (sparkling fruit beverage) and 1919 (draft root beer). Contract brews: Pete's Wicked Ale, Summer Lager, Kilkenny, Auburn, Jefferson, Blue Ridge Mountain
Tours: Memorial Day–Labor Day: weekdays, 3:00 P.M. and 4:00 P.M.; weekends 1:00, 2:00, and 3:00 P.M. Also by appointment, (507) 354-5528. Museum of Brewing open 1:00–5:00 P.M. daily.
Breweriana: Clothing, glassware, wooden boxes, and printed items

★ G. Heileman Brewing Co., Inc., 882 West 7th St., St. Paul, MN 55102
Type: Branch plant of G. Heileman Brewing Co., La Crosse, WI
Tours: Mon.–Sat., 10:00 A.M., 2:00 P.M., 3:00 P.M.

★ Stroh Brewery Co., 707 East Minnehaha Ave., St. Paul, MN 55164
Type: Branch plant of the Stroh Brewery Co., Detroit, MI
Tours: Mon.–Fri., 1:00 P.M.–4:00 P.M.

★ Summit Brewing Co., 2264 University Ave., St. Paul, MN 55114
Type: Microbrewery
Brands: Summit Extra Pale Ale, Great Northern Porter, plus Summit Sparkling Ale (May 17–Labor Day) and Summit Christmas Ale (Thanksgiving–Jan. 15)
Tours: Sat. (except over holiday weekends), 1:00 P.M. Tours last 2 hours, reservations recommended.
Breweriana: T-shirts, pins, coasters, labels, sweatshirts, hats
Slogan: "Beer Is My Life." The mascot is a weightlifter.

KINDRED SPIRITS
Northern Ale Stars, c/o Don Hoag, 5320 Beartrap Rd., Saginaw, MN 55779
Schells Border Batch (BCCA), Jay Smith, Box 305, Minnesota Lake, MN 56068
North Star (BCCA), Don Huntsinger, 3936 York Ave. S., Minneapolis, MN 55410

GREAT PLACES
New Ulm: Goosetown Inn
St. Paul: Johnny's

OF NOTE

Brewing Supplies
Winemakers-Beermakers Semplex, Box 11476, Minneapolis, MN 55411
Braukunst Homebrewers' Systems, 55 Lakeview Dr., Carlton, MN 55718
(RIP) A rich land of standing breweries. Fitger in Duluth has been converted
into retail space. Grain Belt in Minneapolis is a classic piece of American
Gothic architecture.

Great Fermentations
Sherlock's Home, new Pub brewery in Minnetonka.

MISSISSIPPI

★ Kershenstine Enterprises, 401 Industrial Park, Dept. AAB, Europa, MS
39744
Type: Contract
Brand: Rattlesnake Beer

MISSOURI

★ Boulevard Brewing Co., 2501 Southwest Blvd., Kansas City, MO 64141
Type: Microbrewery under construction spring 1989

★ Anheuser-Busch, Inc., 1 Busch Pl., St. Louis, MO 63118-1852
Type: National
Brands: Budweiser, Michelob, Busch, Natural Light, Michelob Light, Bud
Light, LA, Michelob Natural Dark, King Cobra Malt Liquor
Tours: Extensive tour schedule, including the Clydesdale stables. A must
while in St. Louis.
Breweriana: Extensive gift shop at brewery

KINDRED SPIRITS
Missouri Winemaking Society, c/o Bob Bubenik, 7314 Manchester, Maple-
wood, MO 63143
St. Louis Brewers, c/o John Standeven, 7314 Manchester, St. Louis, MO
63143
Small Suds Sister's (BCCA), Marietta Schwend, 2753 Buckingham Dr., Flo-
rissant, MO 63033
Valley of Flowers (BCCA), Jimx Reed, 115 St. Eugene Lane, Florissant, MO
63033
McDonnell-Douglas (BCCA), Jimx Reed, 115 St. Eugene Lane, Florissant,
MO 63033
Gateway (BCCA), Elmer Mick, 4602 Wilcox, St. Louis, MO 63116

GREAT PLACES
St. Louis: Houlihan's/Union Station

OF NOTE

Beer Can Collectors of America, National Headquarters, 747 Merus Ct., Fenton, MO 63026. National headquarters of a sudsy organization that puts out a first-rate publication, holds staggeringly popular CANventions, and whose membership resists taking themselves too seriously.

Brewing Supplies
Bacchus and Barleycorn, 7314 Manchester Ave., St. Louis, MO 63117
E. C. Kraus Sales, Box 7850, Independence, MO 64053
(RIP) Lemp Brewery, St. Louis. Standing in the shadow of Anheuser-Busch, a grim reminder to the fate that can befall the industry's fastest rising star.

BUY 'EM IF YOU CAN FIND 'EM

Budweiser (Anheuser-Busch). If you can't find this one, you're a sick puppy. Arrogantly self-dubbed the King of Beers, Bud deserves its crown, much to the chagrin of the zymurgist crowd. Bud has not been afraid to entrust its reputation to the Beer Drinker's palate. The company is justly proud of its brewing techniques (beechwood aging, kraeusening), as well as its quality control. Full bodied with a dry finish, Bud can call its own. This is America's most reliable beer. Stop fighting it and get on board.

Michelob (Anheuser-Busch). Not up to Bud's standards, with an "eggy" taste that gives an illusion of luxury. Worthy of mention mostly because of its exquisite packaging and marketing, recently retargeted to baby boomers by association with rock stars Eric Clapton, Steve Winwood, and Phil Collins. A sad testament to how the sixties generation has sold out. C'est la vie. At least the beer's all right.

Michelob Dry (Anheuser-Busch). Interesting as the first national foray into the "dry" phenomenon. Most distinguishing characteristic is the complete absence of aftertaste, which can make you wonder why you bothered to drink it in the first place.

Dixie (Dixie). Nothing exceptional about Dixie. A house flavor that is not at all unpleasant; goes down well with the local cuisine. It is hard to judge Dixie objectively without being influenced by the euphoria of New Orleans.

Schell's Deer Brand (August Schell). Another unexceptional beer but one that one feels compelled to buy whenever one is within 100 miles of New Ulm. This brewery is distinguished by the color it adds to the beer drinking scene.

7
THE FRONTIER

LUCKENBACH, TEXAS, TO GOLDEN, COLORADO
71 DAYS, 14,850 MILES ON THE ROAD

LONG LIVE LONG NECKS

Luckenbach, Texas

On the Fourth of July, exactly two years after The Great Beer Trek had been conceived in the salty air off Massachusetts Bay, we sipped on Lone Star from long necks in Luckenbach, Texas (population 3, except on nice days like this). There are no signs to Luckenbach; it is not listed on any state map, but it is famous because some cowboy wrote a song about it. Now it is the capital city for Kozmic Kowboys who have infinite capacity for settin', sippin', and pickin'.

To get to Luckenbach, take Route 290 west from Johnson City. A few miles before you reach Fredericksburg, take a left. A couple of miles up that road, you go down a hill. At the bottom, there's a road off to the right, winding through some hardwoods—big trees for Texas. Turn off the engine of your car (ideally you come in a pickup). If it is a nice day and the wind is blowing just right, you will hear the telltale strum. There also might be a little hootin' and hollerin' and surely the sound of bottle caps being removed from long necks.

On this Fourth of July, the scene at Luckenbach was distinctly laid back. Texas heat ain't so bad if you can get out of the sun, and shade is one commodity (along with music and beer) never in short supply here. Officially Luckenbach is a rundown post office/general store, a couple of foul outhouses, and however many cowboys have made the trip from Austin or San Anton'. Three native beers are sold: Lone Star, Pearl, and Shiner (although only the last truly retains its independence). Each brand has devotees, but all three share the characteristics of the regional taste. These beers are clean and light but with almost a complete absence of hop bitterness. They share the blandness but not the full-bodied maltiness of the midwestern beers.

The hop is the ingredient in beer that awakens the palate with a scream, demanding respect. Texans make up for any lack of gustatorial muscle by serving their beer crackling cold and without a glass. Beer drunk from the container is intentionally gassy. Brewers inject carbon dioxide immediately prior to packaging. Because it is important for beer to retain a nice head after being poured into a glass, beer is overdosed with carbon dioxide to compensate for gas released during the pouring process. The person who drinks directly from the can or bottle has his or her taste buds titillated not by the delicacy of the hop but by the jackhammer stings of a million bubbles exploding on the tongue like the grand finale of a fireworks display. The sensation is made bearable only by the numbing cold.

The cowboy mouth is as well worn as the muzzle on his horse. There's lots of action that's taken place here. This cavity has been filled by vile forms of weed, chewing tobacco being the most common protective lubricant against drying wind and dust. Smoke is a not-unknown habitué of the oral opening, often from a hemp derivative from south of the border. Chili, barbecue, huevos rancheros, tamales, enchiladas, and other fiery fare sustain the cowboy in his pursuit of the American dream—and burn out his taste buds in the process. By the time he is of legal drinking age, his taste buds are worn as smooth as his saddle and in need of all the stimulation they can get.

Hondo Crouch is the legendary guru of Luckenbach. Hondo's dead and gone, but for 75 cents you can buy a cold one from his wife. A brew in hand entitles you to go outside and sit on a stump to contemplate life as a truck drivin' man or honkey-tonk angel. If yer lucky mebbe someun' famous will show up—Willie Nelson, Jerry Jeff Walker, David Allen Coe, or even Ol' Waylon—but nonetheless there will be no shortage of beer and music. After a languid afternoon of both, we found ourselves thinking like cowboys.

"There's only one problem with Alabama cowboys," a Luckenbach regular confided in me. "They don't wear their hats low enough." Style is paramount. The jeans and the boots come off only to make love and then sometimes only the jeans. One hundred degree heat is never a reason to dress down; better to suffer in silence. There is a cowboy hat, a cowboy belt, a cowboy way to dance, a cowboy way to pick teeth, to spit tobacco juice, to howl at the moon, and to drink beer.

The cowboy way to drink beer is from a long neck, the standard returnable bottle that throughout the rest of the country is known as an "export" or "bar bottle." Speedy Beal, sales manager of the Spoetzl Brewing Co., makers of Shiner beer, offered five reasons why the long neck is the vogue in Texas whereas the rest of the world is phasing it out. Only one rings true:

1. Tradition.
2. The brown bottle is light-proof and protects beer from the harmful effects of the sun.
3. Long necks are better suited to pasteurization than any other container.
4. Long necks ice down well and retain their coldness better than a can.
5. 'Cuz they're tall.

Shiner is a perfect Texas beer, bland and agreeable, the ultimate accompaniment to an outdoor barbecue or a chili cookout. Herbert, the bartender at the brewery's tiny stand-up bar, serves more than 250 free beers daily to tourists, visitors, and anyone else who walks in off the street. A mural of

Kosmos Spoetzl dominates the tiny hospitality room, which is a pleasant way station for travelers between Houston and San Antonio. Kosmos bought the tidy little brewery on the banks of Boggy Creek after having tried to carve a niche for himself in Egypt, Canada, San Francisco, and his native Bavaria. Southeast Texas has a surprising number of German/Czechoslovakian settlers who came to raise the cattle and to grow the cotton that has made this section of the state nearly as prosperous as the oil regions. Kosmos built his business on the strength of a handshake and a free beer. He was famous for driving a Model A around the countryside, stopping at every homestead to give the farmer in the field a welcome draught of beer from the iced keg he kept in the back seat.

Spoetzl died in 1950, having run the brewery for thirty-five years. Control passed on to his daughter, Cecelie, who became known throughout the town as Miss Celie. Believed to have been the only female sole owner of an American brewery, she furthered the family image established by her father. To this day there is an atmosphere of friendliness in Shiner that hovers somewhere between southern hospitality, *gemütlicheit,* and "howdy partner." Miss Celie is gone, but if you want to see the brewery, Herbert will be glad to show you around as soon as he has taken care of everyone at the bar. If things are busy, Speedy will take off his sales manager's cap to come over and help out for a while.

The people at Shiner work hard to make friends. No festivity worth going to in this part of the country is not accompanied by kegs of Shiner. Otherwise brewing is big business in Texas. Anheuser-Busch has a Houston plant, Miller one in Fort Worth (where it brews Löwenbräu), Schlitz in Longview, Falstaff in Galveston (now closed), but it is San Antonio that is the heart of Texas beer country.

The brewery tour at the Pearl Brewery has been eliminated, but the free beer remains. The Jersey Lilly Hospitality Center is a handsome, spacious facility at its best with a loud piano, dancing girls, and a thousand men with foam on their mustaches. The new Jersey Lilly was remodeled in 1970, but a replica of Judge Roy Bean's original in Langtry, Texas, is located right across the street. Pearl features manicured grounds and gleaming white buildings with a Spanish motif. It is one of the most attractive places where beer is made in the United States.

The ultimate long neck accolade, however, goes to Lone Star, originators of the "Long Live Long Necks" slogan. In Beaumont I asked for Lone Star at a store, only to be told that they carried it only when the motorcycle races were being held nearby. A cowgirl in Lubbock whose life revolved around life at the roadhouse claimed that Lone Star was to be drunk when, and only when, one was in the mood to descend to the true depths of depravity. With such a lusty image, we expected Lone Star to flow from a squalid factory. Sanitary conditions would be nonexistent, the air clouded with fly swarms. The water would be taken from the San Antonio River just downstream from

Down Mexico Way

Let's set the record straight: there is no urine in Corona Beer. This is a vicious rumor started by beer snobs and microbrewers who find it unbelievable that a bland, fizzy beverage served with a lime wedge *atop its fancy lithographed bottle could vault from nowhere to the number one imported beer in such a short time. The success of Corona defies every theory about the importance of product quality to the taste buds of the American consumer. C'mon. Does anyone really believe that Corona would be anything special if served in a stubby brown bottle? Why isn't it ever served on draft? Because the yuppies in their fern bars wouldn't look so cool if they couldn't lounge around holding those neat-looking clear long necks, wanting to look exotic but not wanting their taste buds to venture much further than Old Milwaukee Light. But urine in Corona? Naw, it's a lie.*

Beer aficionados resent the success of Corona, because for years they had touted Mexican beers as an undiscovered secret. The roots of the brewing business are strictly Germanic, the legacy of one Wilhelm Haase who transported brewing skills from Bavaria to Mexico in the nineteenth century to found the Cerveceria Moctezuma, producers of such robust brews as Superior, Noche Buena, and Dos Equis. These products, in addition to other fine brews like Carta Blanca, Bohemia, and Tecate, were welcome balms to the stimulation-starved taste buds of neighbors to the north. With the burgeoning popularity of Mexican food, Mexican beers had a springboard for more widespread acceptance.

That it was Corona that has reaped the harvest should not embitter the knowledgeable beer drinker. In the homeland, Corona is a simple beer for the common people. In America, increasingly, the common man drives a BMW and values lightness in everything from junk food to fruit cocktail. Who knows? When the Corona wave crests, maybe some marketing sharpie will devise Corona Lite. Now, there's a thought to strike terror into the heart of any self-respecting suds lover.

an asbestos factory. In the hospitality room, *gemütlicheit* would be reduced to a quart bottle passed from mouth to mouth.

With such expectations we were disappointed to see a gleaming white brewery stack spelling out L-O-N-E S-T-A-R. The brewery sits amid lush surroundings on a favored spot immune from the Texas sun. The visitor facilities are impressive. There are fountains, band shells, and the largest selection of overpriced souvenirs south of Milwaukee. For those who choose to skip the Hall of Antlers and other testaments to man's ability to slaughter, there is a History of Texas wax museum and a brewery tour. The appeal is strictly neo-Disney theme park and, as such, of little interest to The Great Beer Trek. This was a great place to bring the kids but hardly the home of the raunchiest beer in Texas. Frankly we were disappointed.

Lone Star is best experienced not at the brewery but at any number of Texas roadside joints, late at night when the locals start getting rowdy. The meaning of country music comes into focus just as someone hits you for no apparent reason. You wake up with a fat lip, a beautiful girl whom you've never seen before, and the taste of Lone Star still in your throat.

The White Elephant in the Fort Worth stockyards, just around the corner from the original Longbranch Saloon, is an excellent place to savor the Lone Star Experience. The house song everyone sings on Saturday night is "Let's Get Drunk and Screw." If that is not your style, you might enjoy a few rounds of "Cotton-Eyed Joe"—a song whose resounding "bullshit" chorus accompanies a raucous tribal dance that confirms the cowboy lack of civility. The cow palaces like Gilley's in Houston mix high-tech urban cowboy style (mechanical bulls and soundproof call-home booths to convince the Old Lady you are still at the office) with the best in low-tech beer drinking. The low-life cowboy experience is infectious, especially when lubricated with enough beer. The outlaw has his own perspective on the world, one with its own rules, morals, and beer drinking style.

I broke down and bought a hat, a raunchy straw affair with a band of exotic bird feathers. Not until we crossed the Oklahoma border, however, did I work up the courage to try it on. The cowboy movement had claimed another convert.

HOME, HOME ON THE RANGE...

THE BEER WARS

Golden, Colorado

Late at night, somewhere in the outback of Texas, I awoke Laura to witness an event of cosmic significance—the passing of the century mark on the van's odometer. We whooped and hollered and sprayed a ceremonial Lone Star over the wheels. The jubilation was swallowed, but not diminished, by the blackness.

The pioneers of the West had no idea what would befall them once they left the womb of civilization. Slow, tedious miles were arbitrarily interrupted by panoramic vistas, Indian raids, and violent storms. The thrill of adventure was tempered by the threat of danger, the exaltation of success counterbalanced by the spectre of ignominious defeat.

The Great Beer Trek, cutting a swath northward and westward, was an emotional roller coaster over the nation's flattest terrain. Blessed by a nobility of purpose and anointed with beer, we always seemed to land on our wheels. A madman drove us off the road in Kansas. Rather than robbery and mayhem, however, it turns out he wanted to present us with a jar of bar sausages, which he claimed to be the world's best accompaniment to beer. (He was not far from wrong.) The van's muffler fell off in Idaho, but a vacationing mechanic cheerfully spent an hour reassembling it with baling wire. We got stuck in a mud hole while in the middle of a Montana wilderness, miles from the nearest human habitation, only to be quickly rescued by an elderly couple who were exploring the back roads and who happened to have a chain. We dented a Good Ol' Boy's beloved pickup in a Wyoming gas station and received sympathy instead of the expected torrent of abuse. In each case beer bridged the gap between unfortunate circumstance and happy resolution. We freely shared the brightly colored cans from Pottsville, Pennsylvania, and Stevens Point, Wisconsin, places that grew more exotic with each passing mile. Our liquid tokens successfully broke down whatever communication barriers exist between Scituate, Massachusetts, and Yankton, South Dakota, or Great Bend, Kansas.

At a dusty flea market we traded a number of empty beer cans from eastern breweries for a beautiful, old Falstaff tray. The flea market operator clearly lusted after our remaining cans and proposed the following deal, which we could not refuse: two full cans of the local brew for each eastern empty. The deal was immediately struck, the implications as clear as a glacial Rocky Mountain lake. These new cans could be consumed, transported west, traded again two for one, and the process continued. By the time we returned home, if we ever bothered, we would need a trailer for the beer. This Beer Trek could go on forever!

Of the many discoveries made by The Great Beer Trek in the Frontier, a mother lode of breweries was not among them. The occasional skeleton was uncovered. Research often revealed a business that had eked out an arid existence for several decades until the founders simply gave up. The exception is the Adolph Coors Co. in Golden, Colorado, a brewery that claims the distinction of being one of the planet's largest. A look at the success of Coors, especially in the light of the company's present plight, illustrates what is best and worst about American business.

First one must comprehend the immensity of the Coors accomplishment.

When the brewmaster at an eastern or midwestern brewery has a problem and needs help fast, he is likely to call up old Gustav, the brewmaster from the rival brewery on the other side of town who graduated with him from the Siebel Institute back in '49. Cooperation between the technical and production branches of competing companies (never sales or marketing) is a tradition in the brewing fraternity. When your brewery is in Golden, Colorado, however, there is no one around to help you. The Coors family realized this very early on and established a self-sufficient brewing operation. From a single plant, they produce and distribute beer to the well-spaced population reserves of the West. What is most impressive is that they have accomplished this while making fewer compromises to the considerations of beer quality than any of their brewing peers. If the Coors family encountered problems, they could rely on no one else to solve them. They had to be smarter, they had to be tougher, they had to be more industrious, and they had to be faster on the draw.

Before long the United States's largest brewing plant was located right in tiny Golden, in the foothills of the Rockies. The company is privately held, able to make decisions without the encumbrances of a bureaucracy. They are well financed, free of strangulating debt. Furthermore, in its quest for independence, Coors has acquired energy resources (gas, coal, and oil fields), raw materials (barley and hop fields), even packaging capabilities. From the grain to the can, Coors controls the process more than any other American brewer.

What has made Coors's situation even more enviable in recent years has been the unbridled demand for the beer. Coors could limit production to a single brand, eschew fancy graphics and expensive marketing, restrict distri-

bution to eleven western states, establish exacting requirements for its distributors, and still sell out the full capacity of the nation's largest brewery. For years Coors had to be rationed, and the beer world was abuzz with stories of crazy easterners paying inflated sums for bootlegged Coors.

The Coors Mystique was the industry phenomenon of the early and mid-1970s. The family bypassed opportunities to exploit the demand by opening up satellite plants or by doing anything that would cause them to lose control of the formula that had brought them so far. Expansion would proceed at its logical pace, and beer drinkers could always be assured that the Coors they drank was just as the family intended. To make a long story short, not many years have passed since those heady days, and now Coors finds itself squarely in the world of reality, down there with the regional mortals, struggling not to be caught in the cross fire of the Beer Wars in which the country is involved.

What happened?

Well, everything and nothing. The company still brews a beer that many regard as the ultimate American quaffing experience. Tourists still file through the thirty-eight (thirty-eight!!) kettle brewhouse as if viewing the crown jewels. The company is still profitable, but there are unmistakable signs of weakness. The company that made one beer now makes five (Coors Premium, Coors Light, George Killian Irish Red Ale, Extra Gold, and Herman Joseph), all designed for individual market segments. Distribution now goes as far east as Florida, and distributors who once regarded carrying Coors as a ticket to a life of leisure now realize they have to hustle to stay afloat. Even with expanded lines and distribution, the company is selling less beer and having to spend more to do it. The pie keeps being sliced into smaller pieces.

Discussing the rise and (relative) fall of Coors is a favorite industry pastime. Everyone has a pet theory, citing Bill and Joe Coors's well-publicized political conservatism or the charges of discriminatory hiring policies that led

A Six-Pack of Ortlieb Light

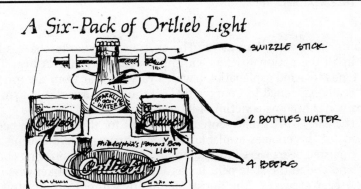

SWIZZLE STICK

2 BOTTLES WATER

4 BEERS

Light Thoughts on Lite Beer

The brewmaster at one of Wisconsin's small breweries was giving our palates a tour of his company's products. We had just finished sampling his most recent bock, a rich, almost chocolaty brew. He gathered our glasses to rinse in preparation for the next round. Midway through the process he held forth a glass of water with a good-natured offer:

"Care to taste this new Coors Light?"

There is nothing new about light beers. The small beer of the Pilgrims was no more than a watered-down version of the real thing. The English coal miner's "mild" is geared so that his customary 5 pints after work will still leave him able to walk home. Meister Braü had failed with low-calorie "Lite" before giving Miller a shot at it, as had Rheingold with its Gablinger brand. Small, independent brewers such as Joe Ortlieb and Fred Huber have put the matter into perspective by recommending that consumers create their own light beers by supplementing their normal brews with ice cubes or mineral water.

Michelob Light has 134 calories, 20 percent less than regular Mich but almost 200 percent more than Pearl Light, which has 1 less than Pabst Extra Light and 31 percent less than regular Pabst Light. Stroh Light and Coors Light claim to be the best tasting of the genre, which is not surprising as both weigh in at over 100 calories, a relatively inconsequential savings over their normal brews. Cold Spring offers perhaps the only truly honest light beer with its Sparkling Mineral Water. Behind closed doors, most brewers will admit that they would avoid them if there were not such an unmistakable consumer demand. The American fetish for lightness has infected a wealth of products ranging from potato chips to canned fruit cocktail. It is fashionable for beer connoisseurs to disdain light beers as the lowest achievement of the brewers' craft. In reality, however, the pale nature of light beer exposes brewing flaws just as fair skin does blemishes and thus is a challenge even to the skilled hand.

There are two ways to make light beers. Some brewers do nothing more than dilute their normal brews (Michelob Light), while others (Miller Lite) employ special enzymes to ferment their beers down to a lower specific gravity. Whichever technique is used, the loss in calories occurs at the expense of flavor and/or alcoholic content. If a more watery brew suits your purposes, don't let the beer snobs intimidate you. But why pay the brewers to do the diluting for you? Try the ice cube/mineral water route. It will raise eyebrows at the local, but it works.

to a bitter feud with the unions. The charges and countercharges have been aired in all the national media with no conclusive victor. A Beer Trek, however, tends to avoid explanations, which vary very far from the product itself. What really happened to Coors is that all the other brewers got smarter. The company has become a victim of its own revolution.

The early 1970s represented a low point for the American beer drinker in terms of the choices available. Regional brewers were closing at a rapid rate, imported beers were limited in number, and home brewing could potentially land one in the state pen. It was a deprived beer drinker who first heard about a beer brewed in the Rocky Mountains without preservatives or additives, a beer so fresh and lively that it was not pasteurized and was kept refrigerated from the moment it left the brew kettle until it reached his lips . . . A brewer with a genuine commitment to quality was worth getting excited about, maybe even sneaking a few six-packs into your suitcase for your friends in New York.

The novelty did not last much beyond the first six-pack. Certainly the beer was good, but it was extremely light and bland, a disappointment to the beer drinker in search of gusto. "Light" beers appeared on the market as well as beers advising the beer drinker to "head for the mountains." The word *natural* became the most overused in the industry. Miller and Bud invaded from the East, spending millions to tout their Coors-like qualities. Olympia pincered in from the West, doing its best to encourage comparison with the original Rocky Mountain High. The subtle advantages of Coors became imperceptible, and the mystique disappeared as inexplicably as it had arrived. The amazing thing is not that it disappeared but that it ever occurred.

THE MIRACLE DOG
Dillon, Montana

We rarely took breaks from our travel and beer routines, but the temptation to fish for rainbow trout in Montana proved irresistible. The spot we found proved as spectacular in reality as it looked on the map—a clear, rushing stream backdropped by snow-capped mountains and a blue sky filled with cowboy-sized cumulus billows, accessible only by hiking along the railroad tracks. On the third cast a flash appeared at my muddler minnow, and soon dinner was assured. This, the most idyllic of moments, was rudely ripped asunder by the chaos of a freight train carrying bituminous coal from Butte to Detroit or some such. We watched horror struck as our black pup, Guinness, leaped to her feet from a comfortable resting place between the tracks and tried a futile escape. The hurtling freight, however, was not to be denied. She was hit. For an instant we saw her tumbling beneath the wheels, but then the rumble and blur of the train overwhelmed everything. After several gruesomely deafening minutes we went to clean up the remaining fragments, only to discover a dazed, but intact, Guinness lying between the tracks.

We carried her to the van and sped 50 miles to the nearest town, Dillon, where a veterinarian confirmed our fervent but tentative diagnosis—bruised but otherwise none the worse for her harrowing experience. Back in the van the jubilation became boisterous. We fashioned a special cushiony bed for a dog who was by this time receiving demonstrations of affection beyond her dim canine comprehension. Later, when she was comfortably asleep, we went to celebrate in the bars that line Dillon's main street. Like most other Montana bars, these feature tables of grizzled cowpokes playing cards, woebegone Indians slumped over their drinks, and a sprinkling of smooth-faced neophytes who want nothing more than to have their own visages creased with the scars of elemental human experience, which somehow seems closer to the surface in this state than any other. No matter, though. That night we bought beers for any cowboy, Injun, or Yahoo in Dillon, Montana, who would listen to our endless repetitions of "Guinness, Miracle Dog of The Great Beer Trek."

There is more to life than beer alone, but beer makes those other things even better.

You Are What You Drink, Part 1

Not a single brewer in the United States admits to brewing an "unnatural" beer. And yet no one can agree on what "natural" is. The all-grain brewer considers himself more natural than the extract brewer, who considers himself more natural than the adjunct brewer. Anheuser-Busch and Miller have waged expensive and protracted war over the definition of natural. A-B accuses Miller of employing microbiological enzymes in the brewing cycle. Miller countercharges that A-B uses enzymes as well. But, returns A-B, our enzymes are malt derived and used during the aging, not the fermentation, stage.

As the brewing titans slug it out, tying up the courts and lining the pockets of lawyers with money that could be better spent on malt and hops, the beer drinker interjects a resounding, "So what?"

In Germany, beer drinkers are protected by a fifteenth-century purity ruling (the Reinheitsgebot*) that defines beer as consisting of barley malt, hops, yeast, and water. That's it. No exceptions, except, ironically, exported beers, which have a need for longer shelf life than locally consumed products. The beer drinker who buys German because of the purity standards may in fact be purchasing a more heavily dosed product than anything brewed in the United States.*

United States brewers have an FDA-approved list of fifty-nine additives that can be used, many of which enhance appearance or stability. Does the use of any of these additives make American beer "unnatural"? Is the domestic product adulterated with chemicals? After visiting scores of breweries, our opinion is no. The brewers we met convinced us of a sincere desire to produce a clean, fresh simple product that will pass the acid test: the palate of the beer drinker. Of the fifty-nine additives, no more than several are used in any given beer and are often used for a specific purpose (to precipitate protein, for instance) and are not present in the final product. Most are organic in nature and, despite scary names, have been exhaustively tested and proved to have no physiological or pathological effect.

Processing methods are of equal importance as ingredients in considering the "natural" question. Pasteurization, a sterilizing procedure in which beer is heated to 145°F for a sustained period, contributes greatly to a brew's shelf life yet is detrimental to its taste. Nearly all bottled beers are pasteurized; draft beers are not. Coors, which is maintained under refrigerated conditions from brewhouse to retailer, is the most notable exception, the extra care in handling undoubtedly being a major factor in the Coors Cult.

Brewmasters tell a reassuring story about the purity of their beer. The defensive, paranoid posture on the part of the brewing industry that resists open labeling and ingredient listing, however, makes us fear the worst.

Trekker's
Guide
to the Frontier ————————————————————————

Cowboys have fared slightly better than Good Ol' Boys, but they too have had a rough decade. Redneckism has taken a beating, and the people doing the kicking are wearing wing tips, not cowboy boots. The real cowboys are holding their own, but there has been a giant shakeout of the weekenders who once packed the ranch-sized bars like Gilley's in Houston and Billybob's in Fort Worth.

For a region dependent on depletable commodities like oil, copper, silver, molybdenum, and water, this has not been a kind decade. For the beer drinker of the Frontier, however, it has been a memorable ten years. Home brewing was legalized, the American Homebrewers Association (AHA) formed, and in their wake came the specialty brewers from Plano to Telluride to Sun Valley. The new beers are geared more toward skiers and backpackers than cowboys, but such is life. You can still get Lone Star in long necks.

Although the fortunes of the Frontier have been as up and down as the Rockies, those of the AHA have been straight up. Boulder is now the center of the zymurgist's universe; his mecca is the Great American Beer Festival (now held in Denver).

Ten years ago the regional dominance of Coors was readily apparent from the passing van, but that phenomenon has been diluted by the brewery's proliferation of brands and increasingly broad distribution. The thought of smuggling a six-pack into the suitcase after a trip to Denver is now quaintly anachronistic. Did we really do that? Whatever for? Still, no big brewer seems to embrace the "new" beer drinker's quest for freshness, purity, and quality quite so much as the folks from Coors.

With the opening of Anheuser-Busch's new plant in Fort Collins, Colorado becomes the highest-volume brewing state in the nation, a fact of increasing insignificance in an era of logistically dictated plant locations. More important is the Frontier's position on the cutting edge of beerdom.

ARIZONA

⋆ Big Stick Brewing Co., P.O. Box 17356, Phoenix, AZ 85011
Type: Microbrewery
Brands: Gila Monster, Big, Stick Ale, seasonal brews

⋆ Christopher Joseph Brewing Co., 125 East 5th Ave., Tempe, AZ 85281
Type: Pub-brewery
Brands: Christopher Joseph Light Cream Ale, Seasonal "Bander Brew," Premium Stout

KINDRED SPIRITS
Brewmeisters Anonymous, c/o Harold Gee, 242 West Ivyglen, Mesa, AZ 85201
A-1 (BCCA), Lanora Neville, 3862 South Donald Ave., Tuscon, AZ 85746

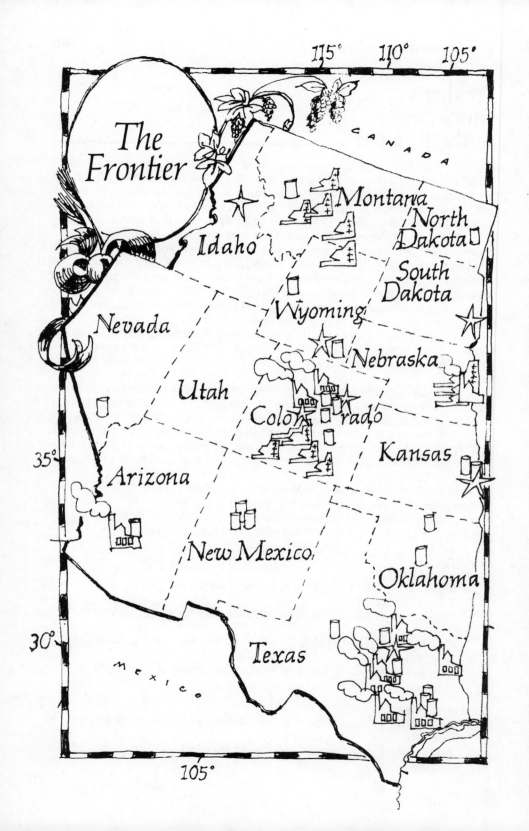

GREAT PLACES
   Arivaca Junction: Amado Cow Palace
   Prescott: Palace Bar
   Tucson: The Shanty

OF NOTE

   Great Fermentations
   The Electric Dave Brewery, Bisbee

COLORADO

★ Boulder Brewing Co., 2880 Wilderness Pl., Boulder, CO 80301
   Type: Microbrewery
   Brands: Boulder Porter, Boulder Extra Pale Ale, Boulder Sport, Boulder
   Stout

★ Rocky Mountain Brewery, P.O. Box 1918, Colorado Springs, CO 80901
   Type: Microbrewery
   Rocky Mountain Brewery is under construction.

★ Carver Brewing Co., 1022 Main Ave., Durango, CO 81301
   Type: Brewery/restaurant/bakery
   Brands: Amber Ale, Pilsner, Stout, Seasonal beers

★ Anheuser-Busch, Inc., 3500 East County Rd. 52, Fort Collins, CO 80524
   Type: Branch plant of Anheuser-Busch, Inc., St. Louis, MO

★ Adolph Coors Co., Golden, CO 80401
   Type: National
   Brands: Coors Original Draft, Coors Light, Herman Joseph's Original Draft,
   HJ Light, George Killian's Irish Red, Coors Extra Gold, Winterfest, Turbo
   1000
   Tours: Mon.–Sat. all day long. Free to the public. VIP tours also available
   to individuals and groups.
   Breweriana: Fully stocked gift shop
   Slogans: Various themes relating to particular brands

★ Valley Brewing Inc., Box 147, 1484 Hwy. 133, Paonia, CO 81428
   Type: Microbrewery
   Brand: Fire Mountain Beer

★ Telluride Beer Co., Inc., P.O. Box 819, Telluride, CO 81435
   Type: Contract
   Brand: Telluride Beer (brewed under contract by Jos. Huber Brewing Co.,
   Monroe, WI)
   Tours: Brewpub under construction in Telluride brewing "dog breath ale"
   Breweriana: Coasters, hats, shirts, cups
   Slogans: "Smooth Old World Quality," "4 Hops and 4 Malts in Unique
   Balance"

★ Vail Brewery Co., 1000 South Frontage Rd., W. Vail, CO 81657
Type: Microbrewery
Brand: Vail Ale

KINDRED SPIRITS
Mile Hi Chapter (BCCA), Chic Runge, 10721 West Berry Ave., Littleton, CO
80127

GREAT PLACES
Boulder: Old Chicago

OF NOTE
American Homebrewers Association/Institute of Fermentation Studies, P.O.
Box 287, Boulder, CO 80306. Well, yes, sometimes they take themselves
too seriously, but look what a bunch of rabid beer lovers have accomplished. All beer drinkers owe a debt of gratitude to Charlie Papazian and
the true believers who have led the renaissance. Lots of services and
publications for the serious home brewer or prospective professional.
Zymurgy, Box 287, Boulder, CO 80306. The bible of the home brewers and
the home of Professor Surfeit. No self-respecting nonworrier misses an
issue.
Wine Works, Barbara Shenfish, 5175 West Alameda Ave., Denver, CO 80219
Wine and Hop Shop, Lloyd Mower, 705 East Sixth Ave., Denver, CO
Buffalo Bill Days, summer, Golden, CO 80203. The celebration is midway
between Oktoberfest and Wild West. The beer could not be fresher.
Great American Beer Festival, Denver, CO. Each year the American Homebrewers Association gathers more good beers under one roof than can be
found anywhere west of the Brickskeller. Contact AHA in Boulder for
details.

IDAHO

★ Snake River Brewing Co., Inc., Rt. No. 5, Box 30A, Caldwell, ID 83605
Type: Microbrewery
Brand: Snake River Amber Lager
Tours: Mon.–Sat., 8:00 A.M.–5:30 P.M.

★ Coeur d'Alene Brewing Co., Inc., dba T. W. Fisher's "A Brew Pub," 204 North
2d St., Coeur d'Alene, ID 83814
Type: Pub brewery
Brands: T. W. Fisher's Centennial Ale, T. W. Fisher's Winter Festival

★ Sun Valley Brewing Co., 103 Garnet, P.O. Box 2598, Sun Valley, ID 83353
Type: Contract
Brands: White Cloud Ale, Sawtooth Gold (lager)
Tours: Brewery under construction; for tour information call (208) 726-
5500
Breweriana: Labels, posters, T-shirts, table tents
Slogans: "Good Head Is Not Hard to Find," "Life Is Too Short to Drink
Cheap Beer"

KINDRED SPIRITS
Ida Quaffer Homebrewers Association, c/o Loren Carter, 3401 Tamarack, Boise, ID 83703

GREAT PLACES
Boise: Litre House
Coeur d'Alene: T. W. Fisher's Brewpub

KANSAS

★ Free State Brewing Co., 636 Massachusetts St., Lawrence, KS 66044
Type: Microbrewery
Brands: Ale, Bock, German Cold-Filtered

KINDRED SPIRITS
Carrie Nation Chapter (BCCA), c/o Jerry Trowbridge, 1734 Belmont Ct., Emporia, KS 66801
Greater Topeka Hall of Foamers, c/o Tom Bennel, 320 Woodlawn Ave., Topeka, KS 66606
Kansas City Pier Meisters, c/o Alberta Rager, 5531 Reeds Rd., Mission, KS 66202

OF NOTE
Brewing Supplies
Palace, Dean Taylor, 704 North Manhattan Ave., Manhattan, KS 66502

MONTANA

★ Montana Beverage Ltd., 1439 Harris St., Helena, MT 59501
Type: Microbrewery
Brands: Kessler Beer, Kessler Bock, Kessler Wheat, Kessler Octoberfest, Kessler Winter, Lorelei Beer

★ Bayern Brewing, Inc., P.O. Box 8043, 100 Railroad St., Missoula, MT 59807
Type: Pub brewery
Brands: Bayern Amber, Pilsner, Wheats, Bocks, and other specialty beers
Tours: Available by appointment (406) 721-8705

★ Stillwater Brewing Co., P.O. Box 1949, Whitefish, MT 59937
Type: Contract
Brand: Melikian Ale

KINDRED SPIRITS
Zoo City Zymurgists, c/o Dan Hall, 6520 Highway 10 West, Missoula, MT 59802
Big Sky (BCCA), Axel Hansen, 2835 Strans, Missoula, MT 59801

GREAT PLACES
Missoula: Northern Pacific Restaurant

NEBRASKA

★ Falstaff Brewing Corp., 25th and Deer Park Blvd., Omaha, NE 68105
Type: Branch plant of Falstaff Brewing Corp., Vancouver, WA. Plant currently inactive.

KINDRED SPIRITS

Cornhusker Chapter (BCCA), c/o Brad Vifquain, 6100 Vine #J53, Lincoln, NE 68505

GREAT PLACES

Columbus: Glur's Tavern

OF NOTE

Brewing Supplies
Homebrewing Supply Co., Karen Hoffman/Annelle Eglehoff, 1324 2d Ave., Nebraska City, NE 68410

NEVADA

★ Union Brewery Beer, 28 North C St., Virginia City, NV 89440
Type: Pub brewery
Brands: Union Brewery Dark, Union Brewery Red
Tours: Museum and brewery open daily except Mon., 11:00 A.M.–5:00 P.M. Call ahead for special tours: (702) 847-0328.
Breweriana: Shirts, hats, glasses, posters, labels, foam scrapers, bottles
Slogans: Naked woman on label. Jasper the Cat is the mascot.

KINDRED SPIRITS

Washoe Zephyr Zymurgists, c/o Bill and Sue Marble, 11670 Fir, Reno, NV 89506
Sierra (BCCA), Bill Davis, 4481 Lomita, Las Vegas, NV 89121

OF NOTE

Reno Homebrewer, Robert and Elaine Bates, 5003 South McCarran Blvd., Reno, NV 89506
Virginia City Camel Races, held each summer. Climb up to 6,000 feet and leave your civilized side at sea level. Not an event for the faint of heart.

NEW MEXICO

★ Albuquerque Brewing and Bottling Co., 637½ Broadway SE, Albuquerque, NM 87102
Type: Microbrewery
Brand: Michael's Golden Ale

★ Preston Brewery, Inc., P.O. Box 154, Embudo, NM 87531
Type: Pub brewery
Brand: Preston Beer

⋆ Santa Fe Brewing Co., Flying M Ranch, Galisteo, NM 87540
  Type: Microbrewery
  Brands: Santa Fe Pale Ale, Santa Fe Fiesta Ale
  Tours: By appointment (505) 988-2340
  Breweriana: Table tents

KINDRED SPIRITS
  Road Runners (BCCA), Daniel McCormack, 12236 Woodland Ave. NE,
  Albuquerque, NM 07112

NORTH DAKOTA

KINDRED SPIRITS
  Dakota Chapter (BCCA), c/o Michael Wolf, P.O. Box 7217, Bismarck, ND
  58502

OKLAHOMA

KINDRED SPIRITS
  Fellowship of Oklahoma Ale Makers (FOAM), c/o Bruce Lemmon, 2627 East
  14th St., Tulsa, OK 74104
  Fellowship Chapter (BCCA), c/o Thomas Hull, 8720 East 86th St., Tulsa, OK
  74133-4320

OF NOTE
  Brewing Supplies
  Wine Craft of Norman, Linda Brooks, P.O. Box 2966, Norman, OK 73070

SOUTH DAKOTA

⋆ Black Hill Brewing Inc., P.O. Box 4009, Rapid City, SD 57709
  Type: Contract brewed by Jos. Huber
  Brand: Black Hills Gold Label Beer

TEXAS

⋆ The Old City Brewing Co., 603 West 13th St., Ste. 1A-306, Austin, TX 78701
  Type: Contract
  Brand: Pecan Street Lager

⋆ West End Brewing Co., 703 McKinney Ave., Ste. 002, Dallas, TX 75202
  Type: Microbrewery
  Brands: West End Lager, specialty brews

⋆ Miller Brewing Co., 7001 South Freeway, Fort Worth, TX 76134-4098
  Type: Branch plant of Miller Brewing Co., Milwaukee, WI

⋆ Anheuser-Busch, Inc., 775 Gellhorn Dr., Houston, TX 77029
  Type: Branch plant of Anheuser-Busch, Inc., St. Louis, MO

★ Stroh Brewery Co., 1400 West Cotton St., Longview, TX 75604
Type: Branch plant of the Stroh Brewery Co., Detroit, MI
Tours: Mon.–Fri., 10:00 A.M.–3:00 P.M.

★ Reinheitsgebot Brewing Co., 1107 Summit, #2, Plano, TX 75074
Type: Microbrewery
Brands: Collin County Pure Gold, Collin County Black Gold, County Collin
Emerald Beer (for St. Patrick's Day)
Tours: First Sat. of each month, starting at 10:00 A.M. and going every hour
on the hour. Tours given by brewmaster and president, Donald Thompson, and Mary Thompson, vice-president. For further information, call
(214) 423-5484.
Breweriana: T-shirts, coasters, posters, mugs

★ G. Heileman Brewing Co., 600 Lone Star Blvd., San Antonio, TX 78204
Type: Branch plant of G. Heileman Brewing Co., La Crosse, WI
Tours: Hall of Texas History, Mon.–Fri., 9:30 A.M.–5:00 P.M.

★ Pearl Brewing Co., 312 Pearl Parkway, P.O. Box 1661, San Antonio, TX
78296
Type: Branch plant of the General Brewing Co., Corte Madera, CA

★ Spoetzl Brewery, Inc., P.O. Box 368, Shiner, TX 77984
Type: Independent regional
Brands: Shiner Premium Beer, Shiner Bock

KINDRED SPIRITS
North Texas Homebrewers Association, c/o Paul Seaward, 6008 Lovers Lane,
Apt. 212, Dallas, TX 75206
Arlington Homebrewers, c/o Herschel Gibbs, 3201 West Division, Arlington,
TX 76021
Bock 'n' Ale-ians, c/o Al Hymer, 1932 West Huisache, San Antonio, TX
78201
Cowtown Cappers, c/o Rob Stenson, Winemaker Shop, 3132 West 7th St.,
Fort Worth, TX 76107
Foam Rangers, c/o DeFalco's Home Wine and Beer Supplies, 5611 Morningside Dr., Houston, TX 77005
Malt Hoppers Beer Club, c/o Lili Lyddon, P.O. Box 9560, College Station,
TX 77840
Bluebonnet (BCCA), Jeff Drinan, 6925 Post Oak Rd., Fort Worth, TX 76180
Grand Prize (BCCA), John Desjardins, 9410 Valverde, Houston, TX 77063
Lone Star (BCCA), Gary Vaith, 1022 Hayloft Lane, San Antonio, TX 78245
Rio Grande (BCCA), Joseph Summerour, Jr., 11833 Dick Mayers, El Paso,
TX 79936

GREAT PLACES
Fort Worth: White Elephant
Houston: Gingerman

OF NOTE

Brewing Supplies
DeFalco's Wine Cellars, 5611 Morningside Dr., Houston, TX 77005
DeFalco Wine and Beer House, Frank H. Brown, 12215 Coit Rd., Ste.
232, Dallas, TX 75251
The Great (Almost) Annual World's Fair, held some summers in Lucken-
bach. Not to be missed if you can figure out when it is held.

UTAH

★ Wasatch Beers, Schirf Brewing Co., P.O. Box 459, Park City, UT 84060
Type: Microbrewery
Brands: Wasatch Premium Ale, Wasatch Gold, Slickrock Lager, Wasatch
Irish Stout, Wasatch Christmas Ale
Tours: Mon.–Sat. For tour times, call (801) 645-9500.
Breweriana: T-shirts, sweatshirts, etc.
Slogan: "We Drink Our Share and Sell the Rest"

OF NOTE

The former brew kettle of the Walter Brewing Co., Pueblo, CO, is now a tree
planter at the Murray Mall, Murray, UT. How the mighty have fallen.

WYOMING

KINDRED SPIRITS

Cowboy Chapter (BCCA), c/o Ken Schneider, 219 Carroll Ave., Cheyenne,
WY 82009-4726

OF NOTE

Frontier Days, Cheyenne, July. Hot and dusty conditions ideal for the pro-
longed consumption of beer.

Great Fermentations
Otto Brothers Brewing Co., new Pub brewery in Jackson

BUY 'EM IF YOU CAN FIND 'EM

Coors Banquet (Coors). The flagship brand of the nation's largest brewing
plant is bound to be good. Its lack of body brings condemnation from
the antilight school of beer drinkers, but Coors should be praised for
what it is—America's premium pale pilsner.
Herman Joseph's 1868, George Killian's Irish Red Ale (Coors). Coors checks
out the specialty markets, hoping to strike a winner. So far, no cigar.
Lone Star (Heileman). An average lager, but stylish. Seems like you get into
trouble when you're drinking Lone Star.
Shiner Premium Beer (Spoetzl). The last of Texas's Bavarian tradition.
That's right—Bavarian tradition. A bland, malty, but flavorful beer.
Sipped from long necks at a barbecue, it will douse the flames of chili.
Boulder Sport (Boulder Brewing Co.). An attempt by a micro to produce a
mainstream lager. Stick to their swarthier porter and stout.

8
HOP
HEAVEN

**PHOENIX, ARIZONA, TO YAKIMA, WASHINGTON
87 DAYS, 18,220 MILES ON THE ROAD**

A DESERT CROSSING

The southern part of the Frontier is a wasteland in its own right, equal parts blue sky, relentless sun, and sand. Shade and beer are precious commodities, and the two almost always coexist.

From Golden we headed due south. In Pueblo we stopped at the Walter Brewing Co., which closed on New Year's Day in 1975. This firm was started by one of the brewing Walters whose family plant in Eau Claire, Wisconsin, still survives. At one time, Walters' was the best-known Colorado beer, distributed over a twenty-state area.

Four Walter brothers emigrated from Germany in the mid-nineteenth century following the well-worn path of industrious predecessors. They continued west until they found places with no breweries. Three Walters stopped in Wisconsin, but the last, Martin, went on to Pueblo. After seven struggling decades, the brewery fell into the hands of General Brewing Co., the company owned by the same people who control Falstaff, Pearl, and Narragansett. Their specialty is distressed concerns, and the ruthless bottom-line orientation often means that a brewery is worth more liquidated than operating unprofitably. The Walter plant provides a familiar tableau, albeit with a southwestern flair, of a scene witnessed too many times on this Beer Trek. The carcass shows the ravages of repeated predators, its bones bleached by the Colorado sun. White bricks glisten, making you squint into the gaping holes ripped in the walls to facilitate the removal of storage tanks. The brewery is off the main drag in a silent setting that features snow-capped mountains on one horizon, plains on the other. The silence brings home what it took for Martin Walter

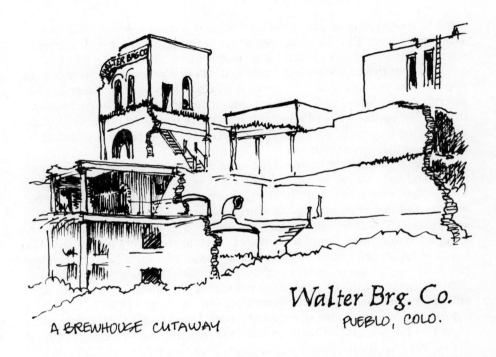

A BREWHOUSE CUTAWAY

Walter Brg. Co.
PUEBLO, COLO.

to launch the enterprise. The stores in Pueblo still sell cans with his name, but the beer is really Falstaff from the Omaha plant. We are touched by the stillness and the majesty. Even though we have experienced this same feeling from New Haven to Potosi and now to Pueblo, one is always touched by the death of a friend.

The culture changes dramatically south of Pueblo, the landscape and society reflecting a Spanish heritage from South of the Border. Mexican beers accompany the native cuisine and provide welcome variety after a diet accustomed to the blandness of Coors.

Phoenix proved to be another beer wasteland—old people, and young people trying to make money off the old people.

We topped off the radiator with the thermometer tipping a Trek-record 114 degrees. A perfect day for a desert crossing. We stopped at a diner for a final dose of air-conditioning before setting out. The van managed the heat quite well, the participants somewhat worse. It was a toss-up as to who was more affected, Guinness with her mat of black fur or Laura, now in her fifth month of pregnancy. Both lay in the back panting as I lowered the windows and put the hammer down to try to make the desert pass beneath us.

The desert, and man's changing relationship to it, illustrates how compacted our twentieth-century lives have become. One can fly over the desert in an hour, the drive takes about 6 hours on Interstate 10, and it is nearly impossible for the prudent traveler to expire. And yet the desert still holds the same foreboding threat that it did for the early pioneers. As people and Beer Treks move from East to West, the desert is the last and hardest barrier to success. The thought of crossing it on foot is inconceivable.

Most of the breweries were now behind us. Moreover, the tradition of English beer brought to our shores by the Pilgrims and that of Bavarian-style lager that dominates the Midwest was now a dim memory at the backs of our throats. For us, as for the Okies or any American who has set out to Hollywood in hopes of becoming a star, the West Coast held the promise of riches as enticing as they were unknown.

After four grueling hours of hot-wind driving, we reached the Colorado River. The wet, warm, brown ribbon is a poor excuse for the remnants of Rocky Mountain snow, but we were drawn to it as if magnetized—man, woman, and dog plunging into its waters alongside scores of like-minded desert crossers. The experience is as gratifying as it is humbling. Simple pleasures often are. But survival was assured. Several sweltering hours later, the lights of LA spread before us. The Pacific was in the air, a balm to parched skins. We treated ourselves to a night of air-conditioned comfort at a Motel 6, even springing for the extra $1.50 to unlock the TV. The choices on the eight zillion channels included such appropriate fare as *Holocaust* and *The Towering Inferno*. We opted instead for mind fodder. Laura took a cool shower while I went to get a bagful of Mexican fast food and the usual selection of local brews, forgettable fare including Burgermeister, Brew 102, Lucky Bock, and Eastside.

The beers were as bland and faceless as the television programs. We stared, munched, and sipped, grateful for survival but wondering why we had ventured forth. The tone was sadly transient—a cheap motel, greasy food, and forgettable beer. Stripped of make-up and bathed in fluorescent light, we stared into the mirror and saw ourselves at our lowest ebb. The hardest barrier, the desert, was behind us, but the Secret of the Suds was still not within our grasp. Time and beer were running out.

The next morning was, by desert standards, cool and dewy. As the rest of the crew slept, I strapped on the trusty Adidases and went for a 4-mile jog through the neighborhood. The haze burned off just as I worked up a sweat. Back at the Motel 6 the van was packed and, save for my shower, ready to go. Moments later we were on the road again, in search of more wisdom. There was a cold Burgie-Light in the cooler, a brew that the night before had been judged to be afflicted with terminal anorexia nervosa. What the hell. I cracked it. Morning beer was against the rules, but this was LA, almost Hollywood, where the rules are permanently suspended. Maybe Burgie-Light will never win any prizes in taste tests, but on that day it provided enough hue to the morning light to make life worth living again.

With three operating brewers (Miller, Schlitz, Bud), LA can legitimately claim to be one of the nation's largest, if least interesting, brewing cities. The beers of southern California are not unlike its residents. Everyone comes originally from somewhere else. After several days of touring the breweries and following up leads for various taverns, The Great Beer Trek found itself, not for the first time on its journey, confused. The problem was hardly a lack of variety; in fact, the watering holes featured selections from the antipodes, an average hostelry presenting a more diversified choice of Oriental beers than the collective beer list of the Holiday Inn chain. But the novelty appeared to be an end in itself. Throughout our journey, beer had provided a window to the regional soul. Here we found windows but with views that gazed into endless space. Instead we looked inward.

Prior to Prohibition, it was common for brewers to tout the healthful qualities of the products. Marketers today must scrupulously avoid any suggestion that consumption of malt beverages might be beneficial for anything more than your social life. Beer is portrayed as one of life's little luxuries, reserved for weekends or after work, whenever reality can be temporarily suspended. Constricted by such artifices, the marketers' concerns inevitably take precedence over the brewmasters'. The clarity of the beer becomes more important than the vitamin B content, and the ability to maintain a stiff, white head supersedes the medicinal benefits of diluted alcohol consumption. Appearance, packaging, convenience, and image are fair weapons for selling beer; issues of content are not. In other words, if you can brew a beer that looks like Farrah Fawcett, you've got a winner regardless of taste.

Brewer's yeast, sold in so many health food stores as a nutritive supplement and a natural by-product of the brewing process, is filtered out of the finished commercial product due to its negative impact on appearance and stability. In our zeal to protect ourselves from false advertising, we are denied access to the truth. Tragically, our prophecies fulfill themselves. Beer has become the leisure beverage it is portrayed as. Its consumption at other times carries stigma. As a nation we live for weekends. We overindulge; then we overcompensate. We counterbalance our pizza with Alka-Seltzer. We drink Lite, which is "less filling" so we can "drink more of it." This, we think, is the American way. And if Los Angeles stands for anything, it is the American way.

Morning Beer

Is morning a proper time to drink beer? Perhaps no other pastime is as stigmatized as drinking before the sun crosses the yardarm. The tests for alcoholism that appear in magazines and Sunday newspapers invariably ask a question about drinking in the morning, the positive answer to which automatically ensures a reserve spot in the alkie ward. While there is ample historical evidence of prominent Britishers starting off the day with a pot or two of ale, the morning imbiber is generally regarded as being only a small cut above the child molester. The occasional morning beer is a mildly degenerate pleasure, which has its well-defined time and place.

Beer was invented as a food, an important element in the diet of the common man. As such, morning consumption has always been considered normal except in societies such as ours where beer has been "elevated" to the status of a luxury beverage. The tradition, however obscured, is not lost. The following case histories illustrate:

Case 1—The Calgary Red. Also known as a Red Eye, this drink sounds horrible but in the right setting tastes great. The morning is gray and damp. You are far enough into the wilderness to be slightly scared. No one else is awake. The campfire is built, but coffee is still twenty minutes off. As you contemplate a way to outwit a trout, mix one small can of V-8 or tomato juice with an equal part of beer. Drink the remaining beer solo at the end to wash out the godawful taste of tomato. Grab your fly rod and attack the stream. (P.S. I tried this drink in a suburban home and nearly threw up.)

Case 2—You are vacationing in St. Maartens, an arid Caribbean island that is duty free and French and Dutch affiliated. Tap water tastes like brine, and a bottle of Heineken costs less than 30 cents. The temperature varies no more than ten degrees off 75, and sunrises are so spectacular as to be required viewing. From the casino you watch the sun rise over the jagged peaks of distant St. Barts. After a long walk on the beach where fishermen haul in sacks of tiny, jewel fish, you return to your seaside bungalow. It is 9:00 A.M.—the time you normally go to work. Instead you breakfast on buttered croissants and Heinekens, then move the chaise lounge so you can nap in the sun.

Case 3—The Orange Plus. This is for early morning joggers, tennis players, golfers—anyone who believes in rigorous exercise before breakfast. Into a 20-ounce mug pour 12 ounces of beer. Note: The low-calorie, tasteless beers like Lite, Anheuser-Busch Natural, Olympia Gold (particularly), and Pearl Light are best. Top off with fresh squeezed orange juice. Drink this and read the morning paper until the rest of the family wakes up. They will think you crazy, but this drink will replenish your body with nutritious fluids more effectively than anything available commercially.

Case 4—The Hair of the Dog. The party was terrific, but you drank too much and fell asleep before being able to fortify yourself with Alka Seltzer. Start the water for coffee, but even before that, check the refrigerator for a cold one to pop. By balancing your chemicals skillfully, you might even feel normal by the time you get to work.

West Coast Living

FERVENT FERMENTERS
San Francisco, California

The Pacific Ocean is probably very nice. It is one of the many prominent features of the American landscape—the Grand Canyon, Mount Rushmore, and Niagara Falls among others—that we did not see on The Great Beer Trek. In most cases the omission was intentional. Our fermentedly defined schedule left little time for sightseeing. In the case of the Pacific, we drove within a stone's throw of the water for the better part of 1,000 miles and never saw more than a grey blur over our left shoulders. The countryside, we understand, is beautiful. We saw only the beer, and have no regrets.

Our inland forays were exercises in pure clarity. We discovered the revolution that we had been seeking, and we learned the Secret of the Suds. And most important, we feel confident in stating that beer is alive and well in America, its future in good hands.

The personality parade started innocently enough by looking up the friend of a friend who worked at the famous Anchor Brewing Co. on Mariposa Street. He broke from his multiple duties in the small brewery long enough to say "hi" and to suggest the next person who could add another piece to the mosaic portrait of beer in America. We progressed from referral to referral.

By now our black book of contacts overflowethed. The common language was always beer. No one failed to find time to break from active schedules to spend time with an often unannounced Beer Trek. What made the journey even more fun is that there was scarcely a stop we made where we were not offered a beer. When we finally crossed the finish line, we were surrounded by the hop fields of Yakima, heading east, with our journey officially complete. But first, the exception that proved the rule.

Paul Kalmanovitz

The Beer Trek was welcomed with open arms almost everywhere, but occasionally our request for an audience fell on deaf ears. Back in New Jersey a call to the Eastern Brewing Co. to ask if we might stop by was met by a firm "no." When we pressed to find if there might be a more convenient day, the response was, "No, not today, not tomorrow, not the next day, not any day after that," followed by a resounding click. Similarly, our attempts to talk to Paul Kalmanovitz, whose signature and personal statements adorn Falstaff cans, were frustrated by stonewalling employees of General Brewing. Although hardly the personification of *gemütlicheit,* this man's role in shaping the course of beer in America is significant, and no Beer Trek can ignore his maverick influence. His reputation is that of a jackal who preys off the carrion of family concerns, and yet his surgical approach to business has resulted in many fine brands remaining on the market. Overall, his contributions enrich the American beer drinking scene, and we wished he had shared his perspective with us.

Fritz Maytag

The savior of Anchor Steam Beer. Steam breweries historically produced the West Coast equivalent of lager without the use of ice. The steam moniker has been explained in any number of ways, from the beer being invented by a man named Harlie Steam to the hissing foam that bellows forth when a keg is tapped. At one time there were twenty-seven steam breweries in San Francisco. Fritz Maytag bought the last one on the day before it was scheduled to close its doors forever. Now he has resuscitated it and in the process become the symbolic patriarch of America's beer renaissance.

The demise of steam beers came about as a result of the increasing preference for lager, which was regarded as more of a genteel drink than the rock 'em, sock 'em steam beer. Tastewise they were originally similar, but the domestic lager has steadily become more bland and tasteless, while Maytag's steam product has retained its original formulation. The workingman's drink has now come full circle and is the elite of San Francisco quaffers. Mr. Maytag's hard-wrought success with the unique, tiny brewery has made him, at an early age, an unofficial spokesman for the enterprising small brewers of the country. With an annual capacity of 25,000 barrels, he stands as a giant

You Are What You Drink, Part 2

"Beer is fattening," goes the adage.

"Only if you drink it," answers the sage.

Many nonbeer drinkers give as their primary reason for such behavior beer's contribution to the waistline. Prior to prohibition many brewers made proud claims for the caloric content of their product. In a contemporary society where one can never be too rich or too thin, it is important to reiterate some basic nutritional facts about beer.

Beer is not *fattening. No food is fattening except in relation to the individual's total caloric intake.*

Calories are a unit measurement that tells how much energy foods provide when oxidized, i.e., burned, by the body. The term empty calories is *misleading;* calories provided by alcohol and the other constituents of beer are just as easily utilized by the body as those deriving from any other food source. *"Fattening"* describes a relative concept. If more calories are taken in than the body requires, whether in the form of hot fudge sundaes or celery sticks, they will be stored as fat. Examine the following comparison of foods to judge whether beer is *"fattening":*

Put butter and jam on your English muffin, and you are up to three beers' worth of calories. A bacon, lettuce, and tomato sandwich with mayonnaise, washed down with a glass of milk, has about as many calories as a six-pack.

There are as many misconceptions about the positive qualities of beer as about the negative. Beer is low in protein, lipids, and salt. It is high in carbohydrates. Unpasteurized and unfiltered beers such as home brew contain an abundance of living organisms that nourish the body in physical and spiritual ways. Any home brewer, having consumed 2 pints of his favorite, will expound at length on the beneficial qualities of his libation. Whether you believe him will depend on whether you are sharing his drink.

In summation, beer is not the all-encompassing nutrition source that a die-hard suds-swiller would have you believe. Compared to the utter lack of nutritional value in soft drinks, however, beer has a good story to tell. The question, *"Is beer good for you?"* has no answer. The question, *"Is beer better for you than diet Fresca?"* does. The answer is *"Yes."*

Product	Amount	Calories	Product	Amount	Calories
beer	*12 oz.*	*145*	*butter*	*1 tbsp.*	*100*
beer (light)	*12 oz.*	*96*	*swiss cheese*	*1 oz.*	*105*
beer (extra light)	*12 oz.*	*70*	*bread*	*2 slices*	*150*
cola	*12 oz.*	*160*	*doughnut*	*1 sugared*	*151*
whole milk	*12 oz.*	*249*	*english muffin*	*1*	*180*
orange juice	*12 oz.*	*195*	*honey*	*1 tbsp.*	*62*
prune juice	*12 oz.*	*426*	*jelly*	*1 tbsp.*	*60*
apple	*1*	*120*	*mayonnaise*	*1 tbsp.*	*109*
banana	*1*	*121*	*peanut butter*	*2 tbsp.*	*180*
fried eggs	*2*	*200*	*sugar, refined*	*1 tbsp.*	*50*
ice cream	*1 scoop*	*185*	*yogurt, plain*	*1 cup*	*166*
bacon	*3 strips*	*146*			

among contemporary microbrewers. It is more than coincidental that the microbrewing revival has as its focus neither the top-fermented ales nor Bavarian lagers but rather this varietal hybrid whose origin is uniquely American.

Jack McAuliffe

While others dreamed and schemed, he did it. He opened the first ground-up brewing venture in America since the post-Prohibition era. An ex-Navy man who developed a love for Scottish-style top-fermented ales while in the service, McAuliffe's New Albion Brewery is located in a ramshackle plywood barn in Sonoma, California. With two partners and some part-time help, they turn out four barrels of their ales and stout weekly. The beers look and taste like home brew with just a little touch of class. (A commercial brewmaster described New Albion to us as "awful, just awful." Later, however, the same brewer admitted that his own bland product could not be given away in England or Germany.)

Because this brewery is so small, there was no suitable equipment available commercially. Jack had to engineer everything himself. When something is not working right, wrenches fly and the air is filled with language that does justice to any ex-Navy man. When asked the brewmaster's most important skills, McAuliffe rapidly ticks off, "Welding, plumbing, scavenging. . . . Stubbornness and low initial intelligence don't hurt either." Assistant Suzie Stern wears hip boots and smiles wryly as she starts up the steam hose, "Somehow this is not exactly what I imagined growing up." The future of New Albion is as cloudy as their beers, but their place in American brewing history is assured.

A subtle change had occurred. The West Coast beer fanatics, fervent fermenters all, were not content simply to drink good beer. They had to un-

BREWHOUSE

"PART SCAVENGER, PART FOOL..."
— JACK McAULIFFE

New Albion

EQUIPMENT STOCKPILE

lock its secrets and demystify it by plunging into the mechanics of its creation. New frontiers, unlimited horizons, everybody's a star. The process for these brewers holds as much fascination as the product. By mastering the former, they know they can create a new richer world of the latter.

The trip north was as schizophrenic as it was frantic. Blue jeans at one stop, blue business suit at the next. The Great Beer Trek was equally comfortable swapping gossip with the movers and shakers of the microbrewery world, speculating on the next moves by the juggernauts of the Beer Wars, or discussing with runners the merits of light beer as fluid replenishment. Different worlds, different settings, different subjects, different people, but common ground. And the common language was beer.

THE SECRET OF THE SUDS   Yakima Valley, Washington

If there was a single pivotal moment in the history of beer making, it was when someone cut the bland heartiness of malt and water with the medicinal spice of *Humulus lupulus*—hops. Although the moment is unrecorded, it can

ADOLPHUS I DOGBONE

Who's Who of Brew?

The Great Beer Trek asked the movers and shakers of the beer world, "Who are the movers and shakers of the beer world?" Each respondent was asked to name who, excluding himself, was the most interesting person in beerdom. Not a single ballot cited the individual whose beer-addled brain spawned The Great Beer Trek. Of course, there were others, as well:

Charlie Lieber, Mark Weiner, Scott Morgan, and Frank Morris. We don't know who you are, but someone out there thinks you are pretty interesting.

Two people nominated members of their family—Jim Koch of Samuel Adams, his father ("He knows how beer should be made and has absolutely no romanticism about quality in beer"), and Carol Stoudt, president of Stoudt Brewing Co., who nominated her husband, Ed ("He led me to discover the world of beer").

In the backhanded compliment arena, one brewer nominated August Busch III but qualified his nomination by noting that the Budweiser czar was "not very interesting on a personal basis." At least he makes good beer.

There were a few cop-outs, like the brewer who named his customers, another who found interest in "whoever was standing next to him with a beer in his hand," and finally, the worst response in the survey—"We are all interesting." And all beer is good and nice, so don't bother reading the rest of the book.

Now for the heavyweights. Buy any of these guys a beer if you have the chance:

- *Fritz Maytag, the savior of Anchor Steam and, in the words of Michael Jackson "the Godfather of the renaissance." "He provides a model for all microbrewers," according to Alan Davis of Catamount Brewing Co. Nancy Smith Hall of the Institute of Fermentation put it more succinctly: "He's so cosmic!" (Forgive her. She's from Boulder where they still talk like that.)*

- *John Ahrens, Beer Can Collectors of America member 9, possessor of more than forty tapes of beer songs, one of the few people to have attended every CANvention, and a man of such diverse sudsy interests that he is a veritable Leonardo da Vinci of the beer world.*

- *Jack McAuliffe, founder of the New Albion Brewing Co., and as romantic a figure as exists in the brewing world. His legend has only grown, especially since he has apparently disappeared off the face of the earth.*

- *Will Anderson, author of* From Beer to Eternity *and other frothy treasures. According to George Hilton, editor of the* Breweriana Collector, *Anderson deserves recognition because "if he doesn't talk about beer, he talks about baseball. What more could one ask of anybody." Of course, Hilton's description fits every bleacher bum in Wrigley Field.*

- *Otto Kuhn and Bill Smulowitz of the Lion, Inc. "These gentlemen," says Timothy Morse, brewmaster of the Hope Brewing Corporation, "combine a knowledge of production and process with an instinct for survival." Hear, hear.*

- *Michael Jackson, who combines global experience, technical knowledge, and the ability to articulate with the gusto of a true believer. Everyone associated with the business has occasion to share a brew with Michael sooner or later and emerges with the discovery of a new friend. He, more than anyone, has elevated overall beer quality consciousness.*

There are many others: Ken Grossman, Sierra-Nevada ("a pioneer"); Dr. Michael Lewis; Charlie Papazian ("who gathered us all together"); Mario Celotto, Humboldt Brewery ("because he's my boss and such a good guy!"); and the list goes on. Still, a few of you could have mentioned me.

safely be attributed to King Gambrinus, the legendary patron saint of brewers. Hops have literally been a fixture in beer ever since, as the distinction between "ale" and "beer" in traditional brewing lore has been simply the absence or presence of this herb. (Ironically, in modern jargon, the definition has been reversed, with "ale" describing a more highly hopped beverage.)

Many herbs and spices can be, and have been, used to flavor and preserve brew. In colonial America substitutes included oak boughs, coriander, wormwood, nettles, and horehound. It is probable that the substitutes only compensated for the unavailability of the conelike flowers of the hop vine. While the others supply flavoring or bitterness, hops supply magic. It's that simple.

The Great Beer Trek stopped to speak with an official of the Washington State Lab and Hop Division who provided us with a wealth of information about hops, including the following:

- More than one-fifth of the world's hops are grown in the Yakima Valley, accounting for two-thirds of the total domestic production.

- Other commercial hop-growing states include California, Idaho, and Oregon. Other prominent hop-growing countries include England, Germany, and South Africa.

- Hops are perennials that will thrive anywhere between the 40th and 50th parallels. There are multitudes of wild forms, and it is not uncommon to find cultivated hops growing alongside colonial farmsites throughout the Northeast.

- Commercial hop vines will grow as long as 30 feet. As with marijuana, male plants must be removed from the crop to prevent fertilization. There is no biological connection between hops and marijuana.
- Commercially grown hops are hybridized to attain specific characteristics, such as resistance to mildew and fungus, in addition to flavoring elements. Other important bred-in hop qualities: yield bittering value, aroma, durability.
- Most commercial brewers use hops in processed form (extract or pellets), as they lack the proper storage of the delicate flowers. Notable exceptions are Budweiser, Coors, and Pabst.
- Big brewers use a blend of hops (supposedly fifteen varieties in the Budweiser formula) to protect themselves from regional crop failures, which could cause annual variations in the taste of their brews.
- The hopping rate of a commercial brewer is approximately one-fourth of what the home brewer or microbrewer will use. After decades of reducing hop content, there is some evidence that brewers are now increasing hopping rates in response to consumer demand for more flavorful beers.
- The entire $50 million crop is controlled by five international dealers. If you have illusions of becoming an independent hop farmer or merchant, forget it.
- Home brewers love hops. They will pay outrageous prices for dried-up products, then use them at a rate that would gag the Miller brewmaster. The resulting brew will leave the teeth coated with a bitter aftertaste and will be poisonous to all but the original brewmaster who will consume it

with the enthusiasm of a camel at the oasis. Eastern home brewers accuse their western counterparts of overindulgence as far as hops are concerned. And so it goes.

In addition to their flavoring and aroma contributions, hops assist in the clarification and preservation of beer, as well as improving head retention. Moreover, according to folklore, hops will do everything from toning the liver to reducing fever. The one characteristic of hops that is widely accepted scientifically is its soporific quality, that is, the ability to make you sleep. Two Anchor Steams before bedtime, any beer drinker will tell you, can accomplish more than a fistful of Sominex.

Whenever the first magic moment of hops being added to liquid bread occurred is irrelevant. What is important is that the moment keeps occurring around the world. Although technological improvements in processing have made a range of consistent hop pellets and extracts available, no brewmaster worth his malt, whether at Anheuser-Busch or in his own basement, can resist the sensuous pleasure of working with whole hop flowers.

THE FINISH LINE The Roadside, eastbound, Yakima, Washington

The distance runner trains long and hard for a race. The race itself can be an exercise in tedium as the runner fights to maintain the pace within the context of an unwilling body. Then there is the sprint to the finish line, followed by the overwhelming sensation of the event having taken a very short time. The long and agonizing miles become compacted into a sense of accomplishment that instantly justifies whatever months of pain and sacrifice have preceded.

On either side of the road in Yakima, Washington, the hop vines absorbed the midsummer sun and transformed its energy into the magical spice that gives beer its allure and mystery. The setting was one of silence and serenity. Harvest time and the influx of machinery and migrant workers were still several weeks off. For the time being, the hops rested in the quiet sunshine to perform their conversion magic. We were tinged with sadness because for the first time since our sudsy travels started we were heading east. And for the first time there were no new breweries left to trek to. How quick it all seemed!

Any sadness was tempered with a sense of accomplishment, the same feeling of the runner having crossed the finish line. The final leg of our journey, a clockwise semi-oblong beginning in Golden, Colorado, and ending in Yakima, Washington, had taken us over mountains, across deserts, and along the Pacific coast. Most important, it had altered our perception of beer in the United States in an inspirational way. Even during our brief moment's respite in the hop fields, the dazzling mélange of people, places, and tastes began to

What to do if you sight an MFR

1. Here are two artist's drawings of authenticated MFR beer shapes. Did the object you observed most resemble (circle one):

A

B

A Night in Seattle

Spring for a limo. You do not want your evening of beer drinking ecstasy ruined by parking tickets or a DUI (driving under the influence). Dress for the occasion. Keep in mind that you will be experiencing in one night more variety than was available a decade ago to The Great Beer Trek across the entire nation.

The Original Trek focused on Seattle by portraying the Wild Rainiers—the humanoid bottles of the Rainier Brewing Company that inject visibility and life to the Northwest beer drinking scene. At one time the Rainier Brewing Co. offered the ultimate brewing tour—free beer, lunch for a nickel, and you didn't even have to tour the plant to qualify. Before long, word had spread throughout the rummy population of the Northwest, and the brewery was home to more bums than any other place west of the Bowery. Such a mistake on behalf of the beer drinker is not atypical of Rainier, a concern that has proved that a loss of independent ownership does not have to mean a loss of individuality. These are the same people who give you Rainier Ale in the dark green cans—the original "Green Death." This brew made the mortal mistake of being darker than ginger ale, with more body than Phyllis Diller, and the kick of a mule.

The chest beating paid off for Rainier in the form of a leadership position in statewide sales. This time around, however, we do not have to focus on publicity gimmicks or clever marketing but can concentrate on the fact that Seattle, along with Portland, provides the throbbing heartbeat to the microbrewing movement. This time we can concentrate on the beer.

For company we will select Vince Cottone. We have never met the guy, but as the author of The Good Beer Guide *($8.95, P.O. Box 30156, Seattle, WA 98103), he has become a guru of the Northwest brewing renaissance and should be able to point us in the right directions.*

We begin by bypassing whatever event is at the Kingdome, the world's worst place to watch baseball, and opt instead for F. X. McRory's, 419 Occidental South. The oyster selection is as varied as the suds fare, so we match up shellfish and ales, checking Ballard Bitter, Redhook, Hale's Celebration Porter, and BridgePort Ale off the list before heading on. We realize what an insidious trap we are falling into, and we have not yet left the one spot in Seattle that every Tom, Dick, and tourist already knows about.

Cottone drags us into the limo, and we flash up to the north side of town to Coopers, 8065 Lake City Way Northeast, where we stick exclusively to products from Bert Grant's Yakima Brewery. Grant, a refugee from the commercial brewing world, has combined the spirit of the microbrewer with the methodology of the big guys, resulting in classic varieties that are as clean and well balanced as they are innovative and alive.

Next we make an obligatory stop at Murphy's, 2110 North 45th St., where we get into a grudge match on the dart board with some locals. By now things are getting out of hand. A new and exotic brew appears every few minutes—Thomas Kemper, Kuefnerbrau Old Bavarian, Terminator Stout. The names blur together, but the collective memory of great brews is as clear as a Bud Light.

The evening ends at the Oxford, 1918 First Ave., where the ambiance is a bit less frantic than the cacophony of Murphy's. We are very grateful for the limo. The evening ends not because we have run out of beers or places but rather time and capacity. Next time we will leave a week for Seattle.

take on shape and form. By the time we returned home, we knew the entire experience would have sorted itself out.

Our itinerary completed, we sat in the van awaiting the surge of inspiration that would bring with it the revelation of the Secret of the Suds. It was so quiet one could almost hear the vines grow.

The van was in park, but our mental wheels were still spinning with the maelstrom of the previous weeks' trekking. The spectre of brewery decimation had been saved by the two-out, ninth inning, pinch-hit home run by the West Coast microbrewers. If but a fraction of them follow through on their plans to start breweries, Mendocino County will someday offer more sudsy variety than 1970-era America.

Moreover, with the proliferation of imports and the diversification of product from the commercial brewing giants, the prospects for the beer drinker are exciting. No wonder the ranks of stalwart beer drinkers have swelled to include health fanatics, gourmets, dieters, and lots of women.

Still . . . no Secret of the Suds. I opened a bottle of Blitz, hoping to overwhelm taste buds in malt and hops, in the process bringing forth visible bells or a chorus of angels' voices.

Nothing. Just the sun, the beer, and the hops. But for the miracle of irrigation we would be sitting in a desert. I realized I was stalling.

"So . . . ," I said to Laura, First Lady of the Van and by now a full partner in the quest, if not the consumption, of beer. "What's the Secret of the Suds?"

Her response was a slight shrug. Finally she mustered tentatively, "Maybe beer is too simple to have a secret."

"You mean we made this entire trip, and there is no Secret of the Suds?" The tone of my voice carried the desperation of one whose foundation has started to crumble. Her reply was carried in a slight tightening of the lips and an imperceptible nod.

"Damn," I exclaimed, slapping the dash, hitting the ignition, jerking the transmission into gear, and turning eastward onto the road. "Sure was a good excuse to drink lots of beer!" But I was not worried. Although the Secret defied immediate expression, both of us knew it had been revealed long before.

Back in Los Angeles, after our desert crossing, minds and psyches at a low and parched ebb, we had made all the required research stops, had discovered ample evidence of beer consumption, but had experienced none. Whatever laid-back *gemütlicheit* the city possesses had thoroughly escaped us.

On our last night in town, we went for a long walk on the beach. Right at sunset, still feeling somewhat lonely and displaced, we stopped at a tiny neighborhood bar, clearly a local.

Furnishings were spare, as they are wont to be whenever the priorities are people, conversation, and beer. The place could hold no more than a dozen; luckily the collective demeanor was receptive to passing strangers. I asked the person behind the bar, a young woman in her mid-twenties with the blond streaks of an ex-surfer, to serve me a brew that in her opinion represented the best local beer experience to be had. She brought a can of Tecate with salted rim and wedge of lemon. I accepted and consumed graciously, but by the end of the can, once I had explained the purpose of our travels, confessed that the salt/lemon custom aborted the traditional taste of a pretty decent beer.

"I guess you're right," she replied, flipping back her blond locks in a way that would arouse any beach boy. "But we're not much on tradition here."

"Why?" I asked, but I needn't have, as the answer became self-evident after a few minutes of conversation with locals. Jerry, a flight instructor, hails from Madison, Wisconsin. While sipping on a Michelob, he filled us with stories about attending Oktoberfest in La Crosse each autumn of his youth. Mary prefers Miller Lite and is making a fortune in real estate after escaping Nashville and two bad marriages. Her brothers used to take her to the Gerst House, and she remembers fondly the surly competence of the waitresses. Ed spends a lot of time keeping fit. He rides motocross on weekends and has a Ph.D. from NYU where one favorite professor held court with wide-eyed students at McSorley's Ale House. He was glad to hear that McSorley's was alive and well, with crust on the mustard and bite to the beer. He couldn't remember what the beer tasted like, only that it was good. At present his favorite is Dos Equis, but that will change before long. Even the surfer-girl waitress was an immigrant from St. Louis where she and her high school friends used to tour the Budweiser brewery every Friday afternoon for the freebies. She came to LA for college and hopes of getting into show biz. So far the closest she has come has been delivering singing balloon-a-grams. But she is not complaining. She's a stalwart on the neighborhood volleyball team, her days are free, and life at the local is casual enough that she felt comfortable joining us for a beer. She drinks Molsons, Schlitz, whatever. One of these days, she confided, she's sure to get a break.

The California lack of tradition revealed itself to be simply the presence of all other traditions. This was certainly food, or should I say "beer," for thought. I asked the bartender for another recommendation. She offered a choice of Tsing-tao from China or Beck's. "It's great on the rocks with a twist," she added.

We left feeling good about new friends (whom we would never see again), but also about Los Angeles and humankind in general. The world, thanks to the addition of a little water, grain, yeast, and hops, looked a bit cheerier. Good beer, bad beer, brown beer, warm beer . . . what is important is not so much what is in the beer but what is in the Man. The bottom of the mug is a porthole, and beer, being a fluid subject, provides the lubricant to wipe aside the grime and mire of everyday life. The view, however blurred, streaky, and temporary, is directly into another's soul. That's the Secret.

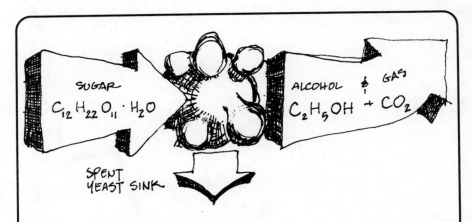

SUGAR
$$C_{12}H_{22}O_{11} \cdot H_2O$$

ALCOHOL & GAS
$$C_2H_5OH + CO_2$$

SPENT YEAST SINK

The Secret of Beer?

Beer yeast, when dispersed in water, breaks down into an infinite number of small spheres. If these spheres are transferred to an aqueous solution of sugar they develop into small animals. They are endowed with a sort of suction trunk with which they gulp up the sugar from the solution. Digestion is immediately and clearly recognizable because of the discharge of excrements. These animals evacuate ethyl alcohol from their bowels and carbon dioxide from their urinary organs. Thus one can observe how a specifically lighter fluid is exuded from the anus and rises vertically whereas a stream of carbon dioxide is ejected at very short intervals from their enormously large genitals.

—by Friedrich Woehler and Justus von Liebig
Published in the Annals of Chemistry, *Volume 29, 1839*
Suggested by the Siebel Institute of Technology, Chicago, Illinois

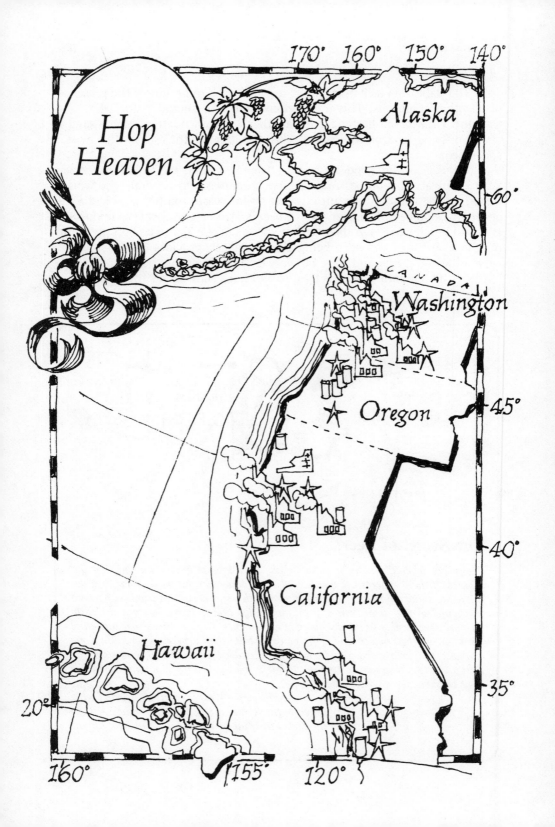

Trekker's Guide to Hop Heaven

There are now more breweries in the three Pacific coastal states than in the entire United States of a decade ago. There is more native beer variety within 10 miles of Chico, California, now than in all of North America then.

Above it all reigns a stately Fritz Maytag who bought the failing Anchor Brewing Company and kept it alive until the rest of the world caught up with his views on the importance of quality to the brewing process. His rival on the legend scale, Jack McAuliffe, had the temerity to start a brewery while survival was the byword among small brewers nationwide. McAuliffe is no longer visible on the microbrewing scene, probably working in seclusion to take on another industry behemoth. Microbrewers everywhere should raise a glass to his courage.

The movers and shakers of the beer business in the Northwest are a new, and irreverent, cast of characters who have great conviction in the styles of beer and beer drinking they have pioneered. The Oregon Brewer's Festival, which debuted in 1988, established that there is more than one great beer festival in the United States. The industry? The AHA? Who needs 'em? They are creating their own industry in the Northwest.

Heileman, Pabst, and General have devoured the scraps of the regional business, but the story here is no longer the Running of the Rainiers so much as the fact that there are enough Oregon brewers to hold a festival (and Blitz was not even included!). Handcrafted beers and ales have quickly become a way of life on the coast.

On the Next Trek, circa 2000, the Hop Heaven brewing scene will be a little outrageous, perhaps a brewery for every dozen or so citizens—just about right.

ALASKA

★ Chinook Alaskan Brewing Co., Ltd., P.O. Box 1053, Douglas, AK 99824
  Type: Microbrewery
  Brands: Chinook Alaskan Amber Beer, Chinook Alaskan Pale Ale, Chinook Alaskan Smoked Porter
  Tours: Tues. and Thurs., 11:00 A.M.–5:00 P.M. or by appointment (907) 780-5866
  Breweriana: T-shirts, posters, hats, buttons, postcards, labels, coasters, aprons, steins, pins, etc.

GREAT PLACES
  Juneau: Red Dog Saloon

OF NOTE
  (RIP) Prinz Brau, Anchorage. A somewhat weird and abortive attempt to create a German brewing tradition, Alaskan style.

CALIFORNIA

★ Humboldt Brewery, 856 10th St., Arcata, CA 95521
Type: Microbrewery
Brands: Oatmeal Stout, Storm Cellar Porter, Gold Rush Ale, Red Nectar Ale
Tours: By appointment (707) 826-BREW
Breweriana: Authentic photos of breweries from the area circa 1800s
Slogan: "Commitment to Excellence"

★ Bison Brewing Co., 2598 Telegraph Ave., Berkeley, CA 94704
Type: Microbrewery
Brands: Amber, Stout

★ Thousand Oaks Brewing Co., 444 Vassar Ave., Berkeley, CA 94708
Type: Microbrewery
Brands: Thousand Oaks Lager, Cable Car Classic Lager, Golden Gate Malt
Liquor, Golden Bear Malt Liquor

★ Triple Rock Brewing Co. Inc., 1920 Shattuck Ave., Berkeley, CA 94704
Type: Pub brewery
Brands: Red Rock Ale, Pinnacle Pale Ale, Black Rock Porter
Tours: Sat. Call for appointment (415) 843-2739
Breweriana: T-shirts, sweatshirts, Black Rock Porter pins, Triple Rock 16-
ounce glasses, brewpub maps, Triple Rock postcards
Slogans: Mascot is "Rocky" (a costume in the shape of a large rock) who
makes surprise appearances at Triple Rock and around the Bay Area

★ Golden Gate Brewery, 1 Bolivar Dr., Berkeley, CA 94710
Type: Pub brewery
Brands: City Lights, Lucky Stars, Bay Island Ales, Imperial Dark

★ Anderson Valley Brewing Co., 14081 Highway 128, Boonville, CA 93415
Brands: Poleeko Gold, Boon Amber, High Roller Wheat, Deep Ender Dark
(Porter)

★ Napa Valley Brewing Co., (Calistoga Inn), 1250 Lincoln Ave., Calistoga, CA
94515
Type: Microbrewery and pub brewery
Brands: Calistoga Pale Lager, Calistoga Dark Lager, Calistoga Red Ale, spe-
cial seasonals
Tours: By appointment only (707) 942-4914

★ Angeles Brewing Co., 10009 Canoga Ave., Chatsworth, CA 91311
Type: Microbrewery
Brands: Angeles Amber Ale, Angeles Lager
Tours: Tours available by calling in advance; brewers not present every day
(818) 407-0340
Breweriana: T-shirts

★ Saxton Brewery, 11088 Midway, P.O. Box 4337, Chico, CA 95928
Type: Microbrewery
Brands: Du Bru Ale, Ivanhoe Ale, Lion-Hearted Ale, Excalibur, Grail Pale
Ale
Tours: By appointment only (916) 893-5637
Breweriana: T-shirts, pins, posters. "We Collect and Trade Labels."
Slogans: "Quality Not Quantity," "Gourmet Ale for the Elite Connoisseur"

★ Sierra Nevada Brewing Co., 1075 East 20th St., Chico, CA 95928
Type: Microbrewery, with pub brewery planned
Brands: Sierra Nevada Pale Ale, Sierra Nevada Porter, Sierra Nevada Stout,
Sierra Nevada Bigfoot Barleywine Style Ale, Sierra Nevada Celebration
Ale, Sierra Nevada Draught
Tours: Call brewery for scheduled times (916) 893-3520
Breweriana: T-shirts, patches, glasses. Available by mail or at brewery.

★ Sherwood Brewing Co., 319 Main St., Chico, CA 95928
Type: Pub brewery
Brands: Sir Robin of Luxley Lager, Gallows Oak Amber, Little John's Spe-
cialty Brew (raspberry ale), Maid Marian Ale (mead).

★ General Brewing Co., Executive Offices: P.O. Box 992, Corte Madera, CA
94925
Type: National
Brands: Lucky Lager, Fisher, Lucky Genuine Draft, Brew 102, Regal Select,
Ballantine, Falstaff

★ Golden Pacific Brewing Co., 5515 Doyle #4, Emeryville, CA 94608
Type: Pub brewery
Brands: Golden Pacific Ale, Bittersweet Ale

★ Bolt Brewery, 302 North Brandon, Fallbrook, CA 92028
Type: Pub brewery
Brand: Bolt Beer

★ North Coast Brewing, 444 North Main, Fort Bragg, CA 95437
Type: Microbrewery
Brands: Schrimshaw Pilsner, Red Seal Ale, Old Number 45 Stout

★ Brewpub on the Green, 3400 Stevenson Blvd., Freemont, CA 94538
Type: Pub brewery
Brands: Gold Coast Lager, California Mission Peak Porter, Amber

★ Butterfield Brewing Co., 777 East Olive Ave., Fresno, CA 93728
Type: Microbrewery
Brand: Bridal Veil Ale

★ Buffalo Bill's Brewpub, 1082 B St., Hayward, CA 94541

Type: Pub brewery
Brands: Buffalo Brew, Billy Bock, Hearty Ale
Tours: A 6-minute tour is given on request, 9:00 A.M.–5:00 P.M. daily
Breweriana: *American Brewer Magazine,* brewpub map
Logo: Buffalo

★ Mendocino Brewing Co., 13351 South Highway 101, P.O. Box 400, Hopland, CA 95449
Type: Pub brewery
Brands: Red Tail Ale, Blue Heron Pale Ale, Black Hawk Stout, Peregrine Pale Ale, Eye of the Hawk Select Ale
Tours: By appointment (707) 744-1015
Breweriana: Mugs, glasses, coasters, T-shirts, posters. At brewery only; no mail orders.

★ Miller Brewing Co., 15801 East 1st St., Irwindale, CA 91706-2036
Type: Branch plant of Miller Brewing Co., Milwaukee, WI

★ Marin Brewing Co., 1809 Larkspur Landing Circle, Larkspur, CA 94939
Type: Pub brewery
Brands: Mount Tamalpais Ale, Alcatraz Amber, Point Beyes Porter, seasonal beers

★ Los Angeles Brewing Co., Inc., 1845 South Bundy Dr., Los Angeles, CA 90025
Type: Microbrewery (brewery under construction)

★ Anheuser-Busch, Inc., 15800 Roscoe Blvd., Los Angeles, CA 91406
Type: Branch plant of Anheuser-Busch, Inc., St. Louis, MO

★ Firestone and Fletcher Brewing Co., P.O. Box 244, Los Olivos, CA 93441
Type: Microbrewery
Brand: Firestone Non-alcoholic Malt Beverage

★ Stanislaus Brewing Co., Inc., 3454 Shoemaker Ave., Modesto, CA 95351
Type: Pub brewery
Brands: St. Stans Amber Alt, St. Stans Dark Alt, St. Stans Fest
Tours: Sun., 4:00 P.M.
Breweriana: T-shirts, hats

★ Tied House Restaurant and Brewery, 954 Villa St., Mountain View, CA 94041
Type: Pub brewery
Brands: Tied House Pale, Tied House Amber, Tied House Dark

★ Nevada City Brewing Co., 75 Bost Ave., Nevada City, CA 95959
Type: Microbrewery
Brands: Nevada City Brew Regular, Nevada City Brew Dark
Tours: Sat. For times call (916) 265-2446.
Breweriana: Available Saturday at brewery
Slogan: "QUAFF"; mascots are Gold Country Miners

★ Under the Oaks Brewing at Ojai, 415 East Villanova Rd., Ojai, CA 93023
Type: Microbrewery
Brands: Irish Red, Pelican Porter, Beacon Barley

★ Gordon-Biersch Brewing Co., 640 Emerson, Palo Alto, CA 94301
Type: Pub brewery
Brands: Export, Marzen, Dunkel, Weiss

★ Pete's Brewing Co., 940 East Meadow Dr., Palo Alto, CA 94303
Type: Contract
Brand: Pete's Wicked Ale (contract brewed by August Schell, New Ulm, MN)

★ Crown City Brewery, 300 South Raymond, Pasadena, CA 91105
Type: Pub brewery
Brands: Mount Wilson Wheat Beer, Arroyo Amber Ale, Yorkshire Porter, Black Cloud Oatmeal Stout

★ Pasadena Brewing Co., 85 North Raymond Ave., Pasadena, CA 91103
Type: Contract
Brand: Pasadena Lager (contract brewed by Xcelsior Brewery, Santa Rosa, CA)

★ Paso Robles Brewing Co., 7320 Union Rd., Paso Robles, CA 93446
Type: Microbrewery
Brand: Dryland Lager

★ Hogshead Brewing Co., Inc., 114 J St., Sacramento, CA 95814
Type: Pub brewery
Brands: Hogshead Lager, McSchleuter

★ Rubicon Brewing Co., 2004 Capitol Ave., Sacramento, CA 95814
Type: Pub brewery
Brands: India Pale Ale, Amber Ale, Extra Stout Porter, Wheat Ale, Ol' Mo
Tours: By appointment (415) 434-3344
Breweriana: T-shirts, hats, pins, stickers

★ Karl Strauss' Old Columbia Brewery, 1157 Columbia St., San Diego, CA 92101
Type: Pub brewery
Brands: Amber, Gold, Dark, Ale, Lager, Pilsner, Stout

★ Anchor Brewing Co., 1705 Mariposa St., San Francisco, CA 94107
Type: Mega-microbrewery
Brands: Anchor Steam Beer, Anchor Porter, Liberty Ale, Anchor Wheat Beer, Our Special Ale (a.k.a. Christmas Ale), Old Foghorn (barleywine-style ale)
Tours: By appointment only, Mon.–Fri. (415) 863-8350
Breweriana: Souvenirs available at the brewery or by mail

★ McKenzie River Corporation, 1750 Montgomery, San Francisco, CA 94111
  Type: Contract
  Brand: St. Ides Premium Malt Liquor (contract brewed by G. Heileman,
    Portland, OR)
  Tours: St. Ides is contract brewed at the Blitz Weinhard Brewery, Portland,
    OR. Blitz operates tours daily.
  Slogan: "St. Ides Premium Malt Liquor. It will blow you away."

★ San Francisco Brewing Co., 155 Columbus Ave., San Francisco, CA 94133
  Type: Pub brewery
  Brands: Albatross Lager, Emperor Norton Lager
  Slogan: "From Grain to Glass"

★ Winchester Brewing Co., 820 South Winchester Blvd., San Jose, CA 95128
  Type: Brewery restaurant
  Brands: Winchester Pale Ale, Winchester Red, Winchester Porter

★ Biere Brasserie, 33 East San Fernando St., San Jose, CA 95113
  Type: Pub brewery

★ Braun Breweries, Inc., 3432A Roberto Ct., San Luis Obispo, CA 93401
  Type: Microbrewery
  Brands: San Luis Lager, San Luis Pale Ale, Western Reserve Malt Liquor

★ Santa Cruz Brewing Co., 516 Front St., Santa Cruz, CA 95060
  Type: Microbrewery
  Brands: Lighthouse Lager, Lighthouse Amber, Pacific Porter, seasonal spe-
    cial brews
  Tours: Possible with notice (408) 429-8838
  Breweriana: Labels, coasters, brochures, postcards, mugs, tap handles,
    sweatshirts, T-shirts, hats, and pen sets

★ Seabright Brewing Co., 519 Seabright, Santa Cruz, CA 95062
  Type: Pub brewery
  Brands: Pelican Ale, Amber Portola Dark, seasonal brews

★ City of Angels Brewing Co., 1445 4th St., Santa Monica, CA 90401
  Type: Microbrewery
  Brands: Angel Amber, Heavenly Gold, City Light
  Tours: The brewery can be viewed from the bar and restaurant. Tours are
    available when no brewing is taking place, conducted by the brewmaster
    or a manager. Call ahead for tours of six or more people (213) 451-0096.
  Breweriana: Bar mats and matches free. Shirts for sale.

★ Kelmer's Brewhouse, 458 B St., Santa Rosa, CA 95401
  Type: Microbrewery
  Brands: Krystal Fine Lager, Klassic Amber Ale, Klout Fine Stout

★ Xcelsior Brewery, Inc., 99 6th St., Santa Rosa, CA 95401
Type: Microbrewery
Brand: Acme Beer
Tours: By appointment. Tasting room open Tues.–Sun., 12:00–5:00 P.M.
   (707) 578-1497
Breweriana: T-shirts, posters, pilsner glasses

★ Truckee Brewing Co., P.O. Box 2348, 11401 Donner Pass Rd., Truckee, CA
95734
Type: Pub brewery
Brands: Truckee, Truckee Dark

★ Stroh Brewery Co., 7521 Woodman Ave., P.O. Box 32, Van Nuys, CA 91409
Type: Branch plant of the Stroh Brewery Co., Detroit, MI

★ Devil Mountain Brewery, 850 South Broadway, Walnut Creek, CA 94596
Type: Pub brewery
Brands: Gayles Pale Ale, Iron Horse Alt, Devil's Brew, Railroad Ale, Red Dog
   Bitter
Tours: Tues.–Sun., 2:00–4:00P.M.
Slogans: "Home of the Brews, Blues and Barbecues," "Nothing But the Best
   . . . and Later for the Rest"

★ Dead Cat Alley Brewing Co., 666 Dead Cat Alley, Woodland, CA 95695
Type: Microbrewery
Brands: Dead Cat Lager, Opera House Ale, Fat Cat Stout

KINDRED SPIRITS
Aztec (BCCA), John Padgett, 6447 Lake Kathleen Ave., San Diego, CA 92119
Golden State (BCCA), Dan Richmond, 15001 Chadron Ave. #D, Gardena,
   CA 90249
49er (BCCA), Warren Hardecker, 611 Sunset Ct., Davis, CA 95616
Foam Heads, c/o Mike Montez, Brewers Mart, 16114 Leffco Rd., Whittier,
   CA 90603
Anza Brewers and Connoisseurs, c/o Al Andrews, 5740 Via Sotelo, Riverside,
   CA 92506
Barley Bandits, c/o Dick Reese, 105 South Glendon, Anaheim, CA 92806
Butte County Brew Crew, c/o Bill Kalberer, Home Brew Shop, 331 Main St.,
   Chico, CA 95928
Clande Stein, c/o Ed and Diane Keay, 183 Nob Hill Lane, Ventura, CA 93003
Fellow Fermenters, c/o MCC Homebrew Supplies, 707 Highway 175, Hope-
   land, CA 95449
Inland Empire Brewers, c/o Sam Wammack, 16490 Jurupa Ave., Fontana,
   CA 92335
Maltese Falcon Home Brew Society, c/o John Daume, Home Wine and Beer
   Making Shop, 22836 Ventura Blvd., Unit 2, Woodland Hills, CA 91364
San Andreas Malts, c/o Brendan Moylan, P.O. Box 40744, San Francisco, CA
   94110

Santa Clara Valley Brewers, c/o Rich Moshin, 1876 West San Carlos Ave., San Jose, CA 95128

Shasta County Suds'ers, c/o Ray Ault, P.O. Box 839, Anderson, CA 96007

Sonoma Beerocrats, c/o Nancy Vineyard, 840 Piner Rd., #14, Santa Rosa, CA 95401

Worts of Wisdom, c/o Dick Bemis, Fermentation Settlement, 1211 C Kentwood Ave., San Jose, CA 95129

GREAT PLACES

Berkeley: Triple Rock Ale House
Hayward: Buffalo Bill's
Hopeland: Mendocino Brewing Co.
Los Angeles: Barney's Beanery
Mountain View: Tied House Restaurant and Brewery
San Francisco: Albatross Pub, Edinburgh Castle, Tommy's Joynt
Santa Cruz: Front Street Pub
Walnut Creek: Devil Mountain Brewery
Hollywood: Barney's Beanery

OF NOTE

Brewing Supplies

Brewmaster, 2315 Verna Ct., San Leandro, CA 94577

Great Fermentations, 87 Larkspur, San Rafael, CA 94901

Home Brewery, 16490 Jurupa Ave., Fontana, CA 92335

R & R Home Fermentation Supplies, Ralph Barnett and Ralph Housley, 8385 Jackson Rd., Sacramento, CA

Williams' Brewing Co., P.O. Box 2159, San Leandro, CA 94577

Shadetree Shop, Mona and Karl Neilson, 3712 Foothill Rd., La Crescenta, CA

Fermentation Settlement, Karen and Dick Bemis, 1211 C Kentwood Ave., San Jose, CA

Home Brewery, Sam Wammack, 16490 Jurupa Ave., Fontana, CA

Suds 'N' Stuff, P.O. Box 6402, Oceanside, CA 92056. *All About Beer's* newsletter.

All About Beer, P.O. Box 6402, Oceanside, CA 92056. Fluffy and frothy but filled with news on the industry and brewery profiles.

American Brewer, 1082 B St., Hayward, CA 94541. Rapidly emerging as the trade publication for microbrewers. Lots of technical information and snippy gossip on the colorful personalities of the brewing business. Useful and fun.

Purple Foot Shop, Ed and Diane Keay, 34 South Chestnut St., Ventura, CA. Wine and beer supplies.

KQED, a television station, sponsors an international beer-tasting festival each summer. For dates and location call (415) 553-2230.

HAWAII

★ Koolau Brewery, Inc., 411 Puuhale Rd., Kalihi-Kai, Honolulu, HI 96819
Type: Microbrewery
Brand: Koolau Lager

★ Pacific Brewing Co., Imi Kala St., P.O. Box 1137, Wailuku, Maui, HI 96793
  Type: Independent regional
  Brand: Maui Lager

OREGON

★ Ashland Ale's Brewery and Public House, 31 Water St., Ashland, OR 97520
  Type: Pub brewery
  Brands: Ashland Ale, Rogue Golden Ale, Ashland Stout

★ Deschutes Brewery and Public House, 1044 Northwest Bond St., Bend, OR
  97701
  Type: Pub brewery
  Brands: Cascade Golden Ale, Bachelor Bitter, Black Butte Porter

★ Oregon Trail Brewery, 341 Southwest 2d St., Corvallis, OR 97330
  Type: Microbrewery
  Brands: Oregon Trail Porter, Oregon Trail Summer Ale, Oregon Trail Ale
  Slogan: "Good at Either End of the Trail." The logo is a covered wagon
  pulled by oxen.

★ Eugene City Brewing Co., P.O. Box 1182, Eugene, OR 97440
  Type: Contract
  Brands: Eugene Ale, Bach's Bock, Eugene Celebration Lager, Eugenier
  Weitzean, Redemption Ale, St. Nick's Dark Barleywine, Auld Lang Syne
  Pale Barleywine

★ Cornelius Pass Roadhouse and Brewery, Rt. 5, Box 340, Hillsboro, OR 97123
  Type: Pub brewery
  Brands: Ruby Tuesday, Terminator, Hammer Head, Cascade Head, Crystal
  Tours: Mon.–Fri., 3:00 P.M. and on weekends by appointment
  (503) 640-6174
  Breweriana: Stickers, T-shirts, and sweatshirts
  Symbol: Mascot is goat

★ Hood River Brewing Co. (White Cap Pub), 506 Columbia St., Hood River,
  OR 97031
  Type: Pub brewery
  Brands: Hood River Full Sale Golden Ale, Chestnut Brown Ale, Porter,
  Stout, seasonal brews

★ Lighthouse Brew Pub, Inc., 4157 North Highway 101, Ste. 117, Lincoln
  City, OR 97367-5050
  Type: Pub brewery
  Brands: Cascade Head Ales, Terminator Stout, Crystal Ale, Ruby Tuesday Ale

★ Blitz-Weinhard Brewing, 1133 West Burnside St., Portland, OR 97209
  Type: Branch plant of G. Heileman Brewing Co., La Crosse, WI

★ Bridgeport Brewing Co., 1313 Northwest Marshall, Portland, OR 97209
Type: Microbrewery
Brands: BridgePort Ale, BridgePort Golden Ale, BridgePort Stout, seasonal
ales, Old Knucklehead Barley-Wine Style Ale

★ Hillsdale Brewery and Public House, 1505 Southwest Sunset Blvd., Port-
land, OR 97201
Type: Pub brewery
Brands: Hillsdale Ale, Crystal Ale, Terminator Ale (Stout), Ruby Tuesday Ale

★ Portland Brewing Co., 1339 Northwest Flanders St., Portland, OR 97209
Type: Pub brewery
Brands: Portland Ale, Grants Scottish Ale and Grants Imperial Stout (both
licensed from Yakima Brewing), Timberline Classic Ale, Oregon Honey
Ale
Tours: Small groups by appointment on Sat. (503) 222-7150
Breweriana: Glasses, T-shirts, table tents, etc.

★ Widmer Brewing Co., 1405 Northwest Lovejoy, Portland, OR 97209 and 923
Southwest 9th, Portland, OR 97205
Type: Microbrewery
Brands: Widmer Altbier, Widmer Weizenbier, plus seasonal beers (Festbier,
Oktoberfest, Bock, Maerzanbier)
Tours: Sat., noon

KINDRED SPIRITS
Cascade Brewers Society, c/o Jim Stockton, 3120 Start St., Eugene, OR
97404
Heart of the Valley Homebrewers, c/o Pat McMullen, 341 Southwest 2d,
Corvallis, OR 97330
Oregon Brew Crew, c/o Jeff Frane, 3652 Southeast Yamhill, Portland, OR
97214

GREAT PLACES
Beaverton: Hall St. Bar and Grill
Hillsboro: Cornelius Pass Roadhouse
Hood River: Hood River Brewing Company
Portland: Bridgeport Brewpub, Brewery Public House

OF NOTE
Willamette Valley, south of Portland, is the second largest hop-growing region in the United States. Many of the small valley communities have
summer festivals where beer, quite naturally, is the featured fare.
The Oregon Brewers stage a summer beer tasting festival that focuses on
the region's more laid-back, West Coast approach to the craft. Check with
regional microbrewers for more details.

WASHINGTON

★ Hales Ales, 410 North Washington St., Colville, WA 99114
  Type: Microbrewery
  Brands: Hale's Pale American Ale, Hale's Special Bitter, Hale's Celebration
    Porter, Hale's Wee Heavy, Hale's Irish Ale, Hale's Harvest Ale, Moss Bay
    Amber Ale, Moss Bay Stout

★ Hart Brewing Co., Box 1179, Kalama, WA 98625
  Type: Microbrewery
  Brands: Pyramid Wheaten Ale, Pyramid Pale Ale, Pyramid Pacific Crest Ale,
    Pyramid Snowcap Ale
  Tours: Call (206) 673-2962
  Breweriana: Labels, coasters, T-shirts, lapel pins

★ Kuefnerbrau Brewery, 112 North Lewis St., Monroe, WA 98272
  Type: Microbrewery
  Brand: Old Bavarian Style

★ Pabst Brewing Co., P.O. Box 947, Olympia, WA 98507
  Type: Branch plant of Pabst Brewing Co., Milwaukee, WI

★ Thomas Kemper Brewery, 22381 Foss Rd., NE, Poulsbo, WA 98370
  Type: Microbrewery
  Brands: Thomas Kemper Helles Lager, Thomas Kemper Munchener Lager,
    Thomas Kemper Bock
  Tours: Sat., 12:30 P.M. and 2:30 P.M.; Sun., 2:30 P.M.; during the week by
    appointment. Taproom is open seven days a week for glasses of beer and
    bottles to go (206) 697-1446.
  Breweriana: T-shirts, glass mugs, sweatshirts, polo shirts, hats, aprons, etc.

★ Rainier Brewing Co., 3100 Airport Way South, Seattle, WA 98124
  Type: Branch plant of G. Heileman Brewing Co., La Crosse, WI
  Tours: Mon.–Fri., 1:00–6:00 P.M.

★ Redhook Ale Brewery, 3400 Phinney Ave., North, Seattle, WA 98103
  Type: Microbrewery
  Brands: Redhook Ale, E.S.B., Ballard Bitter, Black Hook Porter, Winterhook
    Christmas Ale
  Tours: Call (206) 548-8000

★ Falstaff Brewing Corp., 312 West 8th St., P.O. Box 1210, Vancouver, WA
  98666
  Type: National
  Brands: Falstaff, Narragansett Lager, Krueger Beer, Krueger Pilsner, Krue-
    ger Ale, Haffenreffer Lager, Croft Ale, Narragansett Ale, Hanley Pilsner,
    Ballantine Beer, Ballantine Ale, India Pale Ale

★ General Brewing Co., 615 Columbia St., Vancouver, WA 98660
Type: Branch plant for General Brewing Co., Corte Madera, CA. Currently inactive.

★ Smith and Reilly, 3107 Northeast 65th St., #E, Vancouver, WA 98663
Type: Contract
Brand: Smith & Reilly

★ Yakima Brewing and Malting Co., 25 North Front St., Yakima, WA 98901
Type: Microbrewery
Brands: Grant's Ale, Grant's Real Ale, Grant's Imperial Stout, Grant's India Pale Ale, Grant's Hard Cider, Celtic Ale, White Bear Weis Beer, Grant's Spiced Ale
Tours: By appointment (509) 575-1900
Breweriana: T-shirts, pins
Mascot: Scottish lion

KINDRED SPIRITS
Rainier (BCCA), Premium Bill Mugrage, 3819 190th Pl. SW, Lynnwood, WA 98036
Fidalgo Island Brewers, c/o Don Harper, 1218 27th Ct., Anancortes, WA 98221
Brews Brothers, c/o Craig Harris, 324 29th Ave. E., Seattle, WA 98112

GREAT PLACES
Bellingham: Bullie's
Seattle: Cooper's Northwest Alehouse, Murphy's Pub, F. X. McRory's Steak, Chop and Oyster House, Blue Moon
Tacoma: Engine House #9
Yakima: Brewery Pub

OF NOTE
Brewing Supplies
The Cellar, 14411 Greenwood N., Seattle, WA 98133
Chinook Brewing Co., Box 4332AB, Bellingham, WA 98227
Brass Corkscrew Inc., Greg Bujak, 203 N. 85th, Box 30933, Seattle, WA 98103
Cellar Home Brewing, Joseph D. Marleau, 14411 Greenwood Ave. N., Seattle, WA 98133
Jim's Home Brew Supply, Thomas Bellinger, North 2613 Division, Spokane, WA 99207
Good Beer Guide, Vince Cottone, P.O. Box 30156, Seattle, WA 98103. Tells where to drink good beer in the Northwest. The problem is that the book needs to be expanded daily as the number of micros grows.
Running of the Rainiers. A goofy promotional event from one brewery that has not forgotten that beer has a light side, too. Giant humanoid bottles of Mountain Fresh Rainiers stampede the Seattle streets Pampalona-style. To find out when you can have the opportunity to be trampled, call the brewery at (206) 622-2600.

Merchant Du Vin, 214 University St., Seattle, WA 98101. These folks have brought the panache of the wine world to beer and in doing so have done as much as anyone else to educate the American public to the exotic world of brew.

BUY 'EM IF YOU CAN FIND 'EM

All products of the microbreweries. Any beer drinker has to love what these folks are doing—taking our concept of beer and exploding it. Americans used to have beer that tasted great after mowing the lawn; now they have brews to nuzzle, chew, sip, and swizzle. In one short decade the West Coast has become Hop Heaven, the most fertile beer drinking region in the world!

Henry Weinhard Private Reserve (Blitz/Heileman). A lively pilsner that crackles with life. Europeans would deem its body too light to carry the bitterness, but such quibbles should not detract from a successful effort to elevate the concept of an American beer.

Anchor Steam (Anchor). The inspiration for the movement but also a beverage that makes its statement through its taste. Body and bitterness carried to extremes to emphasize how far contemporary lagers have strayed from their roots. Tasted radical until micros showed us what overhopping can be.

9
THE
FLIP
FLOP

YAKIMA, WASHINGTON, TO WEST BROOKFIELD, VERMONT
MANY DAYS, MANY MILES

THE CASE OF THE SEVEN RINGS

Portland, Maine

Not long after the completion of The Great Beer Trek, we shared our experiences with some old friends—over beer, naturally. The setting was in the revived harbor district of Portland at $3 Dewey's, an establishment that features exotic brews from every crevice of the planet, served within an unpretentious context that detracts neither from the taste buds nor the conversation. Still overwhelmed with the stimulation of our recent travels, I gushed forth with the wonders to be discovered within the world of suds. One of the crew was sipping at a pint of Guinness Stout that at $3 Dewey's is served in the strict Irish tradition: in a straight glass (a "pounder") and carbonated with nitrogen, as opposed to carbon dioxide.

My friends were considerate enough to let my enthusiasm run its course as I babbled through a litany of newly acquired beer knowledge. The onyx color of Guinness gave me opportunity to tell about the ingredients of beer, how black patent malt is the source both of the color and the richly burnt flavor. This discourse evolved into "beer types," providing an opportunity to decry the lack of variety in America while simultaneously applauding the indomitable spirit of the beer drinker that has led to the resurgence of the small, independent brewery as well as the enrichment of the current beer drinking scene. After a discourse on the demise of the local brewer, I turned to the strengths of American beers, specifically the cleanliness and consistency of the product. No way, I pointed out, could Miller claim to be "good for you" as Guinness does in its advertising. First of all, the federal agencies would not allow it, and second, a pasteurized product does not contain the living yeast cells as does a naturally conditioned one such as the Guinness that my friend was now halfway through.

My friends, I think, are more polite and indulgent than I am fascinating, even on a subject as rich as beer, for they let me continue. The creamy head on a good stout could reveal many things, ranging from the malt content of the brew to the cleanliness of the glass. The glassware at $3 Dewey's was obviously flawless, you see, because the foamy head clung to the sides, leaving a ring with each sip. When all factors—glassware, carbonation, temperature, company, and environment—are in harmony, it is said that an empty pint of Guinness will have seven distinct rings. I related this bit of sudsy lore just as my friend pointed his glass skyward for the final sip. When he returned the glass to the table, we counted. One, two, three, four, five, six, SEVEN—a perfect seven! I thanked the beer gods and bought the next round.

The "flip flop" is a trucker term for the return trip. An eastbound driver will check out road conditions with his westbound counterpart and promises to return the favor, although not literally, to "catch you on the flip-flop." While our westbound segment had taken more than thirteen weeks, we drove home in five days, pulling into the driveway in Scituate ninety-nine days and 20,000 miles after embarkation.

Our loosely defined mission had been accomplished. We had been to all the breweries, tasted all the beers, met enough people, and seen enough places to feel that we had developed a much more complete understanding of the land in which we lived. The starting point of a Beer Trek, however, is more distinct than the end point, as there is always another beer to sample, a new tavern to check out, a new recipe to try.

The days of boring highway driving let us consolidate our experiences. As a documentation of the contemporary state of beer, however, The Great Beer Trek was quickly obsolete. Even before we arrived home, one of the breweries we had visited threw in the towel and closed its doors. Since then, many other breweries have merged and recombined. Microbreweries have opened on the heels of New Albion's boldness, and before long even some of these had closed. New brands have appeared, others disappeared, still others have been reformulated. Beer is, after all, a fluid subject. The same changes that have made our journey obsolete have firmly and uniquely fixed its place in time, history, and beerdom.

Our optimism for the future for the American beer drinker was marred by one looming cloud—the spectre of consolidation. No brewing concern, in fact no business, willingly sacrifices its independence. The family brewers we met were united in their commitment to pass along the businesses to sons and daughters. Conditions must be close to ideal for the smaller brewer to survive. Management must be strong, finances secure, and the beer good. Only firms with substantial means can comply with dictates of a government that regulates everything from the label on your bottle to the nationalities of your work force. Only firms with substantial means can afford the investments in advertising and packaging that the consumer has been conditioned to need. Of the money spent for a six-pack, a discouragingly tiny proportion actually goes for the beer. While the local brewers scratch and claw, the Buds and Millers of the beer world continue to gain market share.

Consolidation is visible on the distribution level as well. Distributors in one region can sell in truckload quantities to chain stores, taking lower margins and counting on increased volume to make up the difference. Local retailers and distributors cannot compete and are forced to discount products and services. For the local brewer, the economics of scale are clearly working against him. Eventually he will have no way to sell his product. He must either become big enough to play the game or get out of the way. This, too, is the American way.

In the short run, beer drinkers benefit from consolidation in the form of lower prices, but they will eventually be left with a small number of huge breweries that, faced with little competition, may offer less variety of an inferior product at inflated prices. Budweiser will be General Motors, Miller will be Ford, and all the rest will be rolled into Chrysler. For the beer drinker inclined toward doomsday scenarios, consolidation provides the bogeyman.

Our personal observations contradicted this bleak outlook, instead portraying a future for the American beer drinker brighter now than at any other time since the 1840s when the English brewing style of the early colonists was enriched by the first wave of Bavarian immigrants bringing their lager beer traditions. Evidence can be found in the growing interest in, and availability of, imported beers, the birth of the microbrewers, the legalization of home brewing and its subsequent popularity, and finally the belated response to the beer drinker's need for variety by the commercial brewing industry. The existence of a product such as George Killian Irish Red would have been thought dubious several years ago. That it would be introduced by Coors would be unthinkable. As the sophistication of the beer drinker has grown, so has the beer market. More people drinking more beer is something that any industry loves, and the American brewers have learned that they will sell more beer if their product line is not marketed exclusively toward the stereotyped Joe Six-Pack who swills his lager in front of the TV set. Perhaps the vision of a future where the brews available range from Bud in red cans to Miller in green is real, but the consumer of fermented grain beverages, referred to on these pages as "the beer drinker," has historically shown a willingness to fight.

As the English brewers learned from CAMRA, the aroused beer drinker is better appeased than fought.

The big picture, then, is a good one. We sensed this immediately upon putting the van into gear in Yakima and used the tedium of the interstates to formulate our thoughts more coherently. Laura combed through accumulated notes and souvenirs so that we could begin to establish orderliness to the previous weeks. Everything fell neatly into two major categories—the People and the Beers.

Five sudsy subcultures opened their ranks to The Great Beer Trek and contributed greatly to our understanding.

> *The Outlaws.* This group includes renegade beer drinkers and amateur home brewers. Together they lend about 1 percent of the knowledge and 99 percent of the color to beer drinking. Their interest in beer revolves around what happens when people get together to drink it.
>
> *The Zymurgists.* The upper-echelon home brewer and commercial microbrewer comprise a group whose members freely cross boundaries. Their focus is on the process of brewing. Their knowledge is encyclopedic, their adherence to the traditions of brewing total. If they have a drawback, it is that they cannot tolerate second-rate beer.
>
> *The Establishment.* This includes all those in the business of manufacturing and selling beer, ranging from the food-processing expert to the market researcher. Their jobs dictate a devotion to the art of selling rather than experiencing the pleasure of consumption. Happily, the two pursuits can and do coexist.
>
> *The Observers.* These are principally the can collectors (zealots who treasure intrinsically worthless objects) and the breweriana collectors (zealots who treasure genuinely beautiful expressions of commercial art). Both groups are perversely interested in the companies that spawn the objects of their passion. Both groups practice scholarship in its purest form without hope for profit. And both groups could not be more different in character. The brewerianiacs are patricians, civilized and polite. The can collectors are rough around the edges and proud of it.
>
> *The Rank and File.* Anyone who meets on the common ground of enjoying brew is eligible. The steelworker who thinks I. C. Light is the greatest thing to come along since Terry Bradshaw, the college student who bets his Dad he can tell the difference between Michelob and Old Milwaukee . . . these are the final judges of the product and the process. Their opinions count.

Then there are the brews. The most frequently asked question encountered in our travels was, "Which beer is best?" Our competitive national character always wants to condense an experience such as our trip to a one-word summary. The correct answer, alas, is as unsatisfying as a warm, flat Lite. Nearly all beers are good, some are a little better, and each brew has its time and place. Iron City seems to cut the grit of the steel mill in a way that Budweiser never could. Lone Star in long necks is completely at home at a barbecue where Anchor Steam would be hopelessly out of place. Yuengling Porter is terrific, but it is as different from Coors as Pottsville, Pennsylvania, is from Golden, Colorado. Comparison is impossible.

We have tried in "Buy 'em If You Can Find 'em" to spotlight exceptional expressions of the brewers' art. We hope that we have made the point that you, the beer drinker, are the ultimate judge. Our goal is simply to increase awareness of what is available.

Ten years ago, even with more breweries in the United States, it would have been frivolous to classify beer types. Here, one final time, the beers of the nation pass in review.

The Stalwarts

The national brands have achieved levels of quality and consistency that make distinction close to impossible. From Bud to Black Label, the formulations are aimed directly at the paunch of Middle America. As for the new generation of light beers, the blandness is intensified. Some would say you can't go wrong with any of these products; others would say you can't go right.

American beer is often maligned for its blandness and rarely praised for its many virtues. The domestic brew is clean (free of off-flavors), consistent, conveniently packaged, inexpensive, and relatively unaltered by chemical additives. On this last subject the American brewer has a better story to tell than is commonly believed. The post-Watergate public is quick to assume that its institutions—government or business—are foisting inferior swill on the consumer. The Great Beer Trek went into scores of brewhouses, all of which were scrupulously clean, and talked to brewmasters from Schlitz to Shiner. We are not chemists, but if there was a rat to smell, we missed it. The twentieth-century brewmaster is not above using twentieth-century technology to prepare beer, but there is more attention paid to the simple traditions of brewing than a jaded public would suspect. In terms of its impact on one's health, we emerged from our travels feeling confident that, in moderation, the consumption of beer is more advisable than any other available beverage, including mineral water.

The Notables: Bud, Stroh, Coors . . . and the others are right behind.

The Supers

Just as the hop was about to disappear from the American palate, it has made a dramatic comeback in the form of the "super-premium" beers, which the commercial brewers have developed to offer the consumer an alternative to the full-bodied and flavorful imports. In reality the Supers approximate the formulations of lagers before the trend toward lightness began. By creating

Budweiser

Stalwart

Henry Weinhard's

BEER

Super

SIERRA NEVADA BREWING CO.

PALE ALE

ZYMURGIST'S DELIGHT

The Family Gallery

LIGHT

Bolt Upright

Homebrew

light beers (less ingredients but premium pricing), the brewers have successfully elevated price structures without affecting their flagship brands. No matter, though, the beer drinker now has available a variety of well-brewed products that collectively are the best sudsy development since home brewing was legalized.

The Notables: Andeker (Pabst), Augsburger Dark (Huber), Henry Weinhard Special Reserve (Blitz/Heileman), Michelob Dry (Anheuser-Busch).

Zymurgists' Delights

It is unfair to rate these beers, as all of the producers are new enough that their products are still evolving. Freshness is a key ingredient in the taste of these local products so it is unlikely that one could ever achieve a truly fair taste comparison. What is important, though, is not which of these beers is superior to another but rather that an entirely new world of beer tastes is being brought to our shores. Hallelujah! They are too numerous to name.

Seasonals

Modern technology, specifically the advent of refrigeration, caused the brewing world to turn its back on its climatically determined seasonal traditions. Having eliminated the need for seasonal brews, the beer drinker missed the stimulating effect craved by his palate. As with many other aspects of modern life, we are discovering that many physical needs are paralleled by spiritual ones. The suburbanite computer programmer may live a life completely insulated from the harvest or the rites of spring, but somewhere within the animal the primal need to acknowledge the seasons still exists.

Bock beers are making a strong comeback. Brewers as large as Stroh and as small as Sierra Nevada are reviving the seasonal tradition in a serious way. Leinenkugel, Huber, and Dixie have introduced new beers that are fast becoming annual classics. Several micros are producing strong ales designed for wintertime contemplation. Harvest beers are not far behind, as well as summertime weiss brews in which wheat substitutes for barley. As long as the business environment remains competitive, brewers will be motivated to attack the specialty markets, to the delight of the adventurous beer drinker.

The Notables: Christian Moerlein Bock (Hudepohl), Leinenkugel Bock (Leinenkugel), Augsburger Bock (Huber), Anchor Christmas Ale, Frankenmuth Oktoberfest.

Fake Beers

A misnomer, as these beers are as real as the motivation of their entrepreneurial inventors. Some are undoubtedly quick-buck specialties, hoping to strike a responsive chord in consumers through the name alone (Luckenbach, Gilley's, Rock 'n Roll), but others (Sam Adams) represent genuine attempts by individuals to get into the brewing business without having to build a brewery. With the industry's current excess capacity, this approach to beer making has enormous potential to fill in gaps in the national palate.

The Notables: Sam Adams (Pittsburgh), Dock Street Amber (F. X. Matt), XIII Colony Amber (Pittsburgh).

Last of the Regionals

The survivors in this category have carved more solid niches in recent years, but their futures are still tenuous. The locally owned, limited-distribution brewer is a dying breed and knows it. The current generation, displaying a sudsy survival instinct, never wants to be the one to abandon a family tradition. These concerns should be preserved for better or worse, as are all other endangered species. It falls to the beer drinker to support them. Memorize the names and locations so that when in Rome you can do your beer drinkerly duty:

Dixie Brewing Co., Inc.—New Orleans, Louisiana
Geyer Brothers Brewing Co.—Frankenmuth, Michigan
Cold Spring Brewing Co., Inc.—Cold Spring, Minnesota
August Schell Brewing Co., Inc.—New Ulm, Minnesota
Eastern Brewing Co., Inc.—Hammonton, New Jersey
Genesee Brewing Co., Inc.—Rochester, New York
F. X. Matt Brewing Co., Inc.—Utica, New York
Hudepohl Brewing Co., Inc.—Cincinnati, Ohio
Latrobe Brewing Co.—Latrobe, Pennsylvania
Pittsburgh Brewing Co.—Pittsburgh, Pennsylvania
D. G. Yuengling and Son, Inc.—Pottsville, Pennsylvania
Straub Brewery—St. Mary's, Pennsylvania
Jones Brewing Co.—Smithton, Pennsylvania
The Lion, Inc.—Wilkes-Barre, Pennsylvania
Spoetzl Brewery, Inc.—Shiner, Texas
Joseph Huber Brewing Co.—Monroe, Wisconsin
Stevens Point Brewery—Stevens Point, Wisconsin

THE DOGBONE BREWING CO.   West Brookfield, Vermont

Time goes on and a Great Beer Trek—anyone's Great Beer Trek—becomes a page in a date book. Tim Matson still lives in Vermont, but he no longer brews with the conviction and zeal that originally attracted him to the pastime. Will Anderson's collection of breweriana is being sold. Bill Henderson is no longer a member of the Beer Can Collectors of America, and Joe Pickett's beer is now no more.

For each sad passage, there are offsetting positive developments. Jack McAuliffe's New Albion Brewing Co. has met its maker, but the flag has been picked up and carried forward by a dozen new concerns. The American Home-brewers Association, originally a collection of felons and free spirits, is now an active and respectable organization whose numbers continue to grow as rapidly as the number of exotic beers offered at the Great American Beer Festival in Denver, Colorado. George Killian, Christian Moerlein, and Henry Weinhard are becoming familiar names to beer drinkers who continue to de-mand higher standards of quality in their libations. Specialty beers, such as seasonal bocks, are being created by the national brewers, following the paths of success blazed by the Bill Leinenkugels of the beer world.

But for the most part, life in the beer world simply goes on, much as it did before the Beer Trek. Miller sues Bud; Bud sues Miller; Stroh acquires Schaefer; Pabst acquires Blitz; Pabst merges with Olympia; Heileman buys part of Pabst . . . to make a long story short, the Beer Wars continue without change or effect immediately apparent to the beer drinker. In La Crosse, Wis-consin, Jeff still religiously attends Oktoberfest. In New Ulm, Minnesota and

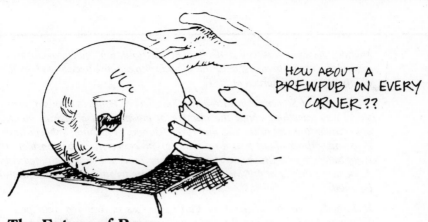

HOW ABOUT A
BREWPUB ON EVERY
CORNER??

The Future of Brew

*This is a subject about which no self-respecting beer drinker is without opinion.
The people surveyed were more than self-respecting; they are respected by their
peers. Almost everyone foresaw a future of more breweries, more brands, greater
variety, more segmentation, and higher quality.*

*What a difference a decade makes! Three regional breweries died during the
Original Trek, and the future seemed to be one of identical light beers in different-
sized containers. There was hardly a bull in beerdom. More consolidation, the disappearance of flavor, variety, and identity—these were the themes that comprised
the background tapestry of the voyage.*

*Now there is not a Mike, Fritz, or Augie not predicting a buyer's market for
beer. Consumption is seen declining, a victim of demographics (an aging wave of
baby boomers), while variety increases. The modes of expression are as varied as
the brews of the future. Here are the authoritative views of the beer world in the
year 2000:*

- *Lew Cady, a lover of seedy dives, author of* Beer Can Collecting, *and champion of beer drinkers' rights, predicts exactly 536 breweries in the year
  2000. His rationale is precise—one firm per half-million in population,
  with a total projected population of 268 million. That's simple. Cady foresees a world of light beers, counterbalanced by a rich world of exotics
  brewed by micros, brewpubs, and the mainstream breweries.*

- *George W. Hilton, a professor of economics at UCLA and editor of the*
  Breweriana Collector, *is hopeful yet pessimistic about the prospects of survival for such familiar names as Stroh, Matt, Pabst, Huber, and Jones.
  Weissbier will catch on as a summer drink, while Miller will be bought
  out by a foreign brewer.*

- *Timothy R. Morse, brewmaster of Hope Brewing Co., Providence, Rhode
  Island, foresees a different future with anthocyanogen-free malt, biomass
  fermentation, and gene manipulation of yeast put into practice at a commercial brewery, as well as new techniques for aging beer in twenty-four
  hours.*

- *Lee Ferrera (Humboldt Brewery) predicts freeze-dried beer for backpackers and the major breweries dissolving into micros.*

- *Michael Jackson foresees a decline in consumption, causing carnage among the major brewers, with the silver lining of more widespread availability of true ales served at 50°F.*

- *John Zappa of Stevens Point Brewing Co., Stevens Point, Wisconsin, considers any questions about the number of independent breweries moot; given the influences of the IRS and BATF (Bureau of Alcohol, Tobacco and Firearms—think about that for a minute), no concern can be considered truly independent. On the positive side, Zappa sees the American Medical Association finally admitting the benefits of moderate beer consumption by 2000.*

- *Richard E. Johnson of the Beer Can Collectors of America anticipates lighter and lighter beers (50 calories per can) from fewer and fewer breweries. Even worse, they will be packaged in plastic containers rather than cans.*

- *Charlie Papazian, founder of the American Homebrewers Association, can see home brew in the White House. But no one has ever accused Charlie of being entirely serious.*

More thoughts on the future of beer from The Great Beer Trek Survey respondents:

- *"The contract brewers will have to put up or shut up, and I assume most will do the latter since none have successfully done the former."—Don't quote me*

- *"Many micro breweries will go broke."—Michael Levis, Santa Fe Brewing Co.*

- *"If you get too drunk, your car will drive you home. Anheuser-Busch will have its own Miss Budweiser Rocket Ship."—Gordon Gammell, Sun Valley Brewing Co.*

- *"The number of micros will grow over the next five years, then shake out and consolidate. There will prove to be too much passion and not enough business judgment."—Don't quote me*

- *"Beer gum will come out on the market. Could be the hot item."—Jennifer Smith, Cornelius Pass Roadhouse*

Beer gum, freeze-dried beer, 536 breweries, home brew in the White House— it all sounds exciting. When The Next Great Beer Trek happens in the year 2000, we will find out who are the true seers.

Stevens Point, Wisconsin, diehard brewers fight to maintain free-board. Schlitz has revived the "gusto" theme in its advertising, and at McSorley's Ale House professors are impressing their students with their wisdom as well as their worldliness on the subject of malt beverages.

Our days as full-time trekkers were brought to a screeching halt by economic realities intensified by the arrival of a new beer drinker (circa 1996) named Jake. Eventually we packed our belongings into the van and moved north to Vermont, not far from where we first discussed Mountain Brew with Tim Matson. This time we called not as pilgrims on a quest to learn the Secret of the Suds but as working blokes.

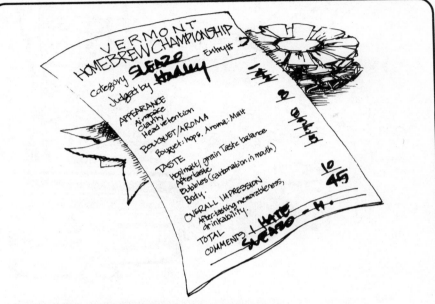

The Fate of the Cram Hill Brewers

The Cram Hill Brewers were spawned on a cold night. In truth, no one remembers, but it must have been a cold night. The initial meeting took place in Vermont, where even a July evening can bring a chill. A group of rank-and-file suds swillers gathered to observe the creation of beer. The demonstration was low-tech, an extract beer brewed with Blue Ribbon Hop-Flavored Malt Extract, but the results encouraging enough to motivate the gathering to regroup once the results could be sampled.

The time was the late seventies, and most of the participants were refugees from the suburbs who preferred the control of home crafts to the standardization of Budweiser. The demographic profile was varied—high education, low income, flannel garb, and political views ranging from liberal to outrageous. Unbeknown to the Cram Hill Brewers, similar groups, unified by beer, were gathering from Boulder to Bangor. It was a movement.

The next few years saw a greening of skills as the members learned about the Secret of the Suds and applied them in new and creative ways. There were the early experiments, using ingredients as far ranging as wild Vermont ginger and birch sap, but gradually tradition and craftsmanship prevailed.

The energy was difficult to contain. A statewide home-brew championship was sponsored, and within two years more than a hundred home brewers had been discovered within the green hills. A celebration of the fiftieth anniversary of the repeal of prohibition caught on with the wire services and was carried coast to coast. More than a half-dozen schemes to begin a commercial brewing venture were brought to the table and toasted with home brews that had improved steadily in quality.

Individuals began to take more specialized paths. Several took the all-grain oath and began producing brews distinguished enough to take top honors in regional and national competitions. Another became a collector and soon had a chichi shop that featured everything from antique beer trays to baseball cards. Two published books on brew. One became a fledgling brewmaster with Catamount, the first local brewery to open its doors since prohibition.

Everyone else worked, raised children, built additions on their houses, and continued to drink good beer. But a funny thing happened along the way—the Cram Hill Brewers stopped gathering. No more state championships, no more National Repeal Day Celebrations. Most everyone is too busy to brew these days. Besides it is too easy to procure the exotic brews that formerly were available only if one brewed them oneself. The Cram Hill Brewers, stout soldiers in the revolution, became, ironically, victims of its success.

We reassimilated to life, but not life as we had known it in pre-Trek times. This was life enriched by the presence of malt beverages beyond the ken of the average man. Our new acquaintances in Vermont led existences in which relative self-sufficiency was an expected way of life. Heating with wood, gardening, and animal husbandry were universal. Our introduction of home brewing was readily accepted by the locals, and before long the Cram Hill Brewers were born. Moreover, in my new job I had acquaintances whose routines include frequent travel around the country. My standing requests for local brews served both to enrich their travels and to create a beer larder for the Cram Hill Brewers more varied than any north of the Brickskeller. Beer had become a way of life.

NOW IF LABATT'S COULD DO IT IN 1936...

The Next Trek

The Next Great Beer Trek is scheduled for the year 2000. By then the renaissance will be in a mature phase. The national breweries will have completed their consolidation, their numbers reduced to a manageable three or four. Budweiser will be in a state of steep decline, its crown taken by Coors Extra Dry-Super Light. Miller and Stroh will complete the set, with all other brands reduced to regional variations of the Heileman theme.

The present regional brewers will give up their namesake brands but will be stronger than ever, buoyed by the contract brewers. Every major corporation, civic organization, and sports team will enter the business with a proprietary brew. Picture Fenway Park serving Lansdowne Lager and #9 Splendid Splinter Ale. The micros will chink the wall with specialized beverages for every taste and occasion. There will be seasonal brews for every sliver of the calendar. Pub breweries will be omnipresent, with at least a dozen in each major city. Many will be cleverly franchised so that uniformity of equipment and economies of scale will make the achievement of local identity financially feasible.

On the sociological side, penalties for drunk driving will be more severe than for armed robbery. For this reason I will let my sons (who will be twenty-one and eighteen by this time) chauffeur us around the land, from sea to foaming sea. The legal drinking age will be about thirty by then, so they will have to be content with hearing me wax eloquent about the exotic brews I quaff. Tough luck guys, but I don't make the laws.

The costs of travel, if they continue at their present rate of inflation, will be astronomical, and since my publisher will undoubtedly manage no more than a paltry advance, The Great Beer Trek–The New Century will throw itself at the mercy of the hospitality of brewers, tavern owners, breweriana buffs, and beer drinkers of the Americas. If this trip is anything like the last, we will never have to buy a beer.

See you then.

The van still runs, but Vermont winters have taken their toll, and the slam of a door is often followed by the dull tinkle of falling rust. The bumper stickers have faded and peeled, but a close examination reveals an abbreviated version of our itinerary, "Schultz and Dooley Love New York," "Long Live Long Necks," "If you ain't been to Luckenbach, you ain't shit," "Relax—Don't Worry, Have a Homebrew," and "Forever Beer." The poor beast has hauled hay and sheep and garbage to the dump, and one would never know unless told that this noble steed at one time visited all the nation's breweries. The same can be said for the black dog who lies by the sugar maple in the front yard. From looking at her you would never guess that one day in Montana she was run over by a freight train.

Inside the house a beer drinker sits midway between "blissed" and "fully krauesened." He opens a brew (his current favorite is a coppery mixture of Schlitz and his home brew batch #81 called "Tooferbusher" for reasons too obscure to mention), pours it into his favorite mug, and doodles in a spiral-bound notebook filled with descriptions, statements, and plans for such exotica as the Dogbone Brewing Company and The Great Global Beer Trek. In the Dogbone section of the notebook are diagrams and schematics, lists of materials, charts, and figures. Brands will include Bolt Upright, Dirtball Lager, and Dogbone Ale. The Great Global Beer Trek segment features many crude drawings of yachts, airplanes, railroad cars, and assorted land cruisers, each customized to provide conveyance to the corners of the earth in appropriate comfort and style. On a page marked "Budget" is written simply "a zillion dollars." And on a page entitled "participants" is the line:

"Reservations are now being accepted."

A Beer Drinker's Calendar

The rhythm of the beer business has changed dramatically in recent years. Technology has removed the seasonal variations from the brewing process. Imagine if Budweiser had to lager all its beer in deep caves dug into hillsides as they once did at Yeungling's. There aren't enough hills in Missouri!

The Beer Trekker's itinerary could just as easily be organized according to chronological events as geography. Here are some of the highlights of the malt and suds calendar:

WINTER

Australian Beer Can Collectors Canathon (January). Contact Mike Pinkard, Box 827-H, GPO, Hobart, Tasmania, Australia.

Western States Canvention and Breweriana Show (March). Date and location vary. Contact Jim Thomas, 4084 Pequeno, Las Vegas, NV 89120.

SPRING

American Homebrewers Conference on Beer Quality and Brewing, Boulder, CO. For dates and information: AHA, Box 287, Boulder, CO 80306.

Great American Beer Festival, Denver, CO. Contact AHA for details.

American Breweriana Association, National Convention. Contact Dan Potochniak, 1610 Celebrity Circle West, Hanover Park, IL 60103.

Antique Advertising Show, Indiana State Fairgrounds, Indianapolis, IN (June).

SUMMER

American Breweriana Association Convention, time and location vary. For information contact ABA, P.O. Box 11157, Pueblo, CO 81001.

National Association of Breweriana Advertising (August). For information, write to Robert Jaeger, 2343 Met-to-Wee Lane, Wauwatosa, WI 53226.

California State Fair Homebrew Competition (August). Sponsored by Gold Country Brewers and California State Fair.

Great British Beer Festival (August). Dates and location vary. For information, write to Campaign for Real Ale, 34 Alma Rd., St. Albans, Herts AL1 3BW, England.

National Microbrewer's Conference (August or September). Association of Brewers, Box 287, Boulder, CO 80306.

CANVENTION, annual gathering of the BCCA clan. Information on dates and location from BCCA, 747 Merus Court, Fenton, MO 63026.

FALL

KPBS International Beer Festival, San Diego, CA (September). Call (619) 265-4051.

Common Ground Beer and Wine Competition, Maine (September). Call John Seckler (207) 967-5758.

Antique Advertising Show, Indiana State Fairgrounds, Indianapolis, IN (September).

Master Brewers Association of the Americas Convention. Write MBAA, 4513 Vernon Blvd., Ste. 202, Madison, WI 53705.

Brewers' Association of America Annual Convention. For information, BAA, 541 West Randolph St., Chicago, IL 60606.

OKTOBERFEST, the big one on the river, La Crosse, WI. Contact La Crosse Chamber of Commerce, La Crosse, WI 54601.

Thomas Kemper Brewery's Octoberfest. For information contact brewery at 22381 Foss Rd., N.E., Poulsbo, WA 98370.

Contra Costa Chorale's Annual Micro-brewery Beer Tasting, Orinda Community Center, Orinda, CA. Call (415) 268-2581 or (415) 655-9621.

Dixie Cup Homebrew Competition, Houston, TX. Contact Scott Birdwell, (713) 523-8154.

Mid-Atlantic Regional Homebrewing Competition (November). c/o Rich Gleeson, 344 South Taylor Ave., Crum Lynne, PA 19022.

New England Regional Homemade Beer Competition, Old Deerfield, MA (November). Contact Charlie Olchowski, 473 Main St., Greenfield, MA 01301.

Guzzle 'n Twirl, trading session and social (November). Sponsored by North Star Chapter, BCCA, c/o Jack Isacson, 97 16th Ave., SW, New Brighton, MN 55112.
    Face it. You can't make them all, but if you die trying, what a way to go!

INDEX

ABOUT THE AUTHOR

STEPHEN MORRIS' professional world has touched on beer, baseball, rock and roll, and cast-iron wood stoves. He lives with his wife, Laura, and sons, Jake and Patrick, in a small Vermont hamlet that has inspired the setting of his two works of fiction, *Beyond Yonder* and *The King of Vermont*. He is biding time until the next *Great Beer Trek*.

ABOUT THE ILLUSTRATOR

VANCE SMITH has been known to drink a beer or two, although her real passion is wood stoves. She's illustrated two books on solid fuel burning (1976 and 1982). Her design business, Red House Design, keeps her busy when she is not occupied with her latest passion, horses. Raised in Pasadena, she graduated from Wellesley College in 1970, took her Master of Architecture from Harvard University in 1974, and lives in Vermont.

•